LIFE PRINCIPLES FOR
## CHRIST-LIKE
## LIVING

# Following God

## LIFE PRINCIPLES FOR
# CHRIST-LIKE
# LIVING

## JENNIFER DEVLIN

Advancing the Ministries of the Gospel
**AMG** *Publishers*

*God's Word to you is our highest calling.*

# *Following God*

## LIFE PRINCIPLES FOR CHRIST-LIKE LIVING

© 2006 by Jennifer Devlin

First Printing, 2006

ISBN 10: 0-89957-339-8
ISBN 13: 978-0-89957-339-7

Editing by Rick Steele
Layout by Rick Steele
Cover design by ImageWright Marketing and Design, Chattanooga, Tennessee

*Printed in the United States of America*
18 17 16 15  14 13 –US– 8 7 6 5 4 3 2

**This book is dedicated to:**

Those who want to live a life
that reflects Christ in all they do.

Don't waste another minute!
Run after Him with all
you've got!

# Acknowledgments

I thank the Lord with such a humble prayer of praise as this study is part of my Romans 12:1–2 worship that is dedicated to Him. As an offering, the cry of my heart has poured out on these pages. I am reminded of the fact that this study is an extension of who God is molding me into; through the transformation of a renewed mind focused on Him and His will. My prayer is for each and every one of you who will read this study, that God will do a mighty work of transformation in your life as well. What a mighty God we serve!

I thank God for my tremendous family. Bob, God has deeply blessed me with your love and the way you complete my life. Truly the two of us have become one, and I praise God for you each and every day. Thanks for supporting me as I follow God and His call on my life, and for the understanding and patience you have shown as I have worked on this study. I also want to thank our wonderful son, Owen. What a heart for God you have! I praise God for who you are, and who you will become. Remember to "follow in His footsteps." I love you both very much! Also, to my mom, Bonnie, thank you for your love and the foundation of faith you instilled in us growing up and for faithfully supporting me during this season of writing. Thanks to George, Judy, and the Devlin clan for always encouraging me to follow my dreams. What a blessing the rest of our family is as well. May we all celebrate God's goodness!

A special thanks to Gloria and Dan Penwell; what sweet friends you are! Thanks for your encouragement and friendship. Thanks also to Rick Steele for your patience with my editing questions. You have been such a wonderful editor and mentor. I praise God for AMG's dedication to proclaiming the gospel around the world, and for providing solid studies, books, and references that lead others straight to Jesus. What an honor it is to work with you all.

Tonie—your continuing support and long talks while preparing this study have been so special. Your passion for syntax error and technical editing has found a home in this manuscript, and I thank you. There isn't enough coffee in the world to repay you. What a friend indeed: sister in Christ, and fellow Bible nut. There is no one I'd rather search answers to questions with; chasing rabbits, doing research, and loving God.

I am grateful to our military family who support each other through every situation and to the service members who protect our country's freedom every single day. The PWOC family I love so much will always have a special place in my heart. I thank all the prayer warriors who have prayed for and encouraged me and my family during this process; the prayers were felt and appreciated. And finally, thanks to our Mount Zion family for your sweet spirit and open arms. We feel right at home.

 JENNIFER DEVLIN

## About the Author

Jennifer Devlin is a Bible study teacher, published author, and speaker. Jennifer has served within many community organizations and in women's ministry at local and regional levels, including a stint as the Southeast Region Coordinator for the Protestant Women of the Chapel, an international ministry, serving women of the military chapel system. Mrs. Devlin has served as contributing author for two titles in the successful **God Allows U-Turns** series: *God Allows U-Turns for Teens* and *God Allows U-Turns for Women*, both published by Bethany House (March 2006). Other publishing efforts include serving as collaborating editor and contributing author of *God Answers Prayers: Military Edition* (Harvest House 2005). Jennifer currently serves as Director of **Ministry for Life,** a speaking, writing, and training ministry designed to strengthen and motivate Christians in their relationship with Jesus Christ. Jennifer lives in Huntsville, Alabama, with her husband Bob (retired Army Colonel) and son Owen. To learn more about Jennifer, visit her Web site at:

www.ministryforlife.com

# About the Following God Series

Three authors and fellow ministers, Wayne Barber, Eddie Rasnake, and Rick Shepherd, teamed up in 1998 to write a character-based Bible study for AMG Publishers. Their collaboration developed into the title, *Life Principles from the Old Testament.* Since 1998 these same authors and AMG Publishers have produced six more **character-based** studies—each consisting of twelve lessons geared around a five-day study of a particular Bible personality. In 2001, AMG Publishers launched a series of topical studies called the **Following God™ Discipleship Series**. This release of *Life Principles for Christ-like Living* becomes the third title released in the Following God™ **Christian Living Series,** which is also topical in nature. Though new studies and authors are being introduced, the interactive study format that readers have come to love remains constant with each new Following God™ release. As new titles and categories are being planned, our focus remains the same: to provide excellent Bible study materials that point people to God's Word in ways that allow them to apply truths to their own lives. More information on this groundbreaking series can be found on the following web page:

www.amgpublishers.com

# Preface

Welcome to *Life Principles for Christ-Like Living!* What an honor it is to know you have chosen this study to journey into the Word of God. Be prepared to know God better and to understand how awesome His Word is, from Genesis to Revelation, from beginning to end. God is mighty, and His Word brings us life, as it teaches us to live a life that honors God and reflects Jesus Christ.

This study is not meant to teach some type of mystical numerology, nor is it designed to prove any type of secret code in Scripture. The only code in the Bible is this: everything foreshadows Christ, portrays Christ, or refers to what Christ gave us as an example. Jesus Christ our Lord is the code! Nothing more, nothing less.

All things that our God has set for us in His Word are open to all, and the revelations given by the Holy Spirit will always be consistent with the message Jesus Christ spoke while on earth. As we go through selected 3:16 verses of the Bible, mostly found in New Testament books, we will see the theme and purpose of Christ's life. Over and over, these Scriptures will enlighten us, and cause us to grow in our relationship with our Savior. Every believer should set the goal of having a deeper relationship with Jesus Christ. What better way to do this but through the study of God's Word!

What is a deeper relationship exactly? What is being Christ-like all about? We will study together what God has laid out in His word for us to learn by. As we learn more about the Savior that died for our sins, we will naturally become closer to Him through our increased understanding. The more we realize who our God is, the more we are capable of worshiping and serving Him!

I look at all the years in my life I spent as a "passive Christian" pinning the title of Christian on my sleeve but not wearing it etched on my heart. I shake my head at how many years I've wasted. Sure, I was saved, but was God happy with His end of the deal? Remember, this is as a "Christian"—one who had genuinely accepted Christ, and lived a life as a believer. I had my "fire insurance"—just enough of God to stay out of hell, but just too little to know why I should bow down and worship Him for who He is every moment of my life.

*Life Principles for Christ-Like Living* is designed to help every believer see the strength of the message of Christ throughout the New Testament and how that message relates to our daily lives today. The timelessness of Scripture gives a tremendous opportunity to apply the same Christian values that were held at the beginning of Christianity to our current situation. God is the same, from the beginning of the world shown in Genesis 1:1 to the end-time events predicted in Revelation.

You will notice that the Scriptures examined are not necessarily in the same chronological order as they appear in the Bible. To get a deeper understanding of the progression of Christ's foundation, actions, and life application, we will shift the chapter portrayals to reflect the right timeline. You may also wonder why I have explained much more of the third chapter than just the sixteenth verse. While the sixteenth verse is the focus verse, or the verse that intoduces the topic of the Bible chapter, it is not as useful unless it is seen in the context of the entire passage. You will also see where other Scriptures relate. Whatever will help bring a deeper understanding to God's Word is great, and it is best when we can compare Scripture with Scripture.

The bottom line message for us in this study is simple. Find a passion for God. Find a passion for Christ. Change your life by reading what God has already promised and provided for you. As I have attempted to honor God with completing the task given me, I pray that all who read this will walk away with a better understanding of who God is, just what Christ did for us, and how to live a Christ-like life. I pray that everything written in this study will honor God, and will accurately portray all He is, all He does, and all He says we are in Him. May God bless you as you read and apply these chapters and learn what God has purposed for every believer. Enjoy, and grow in Christ!

# Table of Contents

# ONE

# *Powerful Breath*

## WHY WE SHOULD STUDY GOD'S WORD
## 3:16 VERSE: 2 TIMOTHY

Following God includes following His Word! Throughout these twelve lessons we will discover many important verses in the New Testament that will give insight into how to like a Christ-like life. Our first focus verse in this study will lay the foundation for much of our discussion, as it will convey why we hold the Bible as a reliable source of who God is. We as Christians must believe that the books of the Bible give us a blueprint for our existence as Christians, and that God's hand of protection and influence is on every page. There is no fallible aspect of any part of the Bible in the original texts, for if there were, then God would be fallible, and He is nothing of the sort!

As we go through this first week together exploring the 3:16s in Scripture, we will discover why the Bible is so important, why it can be trusted, and how we can apply it to our own lives today just as wonderfully as the early Christians applied the original texts to their lives. There is no better book out there, and there is no other book that is totally inspired by the Holy Spirit. The Holy Spirit reveals the truths in Scripture to all believers who ask Him to and who read with a belief that the Bible contains the words of God to His people.

Our goal for this week, and for the entire study, is to not only get you interested in the Bible, but to get you so excited about what was written on each and every page that it would become your favorite book. The Bible has such depth and life for us that it should be the one book we can't resist reading, every spare moment of our lives. For if this happens, we will also know the God of the Bible, and will seek Him daily as well—the result of this is a life transformed, a life renewed, a life passionate about God!

*Following God includes following His Word.*

# OUR BASIS FOR TEACHING
# 3:16 VERSE: 2 TIMOTHY

*"All Scripture is inspired by God and profitable for teaching, for reproof, for correction, for training in righteousness."*

**APPLY** Have you ever read a book that was so good, so intriguing, so enlightening, that you literally could not put it down? You know, your favorite book of all time. What is the name of it?

> There have been many.
> can't remember.

Briefly describe the plot sequence.

> Intense
> Mysterious
> intreaging

What details or descriptive elements kept your attention?

> wondering what was going
> to happen.

Look at your responses to the above questions. I challenge you to look for those same story lines that intrigue you within the pages of Scripture. Interested in murder mysteries? It's in there. Good old-fashioned drama? The Bible's got it. How about comedy scenes? Scripture is full of humanity at its best. Enjoy love and relationship scenarios? It's in there too. More of an action adventure buff? Yep, you guessed it! The Bible has scenes that will capture your attention as well.

The Bible is so much more than an all time bestseller! It can also be the book on our shelf that we pick up and read, over and over. The modern day application of the timeless treasures in Scripture becomes a story that never ends!

To attempt to explain Christ and our life in Him would be useless without explaining the basis for our teaching, which is the Holy Bible. The Holy Spirit leads us through Scripture for a better understanding of what we have read. Those of us who live in the United States are very blessed; we can go in to any number of stores, both Christian and secular, and purchase our own copy of the Bible. In other countries in our world, people do not have such ready access to a Bible, let alone a Bible in their native language. Great efforts are being made to translate and distribute Bibles for each and every tongue and nation. Praise God for His call on the lives of people who have a passion for the provision of the written Word for all peoples!

In past centuries, this luxury of a personal Bible was not there, and people were even willing to put their lives in danger in order to have a copy of the Bible, to print copies, and to read the written Word. God graciously provided scribes and writers who would spend their lives copying the Scriptures over and over again, making Bibles by hand in order that others could have their own copy. After the printing press was invented, there were more Bibles in circulation, but nothing like we have today. The average Christian household has numerous Bibles and often a variety of translations. We as Christians are blessed to have our own Bibles to read and study from.

**APPLY** Think back to the time when you received or purchased your own Bible. Record your thoughts here as well as the date or year that it came into your possession.

*I was gifted mine by my parents when I did profession of faith.*
*bought one w/ Amanda.*

Do you still have that Bible? Have you acquired additional Bibles since that time, and have you spent time studying the Word of God?

*Yes. I have two. Also had one from LC.*
*Yes I try to*

What a memory! The day we received our Bible was the day we received our roadmap for life; our instruction manual for every situation we would face.

With all the variety of translations, it always amazes me how God is able to preserve His Word and guide men and women in the translation of modern English versions, so that the gospel remains protected. Below, we will compare a single verse in three translations to see the types of similarities that can be seen throughout most translations on the market.

📖 Write out Psalm 90:1 in the following translations:

New International Version

*Lord you have been our dwelling place throughout all generations.*

King James Version

*LORD, thou hast been our dwelling place in all generations.*

> **The day we received our Bible was the day we received our roadmap for life; our instruction manual for every situation we would face.**

New American Standard Bible

*Lord you have been our dwelling place in all generations.*

In all three verses we studied here, the Lord has been our dwelling place for all generations. This has been an interesting verse to use as our example, but also a great verse to remember. God is God, and has been God long before our creation. Praise Him for who He is!

In this comparison of Scripture, we witness the similarities between three trusted translations used throughout the world today. While the three we compared are trusted, our best source for Biblical accuracy is found in the original manuscripts and also in the original Greek and Hebrew translations. As we read the Bible, the Holy Sprit will guide us into all truth, revealing God's promises, and protecting the gospel.

In our discovery of different translations, we must be careful. A **paraphrase** is *not* the same as a **translation**. A paraphrase is just that; someone's explanation of Scripture instead of the exact Scriptures themselves. We are closest to the original intent of the authors of Scripture when we study from a translation that is as literal, or close to the original language it was written as possible. The New American Standard Bible (NASB) is a wonderful example of this, and is the translation we have chosen to focus on in this study.

Have you ever considered the fact that Jesus taught the people from the same Old Testament Scriptures that we use today? He was a Jew, and taught in the synagogues and communities where Jewish people lived. He was brought up in a home where the Scriptures were known. Jesus was circumcised on the eighth day, according to the Law, and He was dedicated in the Temple. In fact, we know that Jesus and His family observed the feasts that are outlined in the Old Testament, and we also know that Jesus spent time in the temple as a child.

Read Luke 2:41–52. What happens in this passage? Describe the scene:

*Jesus stayed behind in the temple even after his parents left. He wanted to hear His teachings.*

How old was Jesus?

*twelve*

How many days was it before they found Jesus? Where did they find Him?

*1 traveling, 3 in town. In the temple listening.*

What was He doing there, as referenced in verses 46–47? What is Jesus' response as shown in verse 49?

*Learning God's word and sharing. "He was in God's (His fathers) house"*

*Did You Know?*

**JESUS AT AGE 12**

Jesus at age 12: Boys in the Jewish culture would be prepared for adulthood at age 12. They would experience what we know as "bar mitzvah." With Jesus' special event at hand, we can imagine why Mary was upset by His disappearance. With this scene, we are given a first glimpse at Jesus' role as Messiah, as He stays with the best teachers in the Temple who had congregated for the celebration of Passover.

Even at the age of twelve, as Jesus was beginning to approach manhood, His role as Messiah was being established in their society. In a very subtle way, this scene leaves clues for Jesus' ultimate role on earth, to be with the Father, to share with others the will of the Father, and to "be about His Father's business." Jesus was in the Temple discussing Old Testament Scriptures, not only listening to the teachers, but asking probing questions. Jesus was engaged in conversation with them.

As an adult, Jesus quoted the Old Testament many times; fulfilling prophecy that was given in days long before He came to earth. Compare the following verses.

📖 Read Mark 12:10–11 and write it out below.

> "Haven't you read this passage in the scripture:
> 'The stone the builders rejected has become the
> cornerstone; the Lord has done this, and it is
> Marvelous in our eyes".

Compare this to Psalm 118:22–23:

*The stone which the builders rejected Has become the chief corner stone. This is the LORD'S doing; It is marvelous in our eyes.*

In this account in Mark's Gospel, Christ quotes a part of the Old Testament. He was very effective at taking the very Scriptures that the Jewish rulers and leaders knew and showing them how He was the Messiah they had been looking for. Unfortunately, like in this example (see verse 12), they ultimately rejected Him, rejected the truth, and rejected the marvelous nature of the gift God gave them with His Son.

Do you see how the message of Christ is consistent with the Old Testament, and how He would have been well versed?

_____

_____

_____

Take time right now to pray for God to show you Jesus' presence in the Scriptures of the Old Testament. Pray for clarity and wisdom as you go forward in this study. Praise Him for giving us His Word!

*Did You Know?*

**SEARCHING FOR JESUS**

The family came to Jerusalem to celebrate the Passover, and must have traveled with a large group, or caravan. Because of the number of people, it may have been easy to think that Jesus was with another part of the group they were traveling with. We see that it was three days before Jesus was found in the Temple. In Luke 2:44, we see that the caravan had traveled a day's journey, which would have caused a second day to be needed for the return to town, and the third must have been used looking around the town of Jerusalem.

# MEMORY LANE
# 3:16 VERSE: 2 TIMOTHY

*Powerful Breath* DAY TWO

*All Scripture is inspired by God and profitable for teaching, for reproof, for correction, for training in righteousness.*

When I was a newborn, the church that our family attended gave my mother a Bible for me, six weeks after I came into this world. This is a tradition with many churches, to "start you off right" and celebrate the newborn as God's child. I attended countless Sunday school classes as a child where the very promises in this small Bible were taught and explained. Over the many years of my life, this particular little New Testament Bible has not been used much, but it has always gone with me. I grew, and so did the size of the Bible I carried and studied, but that original gift never lost its sentimental value. The church valued my little life, and I have valued their gift all these years.

📖 Read Luke 18:16. What did Jesus say about the children? Does Jesus value children?

_Do not hinder them_
_Heaven belongs to them._

Even as an adult, being a military wife and moving numerous times, this little white leather book has safely gone in a file box of memories. For some reason, I came across this wonderful gift a while ago, and opened it to the page that the silk bookmark had been resting all these years. That silk bookmark has been resting on the very page of this week's focus verse! Now, not every Bible can say that their little silk ribbon has lain atop the very promise in Scripture that validates that the Scriptures themselves are the breath of God. The more exciting thing in my perception is that this little Bible was kept safe all these years and God knew the very moment I would open it up. He knew the verse HE wanted me to see. I'm sure He smiled to see that I caught His idea.

📖 Look up 2 Timothy 3. Take your time, and read verses 10 through 17. Ponder the meaning of these verses. Think about the power there is in the Word of God. Think about the strength and perseverance that Paul had, as a result of being rooted in the Word of God. Scripture is our basis for truth.

As we look over this entire passage, let's focus on verse 15 first. The whole passage is wonderful, as we will discuss in a minute, but in light of this experience I had with my little white Bible, I have to take the wonder of God one step further.

📖 What does 2 Timothy 3:15 say?

I believe that God knew since the beginning of my life that someday He would ask me to attempt to write this Bible study for Him. Verse 15, in my little Bible (KJV) states

*And that from a child thou hast known the holy scriptures, which are able to make thee wise unto salvation through faith which is in Christ Jesus.*

The New American Standard Bible mentions that it is "from childhood," and the New International Version makes the distinction "from infancy"— what an impact! What a wonderful way to see God's hand in this season in my life. . . . the Bible I received as a child literally pointed to the promise of salvation that has been taught to me since my childhood.

This little Bible has been a tangible example of a life-long relationship with Christ that my mother and father started nurturing in my life almost from the moment I was born. While Bibles hold the same promises, God used this vivid visual reminder of my life to bring this point of Scripture home to me in a very personal way. Those who have grown up in a church family know what they have been taught. They know what they know. When you are certain of who you are and *whose* you are, it is easier to persevere during times of persecution.

 **APPLY** Think about your life. Do you remember when someone shared Christ with you or invited you to church? Who has impacted your life with the message of Christ? Write your thoughts.

_____

_____

_____

_____

_____

_____

Take a minute to thank God for putting people in your life who have shared the message of Christ with you. As you pray, ask Him to show you how you can share Christ with others around you. Thank Him for the gospel and His Word.

📖 Re-read 2 Timothy 3:16. Pray that God would reveal just how strong a promise this verse is to you as a believer. Write the name of someone special that has had an impact on your life with regards to sharing the Bible with you and take a moment to praise God for them.

# THE QUESTION OF HOW
# 3:16 VERSE: 2 TIMOTHY

*All Scripture is inspired by God and profitable for teaching, for reproof, for correction, for training in righteousness*

As we continue to study 2 Timothy 3, the next step to explaining that the Scriptures hold the promise of truth for us is to answer the obvious question of "How?" God so eloquently and unmistakably describes the infallibility of Scripture by answering the question in our focus verse, 2 Timothy 3:16.

**APPLY** Write out 2 Timothy 3:16, and think about it for a moment. How do you feel seeing such a verse as this?

_____

_____

_____

## PAUL AND TIMOTHY

Paul was very fond of one of his fellow missionaries, Timothy. Paul even regarded Timothy as being like a son. Timothy was entrusted with serving the church at Ephesus, and Paul communicated with him formally at least twice in letters about leadership. These two letters are epistles in our New Testament, and bear Timothy's name. The second letter is where we find our focus verse for this week.

*"Theopneustos"* is the Greek term used in the original manuscripts that is translated "inspired" or "given by inspiration of God," and it literally means "God breathed." Paul, a man powerfully used by God in ministry and in writing the Scriptures, describes this passage about the authority of Scripture to his apprentice Timothy as he gives the young man a charge to ministry. The apostle Paul instilled a confidence of the Scriptures in Timothy that applies to our lives as well. Having an understanding of the authority of Scripture is essential for those who disciple others in the word of God, so we will be able to teach from Scripture with assurance that we are sharing trusted and valuable information.

When given a task, do you want to know that what you are doing is based on truth?

_____

_____

What happens if you are representing something that is based on a lie?

_____

_____

_____

Do you see how important it is for us to prove Scripture as truth before we can apply it to our lives?

_____

_____

_____

Have you ever talked with someone who didn't believe that the Bible was true? What was your reaction?

_____

_____

_____

## For some of it to be infallible, it all has to be considered infallible.

If God's Word is **not** infallible (without error), then how can we expect His promise of salvation to be infallible? For some of it to be infallible, it **all** has to be considered infallible. God's word, as written in the original autographs, holds that very status. God's hand of protection has covered the translation process through the ages. Even though modern translations may lack the highest level of accuracy experienced from the original writings, we are still able to learn the truths of God through today's literal translations with confidence, knowing that God, through His Holy Spirit, will lead us into all truth. God is trustworthy, and able to protect His truths even today as they are shared through the written word. With the statement of Divine inspiration given, we can press on with confidence.

As believers in the Word of God, we must believe all truths taught in Scripture, and not just the segments we like. We cannot water down the Word, or omit uncomfortable passages, and claim that we believe the Bible. It just cannot happen. We will have times in our lives where people challenge our convictions and our intensity for defending the integrity of the

Scriptures. We must be ready to give an account for why we believe, and who we believe in. God is honest, consistent, faithful, and true. There is nothing false about Him, so we can press on in any situation knowing that God and His Word is trustworthy.

📖 Read Numbers 23:19. Write the verse here.

_____

_____

_____

What does this tell you about God? Is He honest?

_____

_____

_____

Yes! God is honest, and does not change His mind. God knows who He is, and what He wants us to know. He has made sure to include everything He wants us to know in Scripture, and has given us the Bible as our guide to Christianity, and how to apply it to our lives.

Take a moment to pray to the Lord, thanking Him for His honesty and His character. Thank Him for giving us His Word, and for leading us to the truth of the Bible. Re-read 2 Timothy 3:16, and commit it to memory.

> **For the Word of God to be true, God must be honest, and without any misleading nature about Him.**

*Powerful Breath*  DAY FOUR

# THE FUNCTION OF SCRIPTURE
# 3:16 VERSE: 2 TIMOTHY

*All Scripture is inspired by God and profitable for teaching, for reproof, for correction, for training in righteousness*

So we know that Scripture is the truth, and that it came directly from God's inspiration, but now what? What is the function of Scripture? With Paul's concern to Timothy, the 2 Timothy 3:16 verse begins with the explanation of inspiration, and continues with the function of Scripture. Yes, it is "God breathed" as the New International Version states, but what is the rest of its relevance? Scripture is not only a book of historical events, law, and parables; it is our "Christian instruction manual." Much like our new car's manual, there are explanations and requirements in the pages that are critical for maintaining our relationship, and understanding the "why" and "how" of its purpose, and our responsibility to it.

 Have you ever needed to look at an instruction manual for reference on how to repair or maintain the life of something? Think about this in relation to the Bible as our guide, and record your thoughts.

_____

_____

Paul describes this relationship that Timothy and all Christians should have with the Holy Scriptures. 2 Timothy 3:16 teaches us that the passages of the Bible are used for reproof, correction, and training in righteousness. The New International Version states that God's Word is "useful for teaching, rebuking, correcting, and training." Instruction is the basis to growth, and as we study the Bible, we will certainly grow as Christians.

Let's look at the distinct areas mentioned by Paul in this verse.

*Reproof (teaching)*: This is a term that is used to show the benefit of believing, as well as the warnings of disobedience. The purpose of reproof is to bring about persuasion in the area of the teaching, to change the heart of the ones being taught so that they see the benefit of their new mindset. This type of reproof can be thought of as boundary setting. Through the teaching of the Bible, we see the ways in which we should follow the Lord, and the ways in which we should live. We learn how to live a Christ-like life.

Take time to write a journal entry concerning the types of reproof you have experienced through your times of studying the Bible.

_____

_____

_____

_____

_____

_____

_____

_____

_____

*Correction (rebuking)*: Correction or a rebuke in some area of our life is not meant to condemn us, but rather to set us on the right course again; to make us turn back to the right path for our lives. This term is only used in this verse, and refers to the sanctification process we go through as believers—or the process of becoming more Christ-like.

How have you become more Christ-like since you accepted Jesus as your Savior? Has God corrected you in some way—in regards to past behavior or sinful habits? Describe:

_____

_____

_____

*Training in Righteousness (training)*: This term involves teaching, and if necessary, correction, with the intention of bringing forth righteous living in the one being corrected. It is through this term we see how a godly life, based on the Scriptures, will be a disciplined life. Not a legalistic life built on restrictions and limitations conjured up by man; but rather, the adherence to the will of God as seen through the Bible, and His commands as spelled out in Scripture. It is through the correction from the Word that we live a life based on the Word.

When the second letter to Timothy was written, the New Testament had not been written and compiled as a single compilation. The Scriptures that Paul mostly refers to here are the Old Testament Books that they would have already had in scrolls. This confirms the fact to us today that the Old Testament is relevant under the teachings of Jesus. While we, who have the New Testament, focus on Jesus, we must never downplay the importance of the Old Testament as well. The two testaments become one Bible, showing the complete story of God's interaction with man, and His provision of our Savior, Jesus Christ of Nazareth.

**APPLY** Looking at your life, can you see how you have grown as you have implemented the principles outlined in the Bible to your life?

_____

_____

_____

In the *Complete Word Study Dictionary: New Testament,* Spiros Zodhiates writes the following about the terms used in 2 Timothy 3:16:

> First of all, the word of God is presented as doctrine (*didaskalia* [1319]), instruction, authoritative teaching, i.e., truth. Secondly, as truth it is ethically persuasive (*elegchos* [1650], proof, conviction) convincing us of our error. Third, it then places us in a correct moral posture. Fourthly, the word of God continues to provide discipline (*paideia* [3809], training, discipline, chastisement) in righteousness. (613)

The focus verse for this week, 2 Timothy 3:16 is one of the most wonderful verses we have to build ourselves up in the truth. While it confirms the authority of Scripture, it also shares the transformational power that the Word of God has on one who studies and lives by it. Through living a life based on the Bible, we live a life based on God. Christ lived a life based on God's will, and He obeyed the Scriptures as well. In turn, as we follow God's will, His commands, and the Scriptures, and surrender to the Holy Spirit's leading, we will follow the example of Jesus Christ, and our lives will become more Christ-like.

Although a church setting is critical to one's life in Christ, the Holy Spirit is also effectively able to instruct us through the verses and promises in Scripture. There is no question or situation in life that cannot be solved through the study of the Word of God. The passages that we have access to will either directly relate to all we will potentially endure, or they will at least give insight to any modern day application for our lives.

Verse 17 conveys this with saying, *"so that the man of God may be thoroughly equipped for every good work."* God would not expect us to use the Bible as our source of teaching, through the Holy Spirit, without providing all we would need. God's goal in our lives is to teach us His ways and to totally equip us to go forth and teach others His ways.

God provides salvation to all who accept it, and this salvation gives us access to eternal life through the shed blood of Jesus Christ. We are saved (provided salvation) in order to worship God, to show His glory in our lives to others, and to teach others His ways. We do not have a selfish faith; our faith should be evident to all, and should impact the lives around us.

Conviction is a wonderful way that the Holy Spirit is leading us through the Bible. It is incredible how we can see our sin, and the sin of others jump off of the pages as we read the requirements of holy living, and the expectations God has for His children. Right next to the sin of murder, we find the sins of gossip and lust. A good friend of mine has said, "sin doesn't have a point system." In other words, sin is sin, and there are none that are less sinful than others. That's enough to make all of us think twice about our "perfect" lives!

We will have a life-long challenge of becoming more Christ-like—and *no one* ever finishes the process here on earth! We all have a long way to go, so

*". . . that the man of God may be adequate, equipped for every good work."*

**2 Timothy 3:17**

don't ever feel like you are not as good a Christian as the next person just because there is still growth that needs to occur. We are all inferior to Christ, and He is the only one we strive to be like, not the "Super Christian" at church. That's why there are Scriptures such as the following:

*for all have sinned and fall short of the glory of God* (Romans 3:23)

Even in our shortcomings, we have a Savior that will carry us through and bridge the gap we find ourselves faced with.

How has God convicted you of wrongdoing? What did it feel like?

_____

_____

_____

When conviction has hit our hearts, discipline is not far behind. Our God and Creator will not condemn us, nor will He convict us without showing us the consequences of our actions. Throughout the pages of the Bible we read about numerous characters that have done less than spiritual things, and have reaped the consequences for their actions.

📖 Read 2 Samuel 11:1–5. What did David do?

_____

_____

📖 Read 2 Samuel 11:6–27. What was David's reaction to the situation with Bathsheba?

_____

_____

_____

📖 Read 2 Samuel 12:1–15. What happened between Nathan and David?

_____

_____

_____

Even David, the man after God's own heart, was faced with punishment because of a springtime fling with a girl on a rooftop. If he had only been off at war, like the rest of the warriors, he wouldn't have found himself in such a tempting situation. Once again, God allows us to have a clear glimpse of what will happen to us when we sin—with just about every scenario spelled out for us. He leaves no stone unturned! So even when He reveals our inadequacies, He has already provided the solution. Praise God for His mercy toward our inequities and the gift of forgiveness and salvation.

With discipline given, should we expect God to leave us twisting in the wind? Absolutely not! God will always instruct us and train us as we grow in Him. His goal of conviction and discipline is not to act as a mean-spirited God who loves to strike mere mortals to their knees! He allows situations and choices that we make to have consequences so we will desire to be more Christ-like, as we confess sin and mend our ways through the transforming

*Extra Mile*
## GREAT COMMISSION

Read Matthew 28:19–20. These verses are often referred to as the Great Commission. We are charged with the same duty that the disciples were given that day. God wants us to share the message of Christ with others. He wants us to be a light in the world for Him. This is an honor and a privilege, to be entrusted with sharing the gospel with others. Basically, the Great Commission simply states that as we know Scripture and the message of Christ, we are to share it with others.

power of the Holy Spirit. God's desire for every one of us is to bring us into right relationship with Him.

Romans 8:28 states very clearly that

> …*we know that God causes all things to work together for good to those who love God, to those who are called according to His purpose.*

God's goal for our lives is for all of us to worship and obey Him, and to ultimately join Him in His kingdom. It is up to us to accept His offer of salvation, and once we do, it is our job to allow the Spirit to grow us in our understanding of His Word and guidelines. We are to surrender daily in order to maintain the relationship that we started when we initially chose to believe in Christ and welcome Him into our hearts. Salvation is not just a one-time thing—it's a lifetime thing!

*Salvation is not just a one time thing; it's a lifetime thing!*

# FOR ME TO FOLLOW GOD

*Powerful Breath* — DAY FIVE

Now that we know that the Bible is truth and inspired by God, and that God is honest, how do we apply it to our lives? Scripture will teach us, rebuke us, train us, and correct us, but what is our part of the deal? The truth in Scripture should keep us from sin, and keep us living godly lives—if we apply what we read to our own situations.

How does reading the Bible keep us from sin? Well, with continuous study, and a reliance on God's promises for every aspect of our life, we can confidently claim the following verse,

> *How sweet are Thy words* [Scripture] *to my taste! Yes, sweeter than honey to my mouth! From Thy precepts I get understanding; Therefore I hate every false way* (Psalm 119:103–104—bracketed word added).

With this passage we see that as we understand what God has told us in His Word, we will find the instruction sweet, not bitter, and worth following! When we follow God's will for our lives, we will naturally gravitate away from all that is not of God, and will find ourselves staying on the right path, God's path for our life. To truly obey God, we will stay as far from sin as we can. The book of Haggai in the Old Testament has a wonderful passage about "catching sin."

*"You can't catch holiness, but you can catch sin!"*

📖 Read Haggai 2:10–13. What was the issue that Haggai brought up? What was the response of the priests?

_____

_____

When the priests were asked about their own law, the discussion became a learning lesson from the Lord. They were asked what would happen if something holy was wrapped in a garment, and it brushed up against something sinful—would it cleanse the sin? Well, of course not! The other side of the question was different though. When something that was defiled, or sinful, brushed up against something clean, it would cause the clean thing to become sinful.

This example showed the priests by their own law that you cannot brush up against something and be holy—you can't catch holiness; but by the same process, you could indeed "catch" sin. Sin is contagious, and affects all who come into contact with it.

**APPLY** Have you ever been around others engaging in a sinful activity, while you tried to stay away from the sin? Did you wind up sinning as a result of their presence?

_____

_____

_____

_____

How did the situation and your choices impact your life?

_____

_____

_____

On the other hand, have you ever expected others to "do your faith" for you? What was the result?

_____

_____

_____

We are responsible for building our personal relationship with Christ. The relationship our parents have had with the Lord won't automatically make us a believer, nor will our unrepentant hearts be cleansed without repentance. We must remain distanced from the temptation of sin around us, stay on the right path, and seek God's will for our lives.

This passage in Haggai gives us a useful example for our lives today. We must watch out for those times when we might be tempted to "brush up" against sin—it's enough to dirty our whole faith walk!

**A Final Word on Authority and Scripture:**
There will always be those individuals who insist that the Bible is just a clever collection of stories that mere men wrote down for posterity, and that they are useful for history—but not for authority. There are countless books that go into extreme detail about the preservation of Scripture, the process of canonization, and the "living" aspects of the Word of God. Authors of these books come to one clear conclusion: there is no way that mere man could have written and preserved Scriptures in such a miraculous way. The Bible has not only been on the best-seller list, it has remained the best-selling book over all times and generations.

📖 Read Psalm 33. Write down Psalm 33:11 below.

_____

_____

_____

Can you see how God has preserved His Word over the ages?

_____

_____

_____

Do you see the timelessness of Scripture, and God's plan for our lives?

_____

_____

_____

> ## "The counsel of the Lord stands forever, The plans of His heart from generation to generation."
>
> ## Psalm 33:11

The Bible is THE Book! God's promise to us, and His truth have remained firm forever, and His purposes have been the same throughout all generations. He wants us to know Him and know His ways for us. Just as Moses was given the written Word on stone tablets, we are given the written Word of God in the Holy Bible. We are to treasure it as they did, giving it a place of honor and authority in our lives that is second to nothing else. Although the Israelites placed their sacred tablets in the ark, we are privileged enough to own and study our very own copy of God's promises. Scripture was written to be read and applied to our lives, not to collect dust on a shelf!

The Christian church began with one denomination, consisting of Jesus, twelve apostles, and the crowds that followed. Like the first Christians, we are to follow the complete, unadulterated teaching of Christ. We are to follow the teachings of Christ first and foremost.

No man or religious institution can mandate what God would and would not have intended us to follow. His Word is clear about what is to be considered without flaw and completely inspired! The original writings of Scripture that have always been infallible remain infallible. I encourage you to investigate this issue further in your own study time.

Go discover and explore God's Word. The Holy Spirit will reveal the truth to your heart. At the end of the day, remember that we are one body in Christ, and His example is what each and every Christian should follow! Praise God for His Word!

**APPLY** Think about the Bible, and all you have learned this week. Is your opinion different? Is your respect and impression of Scriptures more solid now that we have taken a deeper look? Record your thoughts.

_____

_____

_____

_____

_____

_____

_____

_____

*Lord,* I know that you are God. I thank You for giving me the opportunity to study Your Word, and apply it to my life. I thank You for our infallible guide, the Bible. I pray that You will reveal Your truths to me in increasing measure, and that I would understand You more. Thank You, God, for using the Scriptures to teach me, rebuke me, train me, and correct my life. I pray that You would use me and allow me to share Your Word with others. Lord, forgive me for the times I have not defended Your truth when others have blasphemed You; I will defend You now. Thank You for being my dwelling place through all generations. Thank You for those You have placed in my path to minister to me and share Your Word. Lord, I pray that You would continue to use Your Word and those who have faith in You to bring others into Your kingdom. Thank You God, for creating the world and our lives, and thank You for sending Your Son as a sacrifice for my sin. In Jesus' name, Amen.

## *Works Cited*

Spiros Zodhiates, ed., *The Complete Word Study Dictionary: New Testament* (Chattanooga, TN: AMG Publishers, 1993), page 613.

# TWO

# Deep Roots

## SEEING CHRIST IN THE OLD TESTAMENT

## 3:16 VERSE: GALATIANS

Now that we have studied the authenticity and authority of Scripture, we can move forward, studying the truths of Scripture; trusting the source, the concepts, and the application to our lives. All Scripture is useful, and all Scripture leads us to a better understanding of Jesus and our relationship with Him. I am excited to be able to share with you some of the most wonderful references to Christ we have in the Old Testament. He has been present throughout history, and He has always been one third of the Holy Trinity. **Jesus is, was, and always will be!** He is the Alpha and Omega, the beginning and the end.

In this week's focus verse, we see reference to a great man of God named Abraham, and the Son of God, named Jesus. What we know of these men (one man; one fully God while fully man) inspire all of us to be obedient to God in all things, and dependent on Him for all guidance. Do you realize just how much God intertwined the foreshadowing of Jesus Christ into His interaction with Abraham and the people of Abraham's time? Prepare your heart and mind through prayer to receive a deeper insight to just how perfect God's plan of salvation through the shed blood of Jesus Christ is.

*Do you realize just how much God intertwined the foreshadowing of Jesus Christ into his interaction with Abraham and the people of Abraham's time?*

*Deep Roots*

# GOD CALLS ABRAM
# 3:16 VERSE: GALATIANS

*"Now the promises were spoken to Abraham and to his seed. He does not say 'And to seeds,' as referring to many, but rather to one, 'And to your seed,' that is, Christ."*

The Old Testament is absolutely full of amazing accounts of people encountering God. Whether they experienced God's wrath or God's blessing, they discovered that God was unequaled and unrivaled in power. Yet during the time of Abraham, not many people had close fellowship with God. Not many were specifically called by God to do great things. Abraham was different. He was chosen, and he was obedient. Before the foundation of the world, God chose Abraham to be an integral part of the lineage of Christ.

Abraham was an ordinary man whom God used in extraordinary ways. When we first read about him in the Bible, his name is Abram (changed later by God to Abraham), and he settles with his father Terah, his nephew Lot, and his wife Sarai (changed later by God to "Sarah"). They had been traveling to Canaan, but Abram's father decides that they would settle in a place called Haran. Abram's father Terah dies there in Haran at the age of 205. After his father's death, while living in Haran with his family, Abram hears from God, and his life is forever changed.

📖 Read Genesis 12:1–5. What did the Lord say to Abram?

_____

_____

_____

## THE ABRAHAMIC COVENANT

*"Go forth from your country, and from your relatives and from your father's house, to the land which I will show you; and I will make you a great nation, and I will bless you, and make your name great; and so you shall be a blessing; and I will bless those who bless you, and the one who curses you I will curse. and in you all the families of the earth shall be blessed." (Genesis 12:1–3)*

The Lord sure told Abram to leave his "comfort zone" didn't He? Not only did Abram need to leave his country, but his people too! Abram didn't know where he was going; he only knew that he was to go where God would show him. And he did. Abram took his wife, his nephew, and his household, and off he went to follow God.

🛑 APPLY · Has God ever asked you to leave your "comfort zone"? What did it feel like, and what challenges did you have to tackle?

_____

_____

_____

_____

Leaving all that is comfortable can be a good thing when it is what God has for you! God promised Abram that he would be blessed, he would have a great name, and he would be made into a "great nation" (Genesis 12:2). Blessings awaited him as he obediently went as God directed. Abram separated from Lot, and he and his wife Sarai followed the call on his life.

At this point in Abram's life, when he had separated from his relative Lot, the two men split the land around them among themselves. Abram let Lot have first choice of the land, and Lot chose the portion more pleasing to the eye, and brimming with activity. Lot chose Sodom, which as we know was laden with sinful actions and sinful people. While Lot was having fun in Sodom, Abram was serving and praising his God in the land that God ordained for him to spend his days. Lot was after the good land that had all the luxuries and was willing to overlook the sin. Abram, who had every right to claim the best for himself, humbly allowed Lot to take his pick of the acreage and then figured out where he would live after that. Abram wanted nothing to do with the sinful area of Sodom—he wanted to live in an area that was pleasing to God. God spared Abram from the sinful situation by empowering him to be humble enough to let the land go to Lot. Lot would suffer his own consequences for his decision, and we will look into these events during another time of study together. God had a bigger plan, one that could not be established by a decision of any man. God's purposes are truly divine and truly wonderful. God connected Abram way back on that day in Canaan to the promise of salvation through Jesus Christ.

**APPLY** If you had the choice between the land that looked good or the land that pleased God, which would you choose? Why, and what do you think the result of that choice would be?

_____

_____

_____

_____

Many challenges and blessings awaited Abram as he followed God. From jumping ahead of God with his wife and trying to start a family according to their own logic, to being tested about giving up his son, to finding his son a wife—Abram had many decisions to make, and sometimes he was better at believing God's promises than at other times. Regardless, Abram was a man who experienced intense and in-depth fellowship with the Lord. He may not have had all the answers from God at the moment he wanted them, but Abram had the faith to know that God would fulfill all the promises in His time.

📖 Read Genesis 15:5–6. What did God say to Abram, and what was the result?

_____

_____

_____

What a promise God gave Abram! His offspring would be as numerous as the stars in the sky, yet he had no children at this point. Abram believed the Lord's promise, and his faith was *"credited to him as righteousness."* This is the type of faith that God looks for in us—the type of faith that believes Him even when God's promises seem impossible.

Abram asked God how this long line of offspring would happen, and God's response was to make a covenant with him. What a glorious scene this is my friend! God not only allows Abram to ask an honest question, but God goes on to prove His point with a lasting covenant. He asks Abram to bring the

*Abraham's faith is the type of faith that God looks for in us—the type of faith that believes Him even when God's promises seem impossible.*

sacrificial animals, long before the sacrificial system in the law is spelled out to Moses, and God has Abram prepare the animals. Usually a covenant between two parties encompassed two people walking through the blood of the sacrifice in agreement, but in this case, Abram was put into a deep sleep by God, and **God Himself** made the covenant, proving that it was contingent on God fulfilling it alone. *Abram was a part of it, but God would fulfill it.*

God explained to Abram that hardships would come to his descendants as well as victories. This covenant was God's vow of commitment to Abram that He would do what He said He would do. God revealed to Abram that He was a God that could be trusted and that what he promised would eventually come to pass. Please read through this beautiful scene in Genesis 15. The magnitude of God walking through a covenant for us is simply breathtaking. Picture the scene! Picture the love of God for this man, and for his lineage—and for us.

📖 Read Genesis 15:18–20. What does God promise to Abram?

_____

_____

_____

Abram knew who His God was and was willing to do and go wherever the Lord led him. He knew that his descendants would inherit many blessings and much land. Abram beat the odds of the world and was given a picture that surpassed any thing he knew in his generation, and the blessings would follow his lifetime and forever. He was the man God used to show the world how to be blessed in the long term and how to be content *without* gaining the blessing solely for self. Abram would never live long enough to see much of the blessing promised to him. In fact, he never personally owned an inch of the land God promised!

📖 Read and memorize Galatians 3:16. What does the word "seed" refer to?

_____

_____

_____

> "On that day the LORD made a covenant with Abram, saying, 'To your descendants I have given this land.'"
>
> **Genesis 15:18**

*Deep Roots*

# ABRAM, A FATHER OF MANY NATIONS
# 3:16 VERSE: GALATIANS

*"Now the promises were spoken to Abraham and to his seed. He does not say 'And to seeds,' as referring to many, but rather to one, 'And to your seed,' that is, Christ."*

Even with this amazing promise of God, Abram and his wife fell into the trap that many of us do; they tried to jump ahead of God and make things happen in their own strength. After the blessing and the land, Abram and his wife took this "child issue" into their own hands. After all, Abram had to live up to the name God had given him! Who would believe Abram was an "exalted father" without any children of his own; without someone to inherit the family blessing? Doesn't it just make you shake your head in amazement to see so blatantly how our impatience and hasty decisions can compete against God's blessing?

📖 What happens in Genesis 16:1–5?

_____

_____

Abram's first son, Ishmael, was the son of an agreement made between two women in a household, his wife Sarah and a servant named Hagar. Sarah agreed to allow Hagar to have her husband's child, and then wondered why she had trouble dealing with the outcome. Who can really understand that one? Sounds more like a TV talk show topic these days, doesn't it? God's plans still stood firm, even with this turn of events. Hagar gave birth to her son, and named him Ishmael. Abram becomes a father, but only a father to a natural son, *not* a son who carried the promise of God! Oh, how merciful God is when we jump ahead of Him. He continues on the path He has for us, instituting ways for His truths to be consistent and applicable.

📖 Read Genesis 17:1–8. What does God promise Abram? What changes?

_____

_____

_____

God changed Abram's name, which means "exalted father" to Abraham which means "father of many nations," showing Abram the promise in a deeper meaning long before he could see the impact he would have upon multitudes of people on the earth. Even as a man without children, and eventually a man with one heir, God showed Abram that HE knew what He had planned for Abraham, even if the world around him couldn't tell by human standards. This was more than a promise of lots of kids, this was a *spiritual promise*; a lineage that would carry the promise of God.

The scene we see in Genesis 17 is incredible! With one visit from God, Abram and Sarai get new names, Abraham and Sarah. God institutes the covenant of circumcision (verses 9–14), and they receive the promise from God that they will be expecting a son—whom they will name Isaac—a son who would carry the promise and the established covenant of God with him. Of course Sarah laughs at the thought of having a child at their age, and the Lord corrects her for her disbelief. Meanwhile Abraham has his sight on the lasting implication of the family line. What an overwhelming moment for Abraham! God was again promising that He would do just as He promised—in His way, and in His time.

📖 Before we leave this passage, look up Genesis 17:17–22. Notice Abraham's reaction to God. Now compare this with Genesis 18:10–15. What is the difference in their reactions to God? What is the difference in God's reaction to them?

_____

_____

_____

*Abram went from being a childless husband, to the husband with a child out of wedlock (conceived with his servant, Hagar), to the "Father of Many Nations."*

Abraham hears God's promise and while worshiping God, he responds with a faith-filled question and request for blessing. Abraham is focused on the generational implication of this promise from God. Sarah, on the other hand, is hung up on natural circumstances, laughing in disbelief of God, and is corrected for her response to God. We will talk about this moment again in Lesson 4, so commit this scene to your hearts and minds!

Now, work on committing Galatians 3:16 to memory.

*Deep Roots*    DAY THREE

# ABRAHAM'S OBEDIENCE
# 3:16 VERSE: GALATIANS

*"Now the promises were spoken to Abraham and to his seed. He does not say 'And to seeds,' as referring to many, but rather to one, 'And to your seed,' that is, Christ."*

Abraham's first son, Ishmael, came as the result of impatience concerning God's promise. Ishmael, while blessed by God, would never experience the benefit of God's covenant with Abraham. God made another covenant with Abraham and his family line; the covenant of circumcision. Abraham, Ishmael, and all of the men of Abraham's household were circumcised on the same day that Abraham heard from God about this covenant. Ishmael was thirteen years old at the time of his circumcision.

It is critical to see that this covenant was established **after** Ishmael was born, but **before** his next son, Isaac was conceived—making Isaac the true first-born son of Abraham under this covenant with God. In her old age, Sarah gave birth to Isaac, the son recognized by God, just as God had said.

Isaac was the child of promise who held the covenant of God. When Isaac had grown up into a young man, God asked Abraham to do something that would seem impossible to him or anyone else!

📖 Read Genesis 22:1–2. What was the request that God made of Abraham?

_____

_____

Abraham was supposed to sacrifice his "only" son (Genesis 22:2), even though he had fathered two at this point. How did the father of two get asked by God to sacrifice his "only" son? God wanted to test Abraham, and Ishmael was sent off with his mom awhile before. With Ishmael out of the picture, Isaac was the only son Abraham had left. There was no "backup" child for inheritance. There was no second chance at blessing. This was it. Isaac was Abraham's only hope, and God could see what Abraham was really made of, on the inside—in his heart. God told Abraham to take Isaac up to a mountaintop and put him on an altar of sacrifice. Even though Abraham was fully obedient, holding nothing back, do you ever wonder if he was tempted to think up an emergency plan to bring a lamb "just in

## Did You Know?

**THE COVENANT OF CIRCUMCISION**

God made a covenant with Abraham and those with him, and the outward proof of this covenant was the circumcision of all males. This would be a sign of their being included in the inheritance of Abraham. This covenant featured the shedding of blood, like other covenants, and was something to be observed until the Messiah arrived. God instituted this covenant <u>after</u> Ishmael was born, but <u>before</u> Isaac was conceived—making Isaac truly the first-born son of this promise. Read more about this covenant in Genesis 17.

## Extra Mile

**CIRCUMCISION**

Read more about the covenant of circumcision in Genesis 17.

case"? We might have been persuaded to do everything as asked, but wouldn't we mentally run "plan B" through our heads for backup?

They had three days to travel; three days for Abraham to chicken out. There were others traveling with Abraham and Isaac, and do you think they knew what was in the works? Abraham surely didn't tell everyone what God had said, but don't you think the attendants were puzzled to discover they were journeying to a place of worship with no animal to put on the altar? Isaac certainly had no idea what was going on. The men traveled to their destination with the exact supplies needed—except for the sacrificial lamb of course.

📖 What does Abraham say to his servants in Genesis 22:5?

_____

_____

Here Abraham tells the helpers that they are going to the mountaintop to "worship" God (Genesis 22:5). This was the first reference to worship in the Bible—and worship in its truest form is giving all you have and are to the Lord you serve. Abraham knew that God would prevail in the situation, no matter what that would mean for him and his family. Here was a man of God so sure of the Lord's power, might, and provision that Abraham was even able to tell the servants that *"we will worship and return to you"* (Genesis 22:5, emphasis added). No overwhelming sense of loss, no obvious reference to the fact that Abraham may have to return without an heir. Abraham had confidence in God and confidence in God's provision. Now that's faith!

What if Abraham experienced doubt? What would the negative thoughts entail? What would those around him say when they learned that he again was fatherless—when his name is Abraham ("father of many nations")? It didn't matter. At that point, only complete obedience was on his mind. When we look at this passage in Scripture, we see that Isaac even helped carry supplies, placing the wood on his back, and carrying it up the mountainside. Isaac carried the wood that would be the vehicle for his impending death. Does this scenario ring a bell about another Son that was sacrificed in obedience to the Father in the New Testament? Isn't God great at giving us parallels to help us understand (in the tiniest measure) in our human minds what He must go through when He acts on our behalf.

So, there they went up the mountain, and the altar had to be made. The altar was to be created out of earth, so that nothing man created would have a part in it; no tool would cut the stone, only the hands God made for man shaped the altar out of the dirt God created. And the dirt is the material God used to make Adam, remember?

> *Then the Lord God formed man of dust from the ground, and breathed into his nostrils the breath of life; and man became a living being* (Genesis 2:7).

So again, what God created with, He is able to use to honor Him, and bring sacrifice to Him. Only God's creation is pure and worthy of giving to the Creator as worship. There are no idols, no praise, and no glory placed in honor of anyone but God himself.

What happened when Abraham was ready to sacrifice Isaac? Summarize Genesis 22:9–14.

_____

_____

*As Isaac carried the wood that would have been the vehicle for his death, Jesus helped carry the wood for His sacrifice—the cross.*

**GENESIS 22:5–6**

"'I and the lad will go yonder; and we will worship and return to you.' And Abraham took the wood of the burnt offering and laid it on Isaac his son, and he took in his hand the fire and the knife. So the two of them walked on together."

As we know from this account in the Bible, Isaac was laid on the altar, and God spared Abraham the pain of losing his only son by providing a ram in the thicket. There was a substitute. Abraham and his faith in God were proven strong once again. Abraham knew his God, and God was pleased with Abraham. And this wonderful man is the first in line of a blessing thru generations that point not to Isaac, nor Abraham, nor anything they could see in their midst. That blessing points to Christ. This potential sacrifice of a son of covenant, an only son, sets the stage for what we would see God give us in the person of Jesus Christ, the Messiah, much later in time.

Continue to memorize Galatians 3:16. Thank God for sending His Son as the Seed of Abraham.

*Deep Roots*

# ABRAHAM'S SEED
# 3:16 VERSE: GALATIANS

*"Now the promises were spoken to Abraham and to his seed. He does not say 'And to seeds,' as referring to many, but rather to one, 'And to your seed,' that is, Christ."*

There is *so* much to discover about Abraham that we haven't yet addressed. My prayer is that you will continue to dive into the Word of God every day, and that God will reveal His truths to you on every page. You should know by now that the focus verse we are looking at this week is in Galatians, and that this verse deals with Abraham's seed. To understand this passage in the New Testament, we have gone through a little background on Abraham, and now we will take a moment to compare passages with specific references that relate to "his seed" in the Old Testament.

📖 What does Genesis 12:7 say?

_____

_____

📖 Now, record what Genesis 13:15 tells us.

_____

_____

📖 Finally, write out what Genesis 24:7 states.

_____

_____

What is the common thread in these three verses?

_____

_____

_____

**"For all the land which you see, I will give to you and to your descendants forever."**

**Genesis 13:15**

In our focus verse of this week, we see very clearly that the promise made to Abram carried a timeline that far surpassed Old Testament days. This was not a promise of immediate return. There was no way for Abram to know what would happen in the future, but He knew that God promised *"all the land that you see I will give to you and your offspring forever"* (Genesis 13:15 NIV). The Hebrew word for "offspring" can also be translated "seed." Here is a blessing that God gave Abraham that would span far beyond his wildest imagination. His lineage, his family line, would go thru eternity. His offspring would have an eternal impact. His offspring would last forever. Abram took God at His word, and knew that the blessing was immeasurable to any human standards.

Many of us already know of the concept of the word "seed" referring to your children or your bloodline. Think for a moment about those paper seed packets at the store with the beautiful pictures on the cover of luscious foliage and produce. Once you open the back flaps, all you find are little hard specks, and lots of them. It is hard to imagine what they will look like after they have been placed in the ground and cultivated. The purpose of those specks is to become the beautiful creations pictured on the cover of the envelope. They *will* become what their "family tree" is made of, and they will be like the others in the packet—whether it seems that way when they are mere seeds or not!

Do you think Abraham could have fathomed exactly what God was up to on that day of blessing?

_____

_____

Again, it truly didn't matter at that moment if Abraham "got it," because he had faith in His God, and that was enough! He had no idea that the Messiah would come from his family line—but God did. Oh, that we would have the faith Abraham had!

How rich the text is in our Galatians passage! The entire epistle is amazing, as is every word and concept in the Bible. But concerning our study of Abraham and his Seed, this passage in Galatians 3 is powerful and explains so much. Paul has just openly opposed Peter (in Galatians 2) because Peter had been asking Gentiles to follow Jewish customs. Remember in Day Three, our discussion of the covenant of circumcision? This is the issue that had come up among the apostles; those who were circumcised, and those who weren't, and the impression of inferiority of those who did not have the signs of circumcision. Peter was afraid of what "others would say" (the religious bullies around him) if they saw him sitting with Gentiles, and he separated himself from the Gentiles in order to please those from the "circumcision group." What a perfect picture of peer pressure! Scary to think that after all they had been through, walking with Christ, that the religious elite would have any hold over him. But look on! The more exciting part of this little tidbit of Scripture is Paul's response.

📖 Read Galatians 2:20, and summarize it here:

_____

_____

_____

*Abram took God at His word, and knew that the blessing was immeasurable to any human standards.*

Amazing, isn't it? Christ is the point of every discussion Paul has, and here, he makes the point that we look to Christ, not to our own works. Paul sure doesn't mince words, does he? Read the first three verses of Galatians 3 with me:

> "You foolish Galatians, who has bewitched you, before whose eyes Jesus Christ was publicly portrayed as crucified? This is the only thing I want to find out from you: did you receive the Spirit by the works of the Law, or by hearing with faith? Are you so foolish? Having begun by the Spirit, are you now being perfected by the flesh?"

Wow! Imagine what would happen if we sent someone a letter with those words today! Not exactly politically correct, huh? Paul was really hitting them hard, wasn't he? But his scolding was not for any other purpose but to bring them into a closer relationship with Jesus their Savior.

📖 Read Galatians 3:6–7. What are the Galatians reminded of in verse 6?

_____

_____

_____

How did that relate to them in verse 7?

_____

_____

_____

📖 Now read verses 8 and 9. Who is blessed along with Abraham?

_____

_____

_____

Paul goes on to explain how the law is a curse, and that Christ became a curse for us, redeeming us from the law so that by faith we could receive the promise given to Abraham. Simply overwhelming, isn't it? **We all should be** taken back with the realization that God loved us so much that Christ and the purpose God had for His death on the cross was in motion before the world began, and long before Abraham ever heard God's voice. God is the God of truth, and He follows through with what He says He will do. Praise Him for His faithfulness!

Why are we a part of this promise that was made to Abraham? Paul reminds us that, *"He redeemed us in order that the blessing given to Abraham might come to the Gentiles through Christ Jesus, so that by faith we might receive the promise of the Spirit"* (Galatians 3:14, NIV).

Paul uses Abraham as an example to teach the Galatians how to see the type of obedience God is looking for. Through Abraham's decision, we see an "example from every day life" (verse 15, NIV) that shows us that our obedience to God also gives honor to God and to Jesus Christ. Paul was showing them Christ in an Old Testament context that they surely would understand—whether they were Jew or Gentile.

## GALATIANS 3:13–14

"Christ redeemed us from the curse of the Law, having become a curse for us— for it is written, 'CURSED IS EVERYONE WHO HANGS ON A TREE'—in order that in Christ Jesus the blessing of Abraham might come to the Gentiles, so that we might receive the promise of the Spirit through faith." (Galatians 3:13–14)

This week we have learned so much about God making covenants with Abraham and his descendants. All of that detail is **key** to understanding why the instruction to the Galatians is so important. They were trying to run back to the old ways of the law and were missing the point of the gospel and of Christ's gift of salvation through His once-for-all sacrifice.

📖 What was the warning in Galatians 3:15?

_____

_____

Paul wanted the people of Galatia to know that a covenant was binding, whether human or with God, and such agreements could not be "set aside" or changed after the fact. Any contract made would be binding and wouldn't be forgotten just because other things were agreed to as well. This was true for the covenants with Abraham as well.

As we read on into verse 16, we see that the "seed" mentioned in Galatians 3:16 is a single Seed; the Seed *"that is Christ."* The fulfillment of the covenant with Abraham is found in Christ. God made a promise to bless Abraham and to bless us with a relationship with Christ at the same time.

Paul goes on to explain that God's promise to Abraham was not forgotten when the law was *"introduced 430 years later"* (NIV) with Moses. (We will go into the law and Moses in more detail in the next lesson.) The law had a specific purpose and filled a certain need in God's overall plan for mankind—as did the promise for Abraham.

📖 Read Galatians 3:18–19. What do you learn in this passage? What purpose does the law serve?

_____

_____

_____

Go on through verse 20 to 25, focusing on verse 24. What strikes you as the key to these verses?

_____

_____

_____

Reading through this third chapter of Galatians, we see that all that occurred in the Old Testament is truly connected to God plan of bringing Jesus to us for salvation. Therefore, the covenant of Abraham, the law given to Moses, and all the other details work together, not apart, to explain our heritage of faith! Paul wanted to explain to the Galatians that we also are to realize that the "seed" of Abraham is Jesus, and that as the body of Christ, we are one with Christ.

📖 Read and record Galatians 3:29

_____

_____

_____

*"Now the promises were spoken to Abraham and to his seed. He does not say 'And to seeds,' as referring to many, but rather to one, 'And to your seed,' that is, Christ."*

**Galatians 3:16**

*"So the law was put in charge to lead us to Christ, that we might be justified by faith."*

**Galatians 3:24 (NIV)**

The bottom line for us as believers in regards to this passage of the "Seed" is this—as found in Galatians 3:29:

> *"And if you belong to Christ, then you are Abraham's offspring, heirs according to promise."*

This means that we also are a part of this fulfillment, if we are in Christ; we are in covenant, and hold the same promise. *"The Lord is faithful to all his promises and loving toward all he has made"* (Psalm 145:13b, NIV).

Do you see yourself as an heir of God's promise to Abraham? Why or why not?

_____

_____

_____

Praise God! We are heirs of the promise. We have access through Christ Jesus. We share in the lineage and the blessings of that lineage *if* we are obedient to God and believe in Jesus as our Savior. Suddenly, we find ourselves sitting in a seed packet with the most glorious picture on the cover—the picture of heaven!

Do you have the focus verse, Galatians 3:16, memorized? Practice the verse by heart and reflect on all that it says.

*Deep Roots*

DAY FIVE

# FOR ME TO FOLLOW GOD

Amazing, isn't it? This short section of the Bible fully explains why we had the Law, how Christ fulfilled the Law, and why the Abrahamic covenant is still applicable to those who are in Christ. Hopefully you have followed along this week, learning the details of God's interaction with Abraham, and now you are seeing so clearly why it was critical to study all those details! There is such depth in the Word of God, and I believe that this is why we can study His Word our whole lives and still have more to learn about the magnificence of God.

We are given this example in Galatians by Paul, who was scolding the people of Galatia for abandoning their faith and relying on the works of their hands. The people to whom Paul spoke knew the promise and the law. They had heard that Christ fulfilled the law and knew they had freedom in Christ; yet they were going back to the law to please those around them.

**APPLY** Can you think of a time when you have "caved in" to peer pressure? When you participated in something you didn't totally believe in anymore simply to keep the opposition quiet? What happened?

_____

_____

_____

_____

Abraham was bold enough to stand in his faith in God, and did things that probably made absolutely no sense to those around him. Abraham is our example of a man whose righteousness came from faith, and not from his own effort. The sacrifice and promise experienced by Abraham came not from the works of his hands, nor was it to benefit anything in his present situation. Abraham's faith was in God and in all circumstances. God's plan was to provide a "Seed" that would redeem believers from the grave. The Seed that is Christ came from the family lineage of Abraham. In this, Abraham truly has impacted generations for eternity, hasn't he? Just like God said.

Friend, see the magnitude of God's faithfulness here. No matter what He says, and no matter who He says it to, God **will** do just as He says, even if it is not seen for generations upon generations. God is trustworthy, God is faithful, and God cannot lie.

God gave the promise to Abraham, and fulfilled the promise through Christ. God ultimately gave Christ for us, giving us access to that promise. We are His, and He provided for us way back in the land of Canaan.

Recite the focus verse by memory—and celebrate the significance of the fulfillment of that covenant through Jesus Christ.

 *God Most High,* how I love You and am honored to be Your child! I thank You for giving me such a rich heritage and such an accurate record of the promises and covenants that You have made with Your people. May I never take lightly the honor I have of being an heir of Your promises. May I never underestimate the significance of all that is recorded in Scripture. I pray that You would reveal Your truths to me in an ever increasing manner so that I may better understand who You are, my position in You, and Your role in my life. May I use what I learn to become a "doer of the Word" and not simply a "hearer of the Word." In Jesus' holy name, Amen.

> **"Do not merely listen to the word, and so deceive yourselves. Do what it says."**
>
> **James 1:22 (NIV)**

# Notes

# THREE

# The Promise

## THE PROMISE OF THE GLORY OF GOD
## 3:16 VERSE: 2 CORINTHIANS

Looking at this verse, you might be wondering just what it has to do with the Abrahamic Covenant we studied last week. Well, prepare yourself to see yet another layer of just how consistent God is and has been through the ages. God's consistency is shown through the working together of every foundational detail that God has put into place to point us to His goal for every believer; eternal salvation through Jesus Christ. The plan of salvation may have been set into motion by God long before the days of Abraham, but the connection of events has occurred over a broad span of time, being revealed through many interactions between God and His people. This week, we will bring together two major concepts of the overall plan of salvation: the concepts of the Law and the Promise; wrapping them up with a beautiful God-sized bow.

Still puzzled? Just think about how your kids react when you start to tell them an incredible truth about life, which they can't quite see at first, and they just look at you with that blank stare—until you sit together, talk about the details, and the "light bulb goes off above their heads" showing their understanding. I trust that this week, and in future weeks that the "light bulb moments" in your life would continually appear as you seek after God and your ever-deepening relationship with Him. May we all take steps to bring us closer to Christ every day. Let's jump in and see what we can learn together!

*Prepare yourself to see yet another layer of just how consistent God is and has been through the ages.*

# MEET ME ON THE MOUNTAIN MOSES! 3:16 VERSE: 2 CORINTHIANS

*"But whenever a man turns to the Lord, the veil is taken away."*

Last week we spent time discovering the details of the Abrahamic Covenant, and how it applies to us today as believers. Do you remember in Galatians where we learned why the law was instituted?

Go back and read Galatians 3:19. Record what it says here:

_____

_____

_____

Now record Galatians 3:24–25:

_____

_____

_____

> **The Law has become our tutor to lead us to Christ, that we may be justified by faith.**

Amazing that this truth is so clearly stated in Scripture, yet is misunderstood by so many. Ok, so I suddenly feel like I am showing you the Bible like the TV trivia game show that posts the answers, and asks the contestant for the right question. Here is the answer about the Law; now, what is the question again?

To understand Moses, and the verse we are focusing on this week, we have to know about his life and the call on his life. He was appointed by God to carry the Law to the people, and He was obedient to do as God says in instituting the new system set forth by God. Moses was a great leader of God's chosen people, and Moses knew the awe and wonder of meeting with God. To save time, let's skip over the early years of Moses' life and fast-forward to his meetings with God on the mountaintop.

In Old Testament days, when Moses received the Ten Commandments, and the Law, he had the chance to speak to God "up close and personal." God called his trusted servant Moses to the mountain and spent time communicating what He wanted the people to know.

Read Exodus 19:18–25.

What happens in verse 18?

_____

_____

What happens between Moses and the Lord in verses 19–20?

_____

_____

_____

What would happen to the priests if they came near to the Lord (verses 21–25)?

_____

_____

_____

Moses went to meet with God, and the mountain shook and was covered with smoke as the Lord descended upon the mountain in awe-inspiring fashion. Moses and God talked with one another. Amazing to think of man and God up on a mountaintop talking away, isn't it? The spoken word of man and the thundering voice of God—what a truly incredible image! After this meeting, Moses went to the people and spoke to them concerning the Ten Commandments and other laws (the tablets had not been created yet). Verbally, God had given them His instructions for them to follow. To confirm the covenant God had made with them, Moses was told to climb the mountain again.

Who went up to the Lord with Moses, as explained in Exodus 24:1–2? What was Moses to do alone?

_____

_____

_____

What was Moses' response (Exodus 24:3–8)?

1. He returned to the people and recounted God's words, and they responded by saying "with one voice" (verse 3):

_____

_____

_____

2. Moses then (verse 4):

_____

_____

_____

3. Moses got up early and _____ an _____ and set up _____ _____ pillars for the _____ _____ of Israel (verse 4).

4. Moses presented offerings to the _____ (verse 5).

5. Moses put half the blood into basins, to be used to _____ on the people, confirming the covenant (verses 6–8).

6. The other half of the blood was _____ on the _____ (verse 6).

After all these things were done, they were off to visit with God on the mountain.

📖 Read Exodus 24:9–11. How amazing is this scene! Moses, Aaron, and seventy-two others went up that hillside, and saw God!

What was under God's feet?

_____

_____

_____

What happens in verse 11?

_____

_____

_____

📖 After they all had seen God, Moses was called for a closer encounter. Look at verse 12—what did the Lord say to Moses?

_____

_____

_____

Did you notice that the Lord was not only going to talk with Moses, but He was also going to *provide the tablets*? This will be an important detail as we learn more about Moses—so remember that fact!

📖 Exodus 24:15–18 tells us about Moses' visit with God. Read that passage, and record your reaction to their meeting:

_____

_____

_____

_____

During this encounter, God presented Moses details about the Tabernacle, the dwelling place for God. The Tabernacle would represent the temple, the church, and Christ, our dwelling place. Every detail and every aspect of the Tabernacle leads to Christ, relates to Christ, and shows us the way to worship our God. There are many studies out there that take an in-depth look into the Tabernacle, including an excellent Following God™ study (*Life Principles for Worship from the Tabernacle*). I encourage you to invest some time into understanding the magnitude of the instruction Moses received from God. Chapters 25 through 31 of Exodus hold the record of the instruction God gave Moses on this visit.

📖 Read Exodus 31:18. Write that verse here:

_____

_____

_____

> "And to the eyes of the sons of Israel the appearance of the glory of the LORD was like a consuming fire on the mountain top."
>
> Exodus 24:17

> Moses wasn't content to be without God—even if God wasn't going to be with the people.

Who wrote on the tablets? What did He use to write on them?

_____

_____

Isn't that simply overwhelming? Back to the fact that God supplied the tablets, we now see that He not only provided them, He wrote on them. The instructions about the Tabernacle, and the way that man could acceptably worship God was written by God Himself, and given to man. God gave this as a gift to Moses and the Israelites. The Law was the very thing that would lead them to Christ (Galatians 3:24).

📖 Memorize 2 Corinthians 3:16: *"But whenever a man turns to the Lord, the veil is taken away."*

What do you think this means?

_____

_____

_____

# THE OTHER SIDE OF THE MOUNTAIN 3:16 VERSE: 2 CORINTHIANS

*The Promise* — DAY TWO

*"But whenever a man turns to the Lord, the veil is taken away."*

The experience that Moses had on the mountain with God is one those around him could only dream of having. Moses received personal instruction from almighty God, and experienced complete fellowship with God. But, on the other side of the mountain, the natives were getting restless. Moses was about to see what he thought he would never see— a covenant people who had turned to unspeakable practices in a moment of impatience.

We cannot possibly cover every angle of the Israelites' rebellion. So let's concentrate on the essence of the passage here. Moses comes down from meeting with God and finds his very own people and priests worshiping a false god—a calf they had shaped from their own jewelry. What's worse is that Aaron, Moses' spokesman, was the one who built the altar and the idol (Exodus 32:2–6)! Those that participated in this false worship were caught red handed. God's righteous anger burned.

📖 Read Exodus 32:7–10, and follow along in verses 11–19 for the questions below.

What is the reaction Moses displays in Exodus 32:11–12?

_____

_____

📖 What does Moses ask God to do in verse 13?

_____

What is the Lord's response in verse 14?

_____

_____

What does Moses have, and where does he go in verse 15?

_____

Who wrote the tablets, according to verse 16?

_____

_____

_____

*"But whenever a man turns to the Lord, the veil is taken away."*

*2 Corinthians 3:16*

Can you imagine? Here Moses has been with God, communing, communicating, and receiving instruction—and the people were not even waiting for him to return with the message from the real God! Moses was crushed, as I'm sure we all would be.

📖 Read verse 19. What did Moses do when he reached the camp?

_____

_____

_____

Can you understand his frustration? Do you think you would have done the same thing, or would you have reacted differently? Why?

_____

_____

_____

The whole situation was just a mess, and Moses dealt with the people and their sin, as did God. Moses was so angry that he destroyed the tablets that God had made and written on. In Moses' anger, he destroyed the work of God's hands, and the record of the law they were to follow. The Lord gave them a bigger problem than broken tablets; He removed His presence from their lives in a season that should have given them such a sweet time of fellowship with their God. Even if only for a short moment in the timeline of mankind, the perceived separation from God that the people felt because of their sin was undoubtedly overwhelming. During this moment of judgment, God had not forgotten His chosen people, but in His anger, He was exercising the principles of truth, justice, and consequences that make Him a righteous God. Our Creator God was giving the people time to make their own mistakes, and make their way back to Him in repentance.

📖 What does Exodus 33:1–3 reveal about God's punishment for the people?

_____

_____

_____

Why didn't the Lord go with them (verse 3)?

_____

_____

_____

Even though he lived with a stiff-necked people, Moses wanted God's presence in his life. Moses wasn't content to be without God—even if God wasn't going to be with the people. So, Moses constructed a place for him to be alone with God.

📖 Looking at Exodus 33:7–8, what did Moses do?

_____

_____

_____

What did the people do when Moses was in the tent (verses 8, 10)?

_____

_____

_____

What happened when Moses was in the tent (verses 8–11)?

_____

_____

_____

How did God speak to Moses, and what was Moses considered (verse 11)?

God spoke to Moses _____ to _____

God spoke to Moses as a _____ speaks with his _____.

Now during this time, before the second trip up the mountain for the Law, as Moses talked with God at the Tent of Meeting, a pillar of cloud resided outside the door for all to see. God spoke to Moses *"face to face, just as a man speaks to his friend"* (Exodus 33:11). The people would worship from their tent doors as the cloud was there, but they never saw God personally.

The people were about to see a visible reminder of just how powerful the presence of God can be manifested in a believer's life. Moses and God had communicated in that tent, but somehow, God shielded Moses from seeing the fullness of His glory in these meetings. As we will soon see, Moses was about to get a clearer view of God.

After all this background information, now we finally get to discuss the glory of God shining all over Moses' face. Think of it! The radiance of God is so strong, that merely being in His presence would change the appearance of anyone in His midst.

Has there ever been a time in your life where you have sought God with such a passion, such an intensity, that it seemed as though your whole appearance and/or outlook had changed after spending time in fellowship with Him? If so, describe that time.

*As Christians, we are set apart because of God's presence in our lives. Just as Moses did, we should also hunger to be different from the world around us.*

_____
_____
_____
_____
_____

📖 Read Exodus 33:13. What is Moses' request to God?

_____
_____
_____

📖 Now look at verses 14–17. What did Moses need God to send with him and his people?

_____
_____
_____

What does the second half of verse 16 reveal to us about what impact God's presence would have upon the lives of Moses and his people?

_____
_____
_____

The Lord agrees to the requests of Moses because God was _____ with him, and _____ him by _____ (verse 17).

With this agreement made, Moses gets bold! Moses asks to see God's glory. Very clearly, in verse 18 we see this brazen request.

📖 Write Exodus 33:18 here.

_____
_____
_____

> "Then Moses said, 'I
> pray Thee, show me
> Thy glory!'"
>
> Exodus 33:18

Wow! The boldness of Moses! Wish you had that kind of gusto? Wish you could just up and ask God to reveal Himself to you? Right there, in front of everyone? Well, He can, and He will, and He does through Jesus Christ—to all who believe. This we will discover more fully in the next few days.

Back to God and Moses though—God told Moses that He would proclaim His own name to Moses, and that He would *make all my goodness to pass before you* (Exodus 33:19). One word of warning came with that wonderful promise. Discover for yourself what that warning was by recording Exodus 33:20 below:

_____
_____
_____

You know, I'm not too sure that I would press on for such an experience with a warning like that! Moses possessed boldness and desire that only comes from a true relationship with God. We sure could learn a lot from Moses, don't you agree?

Work on memorization of 2 Corinthians 3:16. Is the meaning any clearer to you today? How?

_____

_____

_____

# Show Me the Glory
# 3:16 Verse: 2 Corinthians

*"But whenever a man turns to the Lord, the veil is taken away."*

We left off Day Two with Moses boldly asking to see the glory of God.

**Moses.** The guy who spent forty days on the mountain in fellowship with God.

**Moses.** The one who God entrusted with the Law.

**Moses.** The one who spoke with God as man would speak with his friend.

**Moses.** The one who wasn't afraid to ask for more of God.

What does this guy from the Old Testament have to do with living a Christ-like life? Everything. We will see over the next few weeks together that living like Christ means living in continuous fellowship with God. Moses got it, and if we follow his lead as we learn more about him, we can do likewise. I pray that we will all "get it" too. I pray we will all live a life sold out to God.

Who can blame Moses for wanting to see God's glory? However, to catch a full glimpse of His face would have literally killed Moses. To think that you might die by simply wanting to be closer to God is difficult to accept, isn't it? But Moses didn't lose heart, and the Lord made provision for him. The Lord provided protection for Moses.

In Exodus 33:21–23 we see the provision God made so that Moses could have his request granted. What did the Lord tell Moses?

_____

_____

_____

_____

_____

This time, Moses asked to see the glory of God. The Lord told Moses that none who saw His face survived, and explained to Moses that to see His glory, he would have to hide in the cleft of a rock. In this cleft, Moses would be covered by God's hand until His glory passed by. Think about this for a moment. The glory was so much that Moses could only see the back of God, yet this glory would be so powerful that a refuge was needed. A refuge in a rock that would be covered by God's hand—how large is God's hand that it can cover a grown man hidden in a rock? Such a concept is mind-boggling to say the very least. God is limitless, that's for sure. He is the omnipresent (always there), omniscient (all knowing) and omnipotent (all powerful) Lord. He is without boundaries. I can't even begin to imagine just how awesome and overwhelming the glory of the Lord truly was to Moses.

But before Moses could experience all that God told Him would occur, he had some unfinished business to tend to. Remember those tablets Moses broke in a fit of rage? Well, God didn't forget about them, and made Moses cut his own tablets this time for the replacement set.

📖 Read Exodus 34:1–4. What did God tell Moses to do? What was he supposed to carry in his hands?

_____

_____

_____

Moses did as God commanded, and made the new set of tablets. He went up the mountain, all alone.

📖 Look at Exodus 34:5–7. What an awesome scene! Record the things God proclaimed about Himself:

1. He called upon the _____ of the _____ (verse 5).

2. "The _____, the _____ _____, _____ and gracious, slow to _____, and abounding in _____ and _____," (verse 6)

3. "who keeps _____ for thousands, who _____ iniquity, transgression and _____; yet He will by no means leave the _____ unpunished, visiting the iniquity of the _____ on the children and on the _____ to the third and _____ generation" (verse 7).

This is who God proclaims to be. This is who we should proclaim God to be. He is gracious, loving, forgiving, but JUST. He is God.

📖 Now, it is key to see Moses' reaction. Record Exodus 34:8 below:

_____

_____

_____

*"And Moses made haste to bow low toward the earth and worship."*

*Exodus 34:8*

As the Lord met with Moses on the mountain, God came down from His cloud and proclaimed all He was. All Moses could do in response to this was worship and bow down. The magnitude of the moment with God must have been incredible. To be in God's presence, and to hear from God's own voice who He is, **simply commands worship.**

Moses and God stayed on that mountaintop for forty days, and Moses returned to his people with the reproduced tablets containing the Ten Commandments. Keep in mind that the first set of tablets God made, and God wrote. The second set Moses made, and Moses wrote what God dictated. God made sure the people had a written record of the Law, and He wasn't going to let Moses off the hook for destroying the first set!

📖 Read Exodus 34:29. What was different about Moses this time? What happened to his face?

_____

_____

_____

Moses' face was so bright that the Israelites were unable to look at Moses, they were even afraid of him. What an amazing sight this must have been! This was the same people who had recently seen the waters part, the plagues come, the manna fall, the quail satisfy, the rock spill out water, and many other amazing works of God. Even with such things being accepted as "normal," the glory of God, the radiance seen through Moses' countenance, was considered more remarkable and even fearful. The radiance in Moses' face, even in its fleeting measures, must have been incredible. And to think this radiance represented the mere "leftovers" of God's glory!

During this meeting with God, the glory of God shone bright through Moses' face. This time spent on the mountain with God is where we see the first instance of the veil worn by Moses. Moses had to wear this veil to calm the fears of those who were with him.

So, there went Moses, down the mountain with the new copy of the Testimony, and the people were afraid to go near him. He had to speak to them before they would be brave enough to come close! Moses told them what God had spoken and commanded.

📖 Read Exodus 34:33–35. When would Moses put the veil on?

_____

_____

When would Moses take the veil off?

_____

_____

The radiance was too much for the people around him, and he protected them from having to witness such a condition. From that time on, whenever Moses went to speak with God, he would remove the veil. He could not wear this veil in God's presence; yet once he returned to the people, he had to replace it again (Exodus 34:33–35).

> *"When Moses came down from Mount Sinai with the two tablets of the Testimony in his hands, he was not aware that his face was radiant because he had spoken to the Lord"*
>
> *Exodus 34:29,* NIV

📖 Look at 2 Corinthians 3:16 again. Have you memorized it? Continue to work on memorizing it, and reflect on the concept of the veil as discussed today. Thank God for the boldness of Moses.

The Promise    DAY FOUR

# BRIGHT SHINY FACES
# 3:16 VERSE: 2 CORINTHIANS

*"But whenever a man turns to the Lord, the veil is taken away."*

Our focus verse found in the third chapter of 2 Corinthians really explains the boldness of the new covenant we have in Christ. The fulfillment of the Law given to Moses is found in Jesus Christ, the Seed of Abraham, the One who would bring us all to a path of salvation through His sacrifice for our sins.

Now, considering this passage of Scripture, we need to understand the context a bit more. The glory that was seen on Moses was one that faded the longer he was away from God—it was a glory that resulted in a **specific meeting** with God. Only Moses directly experienced God's glory, yet others feared the result of it. Do you remember earlier in this lesson when we learned how the people would watch Moses going to the tent of meeting (the Tabernacle)?

📖 Re-read Exodus 33:8–11. What did the people do when Moses went to the tent?

_____

_____

_____

**With Christ, our meetings with Him are only limited by our own decisions to meet—He is always available to us and dwells within us. We have continuous access!**

The people were content to stand at their own doorway and worship God from there as they saw Moses go to the tent of meeting and meet with God. The relationship Moses had with God was much more intense than theirs. Moses enjoyed fellowship and experienced conversation with the Lord. The nation of Israel as a whole communed with God in accordance with the Law that God established as a result of their disobedience, until the Seed came. We now know that the Seed, who is Christ, did come, and fulfilled all requirements of the Law.

Anyone who comes in contact with the truth of God will react, either in fear or in acceptance of who God is. If the glory Moses experienced was intense, why can't the glory that comes from a relationship with Christ be equally awe-inspiring? With Christ, our meetings with Him are only limited by our own negligence; He is always available to us and dwells within us. **We have continuous access!** Moses hid the radiance of God from others, but as the Bride of Christ, we are to be bold and courageous with our expression of faith. We are not to hide it under a bushel, as the kids song says, or anywhere else for that matter—we are to let our *"light shine before men"* (Matthew 5:16).

📖 Read Matthew 5:14–16. What are we supposed to be as believers?

_____

_____

_____

What is our purpose as light?

_____

_____

Now write out Matthew 5:17.

_____

_____

_____

Reflect on the words of Jesus in this verse. This verse is closely related with last week's lesson, isn't it? Remember that Galatians clearly states that the Law is in place to lead us to Christ (Galatians 3:24).

📖 Now look at 2 Corinthians 3:7–12. Record your reaction to this passage.

_____

_____

_____

How exciting this is! We have such a hope in Christ. We have such boldness in Christ. But here lies our burden—those who are not in Christ do not share such boldness. They do not have such a clear view. They are still behind a veil.

📖 Read further in the passage, covering 2 Corinthians 3:13–16.

How is the old covenant "taken away" according to verse 14?

_____

_____

The veil that is mentioned in the New Testament covers those who do not know Christ when the Scripture of Moses is read (the old covenant). A veil is a covering that hides what is behind it, but does not make the hidden thing disappear. The object or person is still there, behind the barrier of the veil. The veil is not as much a physical covering in this context of 2 Corinthians, but a barrier that keeps the understanding of God from reaching the heart of the unbeliever; a spiritual veil standing between the unbeliever and Christ. Those who are not believers are unable to comprehend the message of the gospel and have a veil of sorts that prevents them from understanding the message. Once someone accepts Jesus as their Savior, all understanding is at that person's disposal; God's message is clear, and His promises are ours. Our focus verse reveals that _"whenever anyone turns to the Lord, the veil is taken away."_

📖 Look up Exodus 26:31–33. What was the curtain, or veil, used to separate, and what was behind it?

> **"Do not think that I came to abolish the Law or the Prophets; I did not come to abolish, but to fulfill."**
>
> **Matthew 5:17**

> **"For if that which fades away was with glory, much more that which remains is in glory!"**
>
> **2 Corinthians 3:11**

_____

_____

_____

The veil in the Tabernacle was the physical barrier that separated the Holy Place from the Most Holy Place. It hid the section known as the Holy of Holies from anyone except the high priest that would perform priestly duties to the Lord once a year. This veil hid the Ark of the Covenant and the mercy seat where God would dwell. This veil would shield people from seeing God's glory.

Isn't it intriguing that when Moses had just received the instructions for building the Tabernacle, he knew about the need for a veil to place as a shield from God's glory? And here he was, a man with the leftover glory of God on his face, and he was making his own type of veil to shield the people around him from that same glory. I just love to see how God shows us over and over how His ways of doing things are so very consistent.

Now, let's fast forward for a moment to the day that Jesus died for our sins on that cross on Calvary.

📖 What happened to the Temple veil in Luke 23:45?

_____

_____

What did Jesus call out at that moment (verse 46)?

_____

📖 Compare this to Mark 15:38. Record this verse here:

_____

_____

_____

📖 What more do we learn in Matthew 26:51?

_____

_____

_____

*"Jesus Christ is the same yesterday and today, yes and forever."*

**Hebrews 13:8**

What an awesome visual reminder and promise this is to us all! Not only do we know that there is no longer a veil for those who believe in Jesus—but we see confirmed in the gospels that the veil was torn the moment Jesus' work on earth was complete. Jesus fulfilled all that He needed to fulfill, and the access to the Father and His glory was given to all who believe. With Jesus' sacrifice for our sins, the veil is no longer needed, and for those who believe in Him, we have unfettered access to the Father through Him. We no longer have the Law as a barrier to God.

📖 Look up Hebrews 13:8. What does it tell you about Jesus?

_____

_____

Praise the Lord! The message does not change, and neither does our God. *"Jesus Christ is the same yesterday and today, yes and forever"* (Hebrews 13:8). The only thing that changes is our ability to comprehend the message given—and this comes through the understanding given by the Holy Spirit to the believer. There is no amount of human logic, training, education, or intellect that alone can give us such insight. Only the revelation given by the Holy Spirit will help someone comprehend the message of Christ and allow that message to reside within their hearts.

With the new covenant, and the indwelling of the Holy Spirit in believers, our veil is gone—and God's light shines through us—and His radiance in us is obvious to all. No one that has accepted Christ is bound by a veil any longer. No one! We **all** have the same opportunity to grow in our faith. The amount we grow is dependent completely on how eagerly we seek Him. God will meet us where we are in the same measure that we meet Him. God waits intently to reveal Himself and the glory of His grace to us, but we have to want to be there. This is not some mandatory requirement that you can't get out of—salvation is a choice! We can choose to accept Christ or reject Him. With this, we are all open to the same relationship, once we have accepted the free gift given by God.

Continue to work on this week's focus verse memorization. Reflect on all you have learned this week.

> ## No one that has accepted Christ is bound by a veil any longer.

# FOR ME TO FOLLOW GOD

*The Promise*  DAY FIVE

Once we accept Jesus as our Savior and seek Him in His Word, we begin to grow in faith. We live in an unveiled relationship with our God, and we cannot help but reflect this relationship in our lives. We do not have to stand at the doors of our tent watching while a chosen leader has face time with the Lord—we have full access to our God and a "season pass" to the Tent of Meeting. I challenge us all to get out of our own little tents. If only we will stop being convenient bystanders to faith and jump in, face first, to all God has to offer us! When we do, the Holy Spirit will come to us, dwell inside us, and empower each of us to serve Christ.

There is something obvious about a person who has been in the presence of God—a true change in their appearance that is visible to all. Those who are without this quality will react to it either in a positive manner, or in fear of the unknown. Either way, it is up to us to wear our mark of Christianity (radiance) for all to see. It's fun to see Christians in a secular environment. People may comment about the "sparkle" in their eyes, or the "special something" about them, when to me, that is a clear indicator of God's glory shining in them.

 Have you ever noticed someone with a special sparkle about them? Were they strong believers in Jesus? Was it easy to tell; were they bold in their faith?

_____

_____

_____

📖 Read and record 2 Corinthians 3:17:

_____

_____

_____

📖 Now read 2 Corinthians 3:18. What do we reflect? What are we being transformed into?

_____

_____

_____

When the love of Christ dwells within us, His radiance can't help but shine through, and we experience freedom. With the Lord, we know that there is much benefit because, *"the Lord is the Spirit, and where the Spirit of the Lord is, there is liberty"* (2 Corinthians 3:17). In the New International Version, the word "freedom" is interchanged with "liberty." We are free to have a life of fellowship and a good standing for eternity. Second Corinthians 3:18 shows us that *"we, who with unveiled faces all reflect the Lord's glory, are being transformed into his likeness with ever-increasing glory, which comes from the Lord, who is the Spirit"* (NIV). As we walk in faith, building our relationship with Christ, we become more Christ-like.

📖 Looking ahead to 2 Corinthians 4:3 and 4, who is the gospel veiled to, and why?

_____

_____

_____

In verse 6, we are told that,

> *For God, who said, "Light shall shine out of darkness," is the One who has shone in our hearts, to give the light of the knowledge of the glory of God in the face of Christ.*

The very God that created light and life gave His light to shine from within us. This thought takes us right back to our discussion from the gospel of Matthew of our being a "light shining before men," doesn't it?

The passage upon which we are focusing gives us insight into the magnitude of Christ's message compared to the old covenant of Moses' time. Yes, we have the same, unchanging God throughout Scripture. Only now, the prophecies given in the Old Testament were now fulfilled with Christ, and the practice of sacrifice would be changed forever. Now, through Christ, our salvation is secured—**once for all**, through the most perfect sacrifice made unto God on our behalf, by Christ Himself. With Christ becoming our sacrifice once for all, we can look to Him to be our complete sacrifice for our sins.

📖 Read Hebrews 9:26–28. What does the writer tell us about our life? How many times will we die, and what do we face when we have passed on?

_____

_____

What will Christ do when He appears again?

_____

_____

_____

In Hebrews 9:26–28 it is written that

> *now He has appeared once for all at the end of the ages to do away with sin by the sacrifice of himself. Just as man is destined to die once, and after that to face judgment, so Christ was sacrificed once to take away the sins of many people; and he will appear a second time, not to bear sin, but to bring salvation to those who are waiting for him.* (NIV)

We no longer have to sacrifice and shed blood for each sin in our life, as was necessary under the law and the sacrificial system; with Christ's blood, we are cleansed of all iniquity—if we chose to accept the sacrifice that was made on our behalf. In Old Testament times, sacrifice was made in abundance, but the person only received benefit from the sacrifice if they participated in the ceremony.

In the same way, we must choose to participate in the relationship and covenant that Christ has offered to us to be able to benefit from the action. We are so very blessed to have a God merciful enough to give His Son for so many unworthy people. There is nothing we can do on our own, and nothing we can do in place of the sacrifice of Christ for our sins. We all fall short, no matter how good the life is that we lead. We all must accept the sacrifice given, for no other sacrifice will do. Praise God for His mercy and gift of His Son.

As we see in the 3:16 verse of 2 Corinthians, the veil has been removed for all who believe in Christ. God Himself gives the insight we need, and we have a "front row seat" for our Savior! What a wonderful gift—to be able to sit at the feet of Jesus and allow Him to minister to us in spirit and in truth. How awesome is our God!

Reflect on your memorized focus verse. Praise God for taking the veil away and giving you access to His glory.

 *Compassionate and Gracious God,* how I thank You for giving the Law, and the fulfillment of the Law through Jesus Christ. I praise You for being slow to anger, and abounding in love. I praise You for being faithful to Your people, whether we deserve it or not. Oh, how I thank You for showing the boldness of Moses and how I can come before You with such boldness every moment of my life. I thank You for removing the veil from my heart when I accepted Jesus as my Savior. I desperately need Your forgiveness and praise You for making Your forgiveness available to all who believe in Jesus and accept His sacrifice for their sins. I worship You and give You all the praise and all the glory. In Jesus' name. Amen.

*What a wonderful gift—to be able to sit at the feet of Jesus and allow Him to minister to us in spirit and in truth!*

# Notes

# FOUR

# The Great Anticipation

## PAVING THE WAY FOR THE MESSIAH
## 3:16 VERSE: LUKE

Now that we have explored the promises and the Law given in the Old Testament, we are ready to transition to a focus on Christ's footsteps on earth. The fullness of time had come, and God began the next phase of His ministry, involving Christ's arrival in the flesh. *Jesus came to minister to us in Spirit and in truth.* Jesus the Messiah came to make a path for salvation for a lost people in His midst and all the people that would come after them. Do you think they could hear the footsteps of the Messiah getting louder in their minds as they read the words of the prophets? Do you think they had any idea He was about to arrive? They had waited so long for Him. But would they recognize Him, or even accept Him?

While our God is the same through all generations, the way that we know Him, interact with Him, and understand Him has slight variations in approach through the ages. We have never seen a change in the gospel message, but we have fine-tuned our mode of worship, as outlined by God Himself.

A lot of things had to be explained. A lot of changes in thought had to occur. God used John the Baptist to *change the perceptions* of the people, moving them in the direction of Jesus. God used John the Baptist to help prepare the hearts of those who would accept Jesus as their long-awaited Messiah.

> *God used John the Baptist to prepare the hearts of those who would accept Jesus as their long-awaited Messiah.*

# ZACHARIAS SERVES THE LORD
# 3:16 VERSE: LUKE

*"John answered and said to them all, 'As for me, I baptize you with water; but One is coming who is mightier than I, and I am not fit to untie the thong of His sandals; He will baptize you with the Holy Spirit and fire.' "*

The focus verse for this week is beautifully tucked into a passage of Scripture where John the Baptist explains his identity and the identity of the Messiah, the One who was coming to bring them salvation. We will find that the people were questioning if **John** was the Messiah, the one who would come to bring them salvation. John would set the record straight, but how did John, a common man, get to the point in a society where people were wondering if he was the Messiah?

Long before the scene of our focus verse, John had met Jesus. They were still in their mother's wombs when their bond began, and the call on John's life as the forerunner to Christ was undeniable. We will spend the next few days traveling back in time, and discovering the pivotal moments of this relationship that changed the world.

📖 Read Luke 1:5–10. What was Zacharias' role in their community at this time? What activity was he selected to perform?

*He was a Priest*
*Instructed to burn incense*

Zacharias (referred to as Zechariah in the NIV translation) was married to a woman named Elizabeth. Zacharias was a priest who had been chosen during this time to perform the Temple duties, which was a literal once-in-a-lifetime opportunity. He was obedient and set apart for that moment in time and continued to serve the Lord in an honorable capacity. As he was in the temple, burning the incense as he was charged to do, there were praying worshipers assembled outside the Temple. They were in agreement in prayer, and the Lord was honored by their corporate cry. The air was filled with praise and supplication along with the aroma of the prayers of the believers as Zacharias entered the Temple and served God with humility and honor.

📖 Read Luke 1:11–14. Who appeared to Zacharias? What did they say?

*An angel of the Lord.*
*His prayers had been heard and*
*answered. Elizabeth would bear*
*him a son.*

As the people outside the Temple were praying to God, and the priest Zacharias was inside the Temple serving God, God chose to answer the

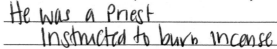

## Word Study
## APPOINTED ORDER

The term "appointed order" found in Luke 1:8 is translated from the Greek "*taxis.*" According to *Strongs Greek Dictionary, taxis,* indicates "regular *arrangement* (in time), fixed *succession* (of rank or character), official *dignity,* order."

From this word study, we gain deeper insight to the honor and anticipation of the moment in which we find Zacharias. This time of service was a once-in-a-lifetime moment for him and a moment that he probably had been waiting a long time to experience. It was his turn to serve, and God had an answer to prayer waiting for him in that moment of obedience to God.

priest's silent prayer, and give him the desire of his heart. This prayer may have been written on his heart a long time before; but God's timing for providing the answer was perfect! The angel Gabriel appeared, and told Zacharias that his wife would be giving birth to a son that he would name John. Not only was he to be called John, but his purpose on earth was going to be mighty! Elizabeth, Zacharias' wife, had waited a lifetime for a child; for she was older, and barren, and in their society, that meant she led a life of dishonor and shame. In the blink of an eye, her status and situation had changed, and she didn't even know it yet—for her husband was still in the Temple.

📖 Read the first part of Luke 1:15 with me: *"For he will be great in the sight of the Lord . . . ."* Here, in this verse, we have a great confirmation of just how favored John would become. The Lord stated this as the promise of this child was given. This statement of fact was spoken over John's life by the angel Gabriel in the Holy of Holies of the Temple. How incredible!

📖 Read verse 17. What would be John's role, according to the angel?

<u>He will go and turn the hearts of parents to their children and the disobedient to the righteous, before the Lord.</u>

Zacharias would not only be blessed with a child in his old age, but this child would be a wonderful child used by God? What an amazing promise. Gabriel promises that *"it is he who will go as a forerunner before Him in the spirit and power of Elijah, TO TURN THE HEARTS OF THE FATHERS BACK TO THE CHILDREN, and the disobedient to the attitude of the righteous; so as to make ready a people prepared for the Lord"* (Luke 1:17).

What an incredible moment! Being a mother myself, I have gone through the anticipation of becoming pregnant; I can imagine the surprise, shock, and general confusion that this moment in his life must have felt like. All rational thought about timelines, ticking clocks, and possibility of conception was no longer applicable. God promised this older couple; they were going to have a child. Naturally, the father-to-be questioned how all this could happen, saying *"How shall I know this for certain? For I am an old man, and my wife is advanced in years"* (Luke 1:18).

Being a wife, I have to say "Praise the Lord" that he referred to his wife's age so much more gently than he referred to his own. That is an example of a good husband! Good and merciful husband or not, Zacharias was a man who questioned the word of God as spoken through the angel Gabriel. Zacharias was doubtful that his wife and he were able to have a child—he was looking at the natural aspect of this situation—not the supernatural power of a promise given by God.

APPLY    Now, take a moment and reflect on this situation. How would you react upon receiving what seemed like a very "belated" answer to your heart's cry—when it seemed like the answer came way too late to be true?

<u>I would be shocked. Scared of my age and the health of the pregnancy/baby. But, elated to be pregnant. Let alone with a child to serve the Lord.</u>

*God chose to answer the priest's silent prayer, and give him the desire of his heart.*

→ prepare the people for the coming of the Lord

*"This is the way the Lord has dealt with me in the days when He looked with favor upon me, to take away my disgrace among men."*

*Luke 1:25*

📖 Look at verses 19–20. What was the response of the angel?

_Reiterated the news was sent from God to be true._

What were the consequences that Zacharias would endure? Why?

_He would not be able to speak until the birth because he questioned the angel of God_

Gabriel told Zacharias that he was not only an angel from the Lord, but that he *"stands in the presence of God."* He makes the point that this was a genuine, bonafide "God moment" that should be trusted! The consequences of Zacharias' unbelief included the fact that he would be unable to talk until after the birth of the child. Think about this for a moment. He was unable to talk with Elizabeth as she encountered each stage of pregnancy, nor could he support her with strong words of encouragement when she became discouraged or filled with anxious thoughts. This left Elizabeth in a situation where she was enduring a difficult pregnancy, without the comfort of a husband's words. This had to cramp their style more than a little bit! Imagine Elizabeth being cut off from society because of her unusual pregnancy, and she can't even communicate effectively with her husband.

📖 Look at verses 24–25. What did Elizabeth do?

_She hid for five months. But then realized she should be proud of her gift from God_

God gave this time of solitude to Elizabeth, and she used it to grow in her relationship with Him, reflecting on the amazing situation that God had placed her in.

Instead of looking at her natural situation as an old woman who finally got pregnant, Elizabeth used this time to be alone and reflect on the fact that the Lord had given her favor. Elizabeth was learning how to live a Christ-like life. She focused on God's hand in her life, even when the world around her seemed very lonely.

🛑 APPLY  Think of a time in your life that was difficult or awkward. Did you spend time with the Lord, thanking Him for that moment, and thanking Him for getting you through that time?

_Yes I spent time with Him. I didn't necessarily thank Him in the moment of struggle because I was confused._
_But later I am thankful._

> **Elizabeth ... was a source of strength for Mary—the mentor, friend, and support that she so desperately needed.**

How could you have better focused on God during that time of your life? Do you see how using tough times to focus on God can actually work for your good? Journal your thoughts here:

I now know God brings us through struggles to help us grow in strength and maturity. He only brings us through what we can handle and is always with us.
I need to doubt/fear less.

Ask God to show you the positive while you are in the thick of it.

Memorize this week's verse. Thank the Lord for how He answers our prayers in His timeline, and in His own way.

# MARY'S TURN
# 3:16 VERSE: LUKE

*"John answered and said to them all, 'As for me, I baptize you with water; but One is coming who is mightier than I, and I am not fit to untie the thong of His sandals; He will baptize you with the Holy Spirit and fire.'"*

About six months or so into Elizabeth's pregnancy, one of her relatives, Mary, was given a message by the same angel—that she would carry the Messiah in her own womb! Mary was young and was promised to be married to a man named Joseph. This pregnancy outside of wedlock would not be easily accepted in their society. The marriage had already been arranged, and the betrothal period simply meant that she was essentially married to Joseph—though they were simply awaiting the formality of the ceremony itself. Thus the marriage had not been consummated. Now, she would be carrying a child that was conceived before their marriage was sealed. This would bring cause for alarm in both families and the society around them. But Mary pressed on in faith, for she would give birth to the long awaited King!

The angel Gabriel merely mentioned to Mary that Elizabeth was also in the midst of a difficult pregnancy, and with that news Mary set off for Elizabeth's house. Keep in mind that this trip wasn't just a walk down the street, but an extensive trek to a distant relative's home, unannounced! I don't know about you, but if I was six months pregnant, and someone dropped in on my doorstep, with the intention of staying a few months, it would be hard to show true, loving hospitality. But Elizabeth did just that. The ladies had no idea what the other one was experiencing, and the only thing Mary knew was that Elizabeth was pregnant as well. She knew that God was giving her a safe place to dwell, and she went to that place of refuge. Elizabeth on the other hand, was a source of strength for Mary; the mentor, friend, and support that she so desperately needed.

Let's compare reactions for a moment. Remember Abraham and Sarah and their reactions to the news of Isaac's conception? There is a great parallel here between their reactions to God and God's reaction to them.

Abraham and Mary—These two react based on faith in the Lord and obedience to His will for their lives. While they may laugh out loud or even question God initially, they in no way question the ability of God to do what He says; rather, they are simply asking questions concerning the details. They reflect a Christ-like response to amazing news that would be hard for anyone to believe. Yet they stand on faith and submit to the will of God.

Sarah and Zacharias—These two wonderful people exhibit our human nature quite well. They both are looking to the natural implications—a child, age, and so forth. They are losing sight of the fact that God has spoken, and God will bring it to pass. They respond in disbelief and are corrected by God for their lack of faith. They have much to learn on responding in a Christ-like manner, although God uses this time to also lead them to a more Christ-like lifestyle.

 Look at the line marked with "disbelief" and "faith" below. About where on this spectrum would *your* personal faith response be if you were faced with the same or similar circumstances as the four characters from Scripture mentioned above? Mark the spot on the line where you think your level of faith would presently be if you were involved in the same issues as Zacharias, Sarah, Abraham, and Mary respectively. Then, think about a significant "faith test" you have had in your own life. Where on the scale between "disbelief" and "faith" did you find yourself then? Mark that point on the line as well. *honestly unsure*

←————————————1————————————————2————————————→

DISBELIEF                                                                FAITH

*Could definitely respond in disbelief but I would try to be faithful.*

*Pray always — for an increased level of faith.*

After evaluating your responses of faith, take a moment to thank God for carrying you through the trials you have experienced. Commit to praying to God for an increased level of faith, one that day by day would bring you closer to the reaction that Abraham and Mary had; a Christ-like response. Through every choice and every situation that God allows us to go through, we have the opportunity to grow in our level of faith, just like Mary, Zacharias, Abraham and Sarah.

When Mary arrived on their doorstep, Elizabeth not only welcomed her into their home, but spoke a blessing over her that only the Holy Spirit could have given her! In Luke 1:42–45 we see the following,

> *And she cried out with a loud voice, and said, "Blessed among women are you, and blessed is the fruit of your womb! And how has it happened to me, that the mother of my Lord should come to me? For behold, when the sound of your greeting reached my ears, the baby leaped in my womb for joy. And blessed is she who believed that there would be a fulfillment of what had been spoken to her by the Lord."*

Now remember, Elizabeth did not know that Mary was coming, or that she was pregnant. The Holy Spirit worked through her to bring forth that message of encouragement!

📖 Look at the passage quoted above. What is the Christ-like reaction that Mary had (see verse 45)?

_Welcoming._

_Knowing she was pregnant_

"Blessed is she who has believed that the Lord would fulfill His promises to Her!"

**God always exceeds our biggest expectations.**

Not only was Mary blessed by what Elizabeth said, Elizabeth was blessed by seeing Mary's faith being shown through her reaction to the words spoken to her. In a sense, God allowed Mary in this moment to see both Elizabeth and God Himself observing her obedience to His will.

This greeting was exactly what Mary needed to hear. Keep in mind that John, who was nestled warmly within Elizabeth's belly, jumped for joy upon being in the presence of Jesus, who was hidden in Mary's womb. Elizabeth welcomed her in with open arms and gave her the comfort she desperately needed. How wonderful God is to provide us with the comfort that we need for every specific event in our lives. God gave these two special women the exact person who could relate to their situation, and they were able to lift each other up in such a difficult season of pregnancy.

Mary's response at this moment of greeting is a famous one, and a critical one to seeing how to respond to the favor of God.

📖 Read Luke 1:46–55. Take notice of what Mary talked about. What was her focus in this moment?

_Giving all glory to God for giving to her the savior of the world._

_For keeping his promises_

Note the topics Mary focused on:

- Praise to God
- Mary's humility
- Greatness of God
- Mercy to those who fear God
- God humbles the proud, and exalts the humble
- God has helped Israel
- God has fulfilled the promise of the seed of Abraham

_When we are in a difficult time in our lives we can turn back to what we know and learn_

Her response revolved around the God she obeyed, not her act of obeying. Her eyes were set on God. Mary praised God for His ways, for His promise being fulfilled, and for the Messiah given. Mary viewed herself as a servant, just as we are to view ourselves as servants of Christ and all we minister to. This is a Christ-like response!

Mary stayed with Elizabeth and her family until the time John was born. At that time Mary returned home and continued the call on her life. Elizabeth had to move forth in her new role, and Mary needed to be with her own mate. Mary went to Joseph, and they traveled to the location of the census. Mary gave birth to Jesus in the midst of God's creation—not in a warm building made by the hands of men, but more likely in a cave, formed by the dirt and rock that only God could have created. He was birthed among the animals and placed in a feeding trough. This setting was among the most humble of situations. God again gives us a picture; as with the altar with Isaac, that only *His* creation is worthy of holding His sacrifice, gift, and promises. Anything made by human hands will always fall short of that which God made!

The new mothers lovingly raised these amazing boys, training them up on the ways of their faith and the customs of the world. To be the mothers of such men; one fully man yet fully divine, the other one who would lead the way for the Messiah, would have been quite a daunting task for them both.

John's display of excitement in the womb was obviously not the end to the bond he shared with Christ; rather, it was only the beginning. With this relationship between the two men formed before birth, God provided a bond that would make sure the plan of salvation would be fulfilled during their lifetime. God took time to prepare John for his work in setting the foundations for Christ's earthly ministry. God waited until the timing was perfect to introduce Jesus as the Messiah to the people of Israel. John and Jesus grew in stature and in favor with the people, and ultimately, Jesus would give the hope of salvation to all.

To be in Christ's presence before He literally set foot on earth as a man must have been incredible. Mary and Elizabeth couldn't have been able to fully anticipate or comprehend what the next thirty-three years would be like for those who walked with Jesus. God always exceeds our biggest expectation. I guess that's why He's God and we're not! Praise God for knowing that human nature would expect someone to confirm the coming of the Messiah, the answer to prophetic Scriptures.

Continue to memorize today's focus verse.

*The Great Anticipation* **DAY THREE**

# PREPARING FOR THE KING
# 3:16 VERSE: LUKE

*"John answered and said to them all, 'As for me, I baptize you with water; but One is coming who is mightier than I, and I am not fit to untie the thong of His sandals; He will baptize you with the Holy Spirit and fire.' "*

Elizabeth wasn't the only one who had a word from the Lord to share with others. Upon the birth of John, Zacharias was able to speak again, and the first words out of his mouth were a prophecy spoken over John, found in Luke 1:67–79.

📖 Read this passage. What is Zacharias' tone now? List some things he prophesies here. What specific role does he see John having during his lifetime?

_He is now praises God_

Out of Zacharias' very mouth came the promise that John would lead the way for the Messiah; the One who would bring salvation. God has such a tender way of using people—even during our moments of disbelief, doesn't He?

John experienced a time of preparation before God was able to place him in a position of ministry. Scripture tells us that John wore skins and ate locusts and wild honey. He lived in the wilderness for a period of time. We see that in his time of solitude, *"the word of God came to John, the son of Zacharias, in the wilderness"* (Luke 3:2).

📖 Read John 1:1–15. Who is the Word? Then, write down who you think is the "word of God" according to Luke 3:2.

_1. God is the word- Made flesh - Jesus_
_2. The word is Jesus through John_

📖 What do we learn about John the Baptist in John 1:6–8, 15?

_He was to tell all about the 'light' that is to come to the world._

Now, we know from the beginning of the book of John (1:1–15), that the word of God was none other than Jesus. We can extend that fact to show that in essence Jesus gave John his charge to ministry, his calling. The term "word" that is shown in Luke 3:2, is translated from *rhema,* which indicates the spoken word or a command. John received his spoken command, or his calling, while he was out there in the wilderness.

Obviously an unadorned man, John was quite different from the elegant, pious priests that led the religion of the time. This is a wonderful example of how God will use the most unlikely vessels of the times to bring the message of the gospel to a lost world. As we see throughout the New Testament, many of the leaders of religion and politics were skeptical of the message of Christ. Utter conviction and determination of purpose filled John in his purpose as minister and baptizer of new believers.

📖 Read Luke 3:2–6. Compare this with the passage in Isaiah that it quotes: Isaiah 40:3–5. What was John's purpose according to the prophecy that he fulfilled?

_To bring the people to the way of the Lord to prepare for Jesus coming_

John had been purposed by God to lead the people to Christ by paving the way for Christ. John would show them in Jesus the fulfillment of all they knew in their Jewish beliefs and their expectation of the Messiah. John's role

> *"And he came into all the district around the Jordan, preaching a baptism of repentance for the forgiveness of sins."*
>
> Luke 3:3

was to explain the necessity of repentance for forgiveness of sins (Luke 3:3) and to share with them that their Savior would bring forth salvation!

As John the Baptist grew into an adult and set the stage for the coming Messiah, he baptized crowds of believers and led them to repentance. In doing this, people wanted to know how to act in this newfound capacity. They wanted to know what was next; what was expected of them. Even while John was "crying out" the truth of the gospel to the people, they still had questions.

John was busy sharing the news that the Messiah was coming, and many people were having a hard time grasping all that John was teaching them. Can you imagine being in their shoes, and hearing that all they had waited for was at hand—but that they would have to change their approach in order to experience all God had for them? Was it really that different from what they knew?

 When you first heard about Jesus, what were the questions in your mind before you fully accepted Him as your Savior? Or, if you have not accepted Jesus as the Lord of your life, what is holding you back? Write your thoughts:

· How do we know he is real?
· How does he speak to us?
· How does he do such harsh things,
   let us get hurt if he always loves us.

I don't actually doubt Him

Have you laid your sins at the feet of Jesus? Have you repented, and asked for His forgiveness for your sins? If not, please, please, please do so now. Don't wait another moment!

 Take a moment to ask God to give you peace about any questions you had in the past, or have at this moment. Ask Him to make His truth of the gospel clear in your heart and mind, bringing you to a clear understanding of why Jesus died on the cross for your sins. Thank the Lord for answering the questions in your heart and for providing you eternal life through the sacrifice of Jesus Christ.

We aren't the only ones who have questions. Neither were the people who spoke to John. In the passage below, we see three different groups of people asking questions, and getting answers from John.

📖 Read Luke 3:10–14. What was the focus of John's instruction?

To the multitudes:

Share food with the ones who have
   none

To the tax-gatherers:

Dont take extra

*What questions were in your mind concerning Christ before you fully accepted Jesus as Savior?*

To the soldiers:

_dont falsely accuse_
_be content w/ your pay_

The three responses John gave were basically the same answer worded in different ways, reaching different situations or places in society. John answered their questions biblically and consistently with all that God had been instructing them to live until that time. (Yes, a Christ-like response!) Regardless of the financial or social standing of those in the multitudes, all of those who were baptized were expected to lead the same quality of lifestyle. Their lifestyle and ours today, should reflect the character of God—a lifestyle based on the Ten Commandments and on the teachings that Jesus would deliver to them in the near future.

📖 Remember the requirements of the Ten Commandments? Refresh your memory by reading Exodus 20:1–17. List all ten below:

_____
_____
_____
_____
_____
_____
_____
_____
_____
_____
_____
_____
_____

The Ten Commandments are wonderful requirements that help us stand firm in our love for the Lord and our love for others. They remind us to honor God and honor others. They remind us to live a life of integrity.

📖 Now look up Leviticus 19:18. What does it say? Record the verse here:

_____
_____
_____
_____

This verse from Leviticus helps us understand another angle of what John and Jesus taught in their ministry—"loving your neighbor as yourself."

All Jews knew these laws given by God, and now, the followers of John the Baptist needed to know if the old laws still applied. Bear with me for a moment as I show you something in Scripture that came *after* this moment with John the Baptist. I want you to see that what John taught these new believers that day was built on God's Word in the Old Testament as well as a reflection of what Jesus would teach them at a later time. As John prepared

*John answered questions biblically, and consistently with all that God had been instructing them to live until that time.*

the way for Christ, he taught in a way that is perfectly consistent with what Jesus would teach as He walked through His ministry. God is all about consistency. A Christ-like life is consistent with *the entirety* of God's Word.

📖 Look at Matthew 22:35–40. When tested, what does Jesus say are the two commandments that the *"whole Law and the Prophets"* depend?

*love the lovd w/ all your heart, son, Mind.*
*love your neighbor*

**How we deal with God and how we deal with people are of utmost importance.**

The first comandment deals with loving God, and the second focuses on loving others. How we deal with God and how we deal with people are of utmost importance. John counsels the crowd concerning this very same subject as recorded in Luke 3:10–14. Since the new believers had already professed their faith through repentance and baptism, they had shown that they knew the law and believed in God. So, John's focus was on showing them the second requirement, that of loving others as themselves.

Take an extra few minutes and pray, giving all your daily concerns and problems to the Lord. Thank the Lord for His faithfulness, and for the freedom we have while we are in the center of His will for our lives. Work on your memory verse, and review the verses we have covered in all of the lessons so far.

*The Great Anticipation*   DAY FOUR

# Now What?
# 3:16 Verse: Luke

*"John answered and said to them all, 'As for me, I baptize you with water; but One is coming who is mightier than I, and I am not fit to untie the thong of His sandals; He will baptize you with the Holy Spirit and fire.' "*

The people John ministered to weren't sure how to do this "Christian thing." There wasn't a church on every corner that had people who worshiped this way. Their repentance was an extension of faith built on the foundation of the Old Testament, but it presented different challenges to them in many ways. Theirs was a faith that believed the Messiah was going to be with them! The fulfillment of the prophecies about the Messiah was at hand. They must have wondered, *Do the commandments still apply? Do the laws have the same effect? Can they still have the same relevance they had before we were baptized?*

The Jewish people of that time had become accustomed to a belief system that was based on the Law, yet they were waiting for the Messiah, the fulfillment of the Law. Now suddenly they are told to repent, and believe? This is a call to action, and a change in all they had known and grown accustomed to. Change is a very scary thing to lots of people, but when our Father in heaven begins that movement of change, we are called to action whether it is comfortable or not. A change that is initiated by God will always be consistent with who He is and what He has taught us through the ages. Such change will be consistent with the Bible in all aspects.

Following God's will, even when it means changing how we do things, or stepping out of our "comfort zones" is living a Christ-like life. Why? Because Christ-like living is a life that follows the will of God over everything else.

**APPLY** Has following God's will in a situation caused you to step out of your "comfort zone"? Describe the situation, and your reaction here:

*yes.*
*Standing up at work. Knowing if they turned*
*down my request I would be okay.*

Do you see how that moment brought you closer to the Lord?

*yes. I have been more connected*

While the people were asking John for guidance and getting baptized, some began to think that maybe John was the Christ (as seen in Luke 3:15). In the 3:16 verse of Luke, they hear John's response and learn that he was only leading the way for Christ. Why would they have such fanciful thoughts? Let's dig into the Jewish beliefs a little more.

The Jewish people of that time were looking for the return of Elijah and the advent of Messiah. The similarities of John and what they knew of Elijah were enough to make them question who John really was.

📖 Read 2 Kings 1:8. How was Elijah described?

*A hairy man*

In 2 Kings 1:8, we see that Elijah *"was a hairy man with a leather girdle about his loins."* With only the written account of this person from their past to go by, the similarities between Elijah and John might have seemed striking, because Mark 1:6 tells us that John wore a garment made of camel's hair and that he, like Elijah, wore a leather belt.

There are so many more similarities between the two men. Though John is **no** re-incarnated Elijah, the two lives and purposes seem to complete themselves in the progress of time. They were close enough in the aspects of their lives that those who were in the presence of John the Baptist sat up and took notice of this man who announced that he was preparing the way for one greater than he!

Without John's ministry, the stage would not have been set for the "main attraction. John's time was a completion of Elijah's time. Christ confirms this in the book of Matthew, both in the eleventh and seventeenth chapters.

📖 Jesus pays tribute to John the Baptist in Matthew 11:9–11. Read this passage and reflect on it for a moment. Write any thoughts that come to mind:

_____

_____

_____

_____

_____

📖 Read Matthew 11:14. What does it tell us about John and Elijah?

*John is fulfillment of old test. expectations of Elijah to return*

_____

In Matthew 11:14, Christ states concerning John, *"And if you are willing to accept it, he is the Elijah who was to come."*

📖 Now compare this verse to Matthew 17:11–13. This passage occurs right after the Mount of Transfiguration moment, where Jesus shows Himself glorified, along with supernatural appearances of Elijah and Moses. What new insight do you have about the Elijah they were waiting for and John the Baptist?

_____

_____

_____

_____

We also see in the passage of Matthew 17:11–13 the following confirmation after the fact:

> *" 'Elijah is coming and will restore all things; but I say to you, that Elijah already came, and they did not recognize him, but did to him whatever they wished. So also the Son of Man is going to suffer at their hands.' Then the disciples understood that he had spoken to them about John the Baptist."*

📖 This passage fulfills the prophecy given in Malachi 4:5–6; the final words of our Old Testament. Read these two verses and write the purpose of the prophecy here:

_____

_____

_____

Through this prophecy we see just why the Jews were so intent on looking for Elijah. We see additional background of the Luke 3:16 verse in the passage of John 1:21–27.

📖 Read John 1:21–27. What was the situation here? Why do you think John responded the way he did?

_____

_____

_____

_____

The people had no idea why this man (obviously not the person they expected) was there doing such things and preparing the way for Christ. John didn't say he was Elijah, or a prophet, or the Christ. John simply quoted from Isaiah 40:3, the prophecy of his ministry, as at this moment Isaiah's prophecy was literally being fulfilled. In this scene, we see John simply being obedient to God, as we are also called to be obedient to His call on our lives today.

John knew it wasn't about him; it was all about the coming Messiah. He was not looking for his own glory, but to bring glory to Christ. Just as Jesus walked on earth, continually pointing others to the Father, we, as Christ's followers are charged to lead others to Christ—just like John the Baptist.

John's wonderful statement and goal that is recorded in John 3:30 is applicable to us all, *"He must increase, but I must decrease."*

Please tuck this verse into your heart—and remember it always. It is the perfect goal of every follower of Christ—for His will to increase in our lives, and for our will to decrease. We will talk more about this in Day Five.

To point others to Christ, we and our egos must step aside to allow **all** of the focus to fall on Christ—no glory should shine upon us and our own strength.

Well, if it wasn't about John and the following he led, than what was all the fuss about? Why was John so intent on leading people to someone other than himself? John so desperately wanted the people to not just claim Christ, but to *"bring forth fruits in keeping with repentance"* (Luke 3:8). They were to live lives worthy of whom they claimed to follow. Once John touched their hearts with instructions on how to live, they were eager to know more. The people wondered if he was perhaps hiding the fact that he was the Christ.

In Luke 3:16 John defuses such fanciful thoughts by saying, *"I baptize you with water; but One is coming who is mightier than I, and I am not fit to untie the thong of His sandals; He will baptize you with the Holy Spirit and fire."*

John was there to bring them to repentance and to pave the way for the complete message that would come from Christ.

When we focus on reading the entire Bible, we witness how God truly has His purpose set out before the foundation of the world, and how each person who walks upon earth plays a role in continuing His plan. God has such a purpose for those He uses in His ministry—we *all* have roles that point others to Christ. Everything in Scripture either provides a foundation for the gospel of Jesus Christ, directly proclaims the gospel, or confirms what the gospel is!

There is only one God, one Holy Spirit, and only one Christ—we are to spend our days not trying to equal them, but to follow Christ's example and bring others to a saving knowledge of Him. We worship God when we love Him, love others, and obey His commands. Repent of your sins, believe in your heart, and confess with your mouth, that Jesus Christ is Lord!

Be sure to work on memorizing the focus verse, and think about the significance of John's statement.

*Did You Know?*
**SANDAL THONGS**

This reference in Luke 3:16 gives us a clue to the humility that John possessed. To bother with another person's sandal, especially in taking it off of their foot, was the type of work normally reserved for a servant—a lowly servant at that! Even in Abraham's day, this was considered a low task, as seen in Genesis 14:22–23 where Abraham refuses to even accept the strap of the king of Sodom's sandal, accepting nothing from him (showing that he wanted to stay as separate as possible). This image that John gives us should bring to mind the moment when Jesus washed the feet of his disciples at the Last Supper, showing that He saw Himself as a servant to all.

# FOR ME TO FOLLOW GOD

Isn't God amazing? Not only is His plan for mankind confirmed over and over throughout the Bible, but His provision of a forerunner is also shown to us. Our understanding of John the Baptist is a little clearer, and our understanding of Jesus and his mission on earth seems to make more sense in the grand story of God's plan.

 Think about your own life and what your life story would look like. At first glance, events in your life may not seem to build on each other, but I believe that all of our stories do just that. I challenge you to take a look at the phases in your life and see if you can see how God has used some significant event in your life to shape who you are and how He can use you in His kingdom, with a specific calling. Journal in the following focuses, pointing out your life shaping details:

**Not only is God's plan for humanity confirmed over and over throughout the Bible, but His provision of a forerunner is also shown to us.**

Childhood specific events:

Sunday school.

_____

_____

_____

_____

Teen specific events:

Camp shiloh was huge.

Youth group.

Chad Vanky

Breakup. Whole life change.

Work specific events:

Kyla

Britany & Hannah

giving all to God will be ok if they get rid of me.

Family specific events:

Marriage.

Having children.

Becoming a mom.

Deciding life decisions

_____

_____

Church background/faith experience events:

Camp Shilon. Aquire the Fire. Multiple youth groups.

_____

_____

_____

_____

With all of these categories, can you see how your life experiences have pointed to the ways you serve, or could serve, God in ministry?

Ministry events/calling on your life (ministering to others, or serving in some way):

Mission trip to Arizona

_____

_____

_____

_____

Ways God can use you to serve that you have not considered:

_____

_____

_____

_____

_____

Genesis 50:20
1 Cor. 1:3-4
Romans 8:28-21

All of these areas have an impact on other areas in our lives. No matter what significant events we have experienced, our lives will show the effects of these events in the roles we play. God is able to use those very experiences to bring forth a calling in our lives, specific to our passion and perseverance. The things we have overcome, we will be able to help others overcome. Through the struggles we battle, we will be able to keep others from battling. God is honored when we take all that we are and all we have gone through and use them to show His presence in our lives.

John the Baptist had a bond with Jesus, and through his upbringing and his training, John's experiences helped him to pave the way for the Messiah. John set out as the forerunner, the one who would step aside when the Messiah arrived. John's role was critical, and specific; and was built on a lifetime of preparation. John was called by God to do the ministry set before him, and John was obedient.

 *Father God,* I thank You for sending John to pave the way for the Messiah two thousand years ago. Lord I praise You for giving Your written Word that I can study and learn from, and I thank You for the gift of Your Holy Spirit who guides us into all truth. Lord, the obedience of John is such an example for me today—may I live a life of obedience and love for You, and may I always bring glory to You in all I do. Lord I pray that I would be a willing vessel ready for service and be willing to sacrifice my conveniences for Your call. In Jesus' name, Amen.

**God is honored when we take all that we are and all we have gone through and use them to show His presence in our lives.**

Prayer Requests:

- Christina's friend in Tennessee
    struggling through chemo
        taking break to find direction

- Lylan rash
    in hospital

- Troy

- Grady lip tie

- Lynden Manor   covid cases

# FIVE

# A Call to Ministry

## COMMISSIONED TO SERVE
## 3:16 VERSES: MATTHEW, MARK

How exciting to finally be at the point of our study when Jesus interacts with the people around Him, revealing His standing as Messiah. We have studied His relationship with John a little last week, but now we will dive into some more details about the beginning of Jesus' ministry on earth!

We will visualize the moment when John baptized Jesus, and we will also watch the Gospels unfold as the disciples are chosen for service. The picture that Scripture gives us of John and Jesus in the river, fulfilling prophecy and bringing forth a new era in our Christian heritage is amazing. The picture of the Trinity is so very clear in this lesson and is a topic that we will cover in detail.

Just as John is baptizing new believers in the river, Jesus begins to bring new believers into God's kingdom as well. Jesus' goal is much broader than any mission that God could have given another man, because Jesus is the Messiah, the One through whom our salvation would come.

After examining the baptism scene, our focus will move on to the appointing of the apostles. Jesus gives us a clear example of how to appoint others to serve with us in ministry, and in turn, gives us a road map for yet another facet of Christ-like living.

*Jesus' goal is much broader than any mission that God could have given another man, because Jesus is the Messiah, the One through whom our salvation would come.*

# TIME TO STEP ASIDE
# 3:16 VERSE: MATTHEW

*"And after being baptized, Jesus went up immediately from the water; and behold, the heavens were opened, and he saw the Spirit of God descending as a dove, and coming upon Him."*

Right on the heels of our study of John comes the baptism of Jesus. What a glorious verse to include in our 3:16s! This is the absolute, undeniable arrival of the Holy Spirit to dwell inside man on the earth, as well as the start of Jesus' earthly ministry. The purpose for the Holy Spirit coming to Jesus was not to get rid of the sin in Jesus' life, for He was already sinless, but rather, to be a sign to believers and to equip and assist Jesus for ministry. It was a sign to the people around Jesus that God would send His Holy Spirit to those who believed in Jesus. The confirmation given that the baptism of Jesus was truly a "God thing" is shown in this focus passage, in Matthew 3:16–17, where God the Father himself speaks from heaven to tell Jesus that He was loved. In that moment, the Father is also telling those around Jesus that Christ is in fact the Son of God and is pleasing to God the Father.

To get the full meaning of today's focus verse, and why it is so pivotal to our understanding of Christianity, we have to remember the setting. God didn't use just *any* man to prepare the way for Christ—he used John the Baptist. As we learned in last week's lesson, John and Jesus first "met each other" while they were still in their mothers' wombs. God gave John and Jesus, the two offspring, a bond that would never be broken. John had helped lay the foundation that brought this moment of the baptism of Jesus into focus, and because of all He accomplished through God's leading; the crowds who witnessed this event knew this was something incredible.

John the Baptist begins his ministry by baptizing many people, giving them a baptism of repentance, and proclaiming that he was preparing the way for the Messiah. When the timing is perfect, God introduces the world to their Messiah, and Jesus' ministry on earth begins.

📖 Read Matthew 3:13–15. What was John's reaction to Jesus' presence?

_____

_____

What was Jesus' response to John regarding his hesitation?

_____

_____

Jesus comes to Galilee, wanting to be baptized by John, but John feels unworthy to baptize the man whom he knew to be the Messiah. Even though John is hesitant, Jesus makes sure that the will of God is going to be done! Jesus knows that in John's obedience would be found the fulfillment of prophetic words from long ago. In response, John surely isn't going to stand in the way of the plans of God.

The example Jesus gives us for following the will of God permeates His message and entire ministry, but let's look at one verse that speaks to this specifically, John 4:34:

*"Jesus said to them, 'My food is to do the will of Him who sent Me, and to accomplish His work.' "*

How much clearer do we need to see this? What a wondrous "mission statement" this is for ministry! If it is good enough for Jesus, shouldn't it be sufficient for all mankind as well? At the moment these words are uttered by the Messiah, He has been busy teaching and serving others and has not had time to fill his own temporal needs. The spiritual needs of a woman he meets at a well takes priority. Praise God He takes the time for us all—even those who have a varied past. May we always be as excited about Jesus' mission as He is.

Speaking of excitement, John the Baptist, who has spent his time in ministry proclaiming the coming of the King, now has the opportunity to announce Christ's arrival. John is excited about the honor he has of introducing the people around him to their Savior.

📖 Read John 1:29–34. What a glorious announcement of Jesus' arrival! Record your observations from this passage:

_____

_____

_____

_____

John boldly proclaims who Jesus is to those around him. There is no doubt in his mind that they are standing in the presence of the very One whom he and many others had been prophesying about. John is a witness to everyone that the one they knew as Jesus is the One who would baptize them with the Holy Spirit.

**Passing the Torch:**
John is a dutiful servant who is more than eager to hand over the "dunking rights" to the true baptizer, even though those who helped John would be jealous at the thought of someone taking over John's ministry—a ministry they worked hard to achieve as well. John knows that as he paved the way for Christ, eventually it would be time to pass the torch of leadership to the Christ. Instead of worrying about *his own* ministry, or being jealous that the Messiah is "taking away" some of his followers, John keeps his eye on the goal. John is there to *serve* Jesus and to prepare a path for Him. He is there to bring the fullness of Christ to others, not bring himself glory. More importantly, John is content and secure in not getting the attention and recognition.

Have you served in ministry or in another type of volunteer work? Describe that experience:

_____

_____

_____

_____

_____

*Praise God He takes the time for us all—even those who have a varied past.*

What was your term of service for that specific position? How long did you serve in that capacity?

_____

_____

Was it hard to let go of that position of service? What emotions did you experience with that moment of transition?

_____

_____

_____

_____

**John shows us a wonderful example of reacting to the changing roles of servanthood in a most Christ-like manner**

Any time we serve others, whether secularly or in a ministry atmosphere, we become attached to those we are serving. When our season of service in that capacity is complete, the transition can be hard for us, and the emotions we feel can be surprising. John shows us a wonderful example of reacting to the changing roles of servanthood in a most Christ-like manner. John, who keeps his eyes on Jesus and his heart set on the will of the Lord, is excited about the new phase of God's ministry that is about to occur. He rejoices in being "replaced" and rejoices in the focus being where it always needed to be—on Jesus.

When the time comes for John to direct those who are following him to now follow Christ, it is okay with John because he sees this transition as a *completion* to his ministry, not a tragedy. There is nothing lost in ministry when we see people shift from one season of ministry to another, because we are all here to lead people to Christ, not to ourselves!

📖 Read John 3:22–36. This is John's last testimony before he was imprisoned. What discussion takes place in this passage?

_____

_____

_____

In verse 26, what are John's disciples upset about?

_____

_____

In verse 30, what is John's response?

_____

_____

John perfectly displays this concept of passing the torch in saying that the focus should be on Jesus and not himself, because leading the people to Jesus Christ is his whole purpose anyway! Christ is the head of *all* ministries and is to be the one that we all follow. John understands that there is nothing better than having people run to the very Savior that he has been pointing them to. He understands the essence of Christ-like living: "Lead others to Jesus Christ. . . . Point them to Jesus Christ so that *Christ* can be their Savior.

John wants to "decrease" in attention, so that the attention can "increase" in Jesus' ministry.

The thing I love about this whole concept: belief, baptism, and so on, is the fact that at some point, human beings are no longer able to complete the task in their own strength. At some point, all of our rituals, religions, customs, and comfort zones reach their limits, and then we are left, once again, needing God to complete the scene. With John, God the Father paves the way, but it is now time for His Son Jesus to "seal the deal" so to speak.

Picture the moment with me. I imagine it a beautiful day, and the crowds are watching the baptisms taking place, rejoicing with each new believer. Some are strolling along talking about the change of heart they have recently experienced concerning their faith, while others sit on the shore, still dripping from the river water that has soaked their clothing and shivering with excitement from their dip with John. They are ready, prepared, and eager for the Messiah. They believed John when he said that the Messiah was coming, and that He would be the One to bring their baptism to a new level . . . a level that John could not take them to. **The Messiah would give them the Holy Spirit.**

Do you think the people listening to John's teaching really understood what he meant about the Holy Spirit? Why or why not?

_____

_____

_____

_____

John makes no mystery out of the fact that he baptizes with water and that the Messiah is coming to baptize the people in the Holy Spirit. John's baptism is for repentance, and Jesus' baptism is complete, bringing the remission of sins and the gift of the Holy Spirit. Paving the way for another person implies that the other person will finish the task. So, what makes Jesus so different? Why should He have to finish what John started?

Prophecies are found throughout the Old Testament that confirm over and over again of the validity of John's claim and the authenticity of the role of Jesus as Savior. They also point to this moment we see in our Matthew 3:16 focus verse; the moment that the Holy Spirit would descend upon Jesus in the form of a dove. This is the moment that the Holy Spirit begins to dwell in the hearts of those who accept Jesus as their Savior.

📖 Look up Isaiah 11:1–2. In this passage in Isaiah, we have an Old Testament confirmation of what occurs with Jesus. In Isaiah 11:1–2, who is mentioned, and what are their distinct roles? Answer the questions below:

Isaiah 11:1 refers to:

_____

Who is the Branch mentioned here?

_____

> *"He must increase, but I must decrease."*
>
> *John 3:30*

Isaiah 11:2 refers to:

_____

What will the Spirit do, according to this verse?

_____

We learn in Isaiah 11:1–2 that Jesus, the One God will send out of the lineage of Jesse, will arrive at the appointed time, and the Holy Spirit will empower Him. Do you see the significance of our Matthew 3:16 focus verse as it confirms the prophecy in Isaiah 11:2? What characteristics are revealed about the Holy Spirit?

_____

_____

_____

The Holy Spirit is omniscient (all knowing), omnipotent (all powerful), and omnipresent (all present), as is the Father and the Son. Some of the characteristics in this verse that describe the outpouring of the Holy Spirit in believers are: wisdom, understanding, counsel, strength, knowledge, and "the fear of the Lord." These attributes are imparted to believers through the Holy Spirit.

Another reference some see to Jesus receiving the Holy Spirit is given in Isaiah 42:1. What new insight about Jesus do you see here?

_____

_____

God delights in Jesus, and we see that Jesus will bring justice to the nations!

So much happened in that moment in the river with John and Jesus. It was more than ceremony. It was more than conversion. It was life changing for more than just those two men. It forever changed the way we as believers see God and the way that we interact with Him. From that moment on, the Holy Spirit would dwell in the hearts of those who believed in Jesus, and Jesus proves once again that He is our perfect example of how to live for God.

> **John and Jesus' encounter at the river forever changed the way we as believers see God and the way that we interact with Him.**

 A Call to Ministry

# DOWN BY THE RIVER SIDE
# 3:16 VERSE: MATTHEW

_"And after being baptized, Jesus went up immediately from the water; and behold, the heavens were opened, and he saw the Spirit of God descending as a dove, and coming upon Him."_

Now that we have more background on the Holy Spirit's descending on Jesus, look at the Matthew 3:16 focus verse again with me:

*"And after being baptized, Jesus went up immediately out of the water; and
behold, the heavens were opened, and he saw the Spirit of God descending as
a dove, and coming upon Him,"*

The Spirit descended, and the evidence to the crowd was undeniable. There
was no question that something magnificent had just happened.

📖 Re-read Matthew 3:16, and then read verse 17. What other occurrences
set the baptism of Jesus apart from the others John performed?

_____

_____

_____

_____

Not only did this scene involve Jesus, but the Spirit of God descended, and
our God's voice bellowed down from the heavens as well. God knows us
(and our human nature) so much more than we'd like to think. He knew
that the crowd would need a visual sign to go along with what was happening—to be able to comprehend the tiniest details of this huge moment for
mankind. What did this baptism truly mean? It was the beginning of Jesus'
ministry. Jesus identified His connection with the human race, leading by
example with a servant attitude.

The important insight from verse 17 is the fact that this seal of approval by
God was given when God said (in a loud, heavenly voice) that Jesus was His
Son, and He was pleased with Him, and loved Him. Who would argue with
that kind of job reference?

The fact that the baptism of Jesus was the **only** baptism John performed that
was followed by the opening of the heavens should have been a clue to those
who witnessed the event. Our human nature will have us (at times) doubt
the truth and talk ourselves out of believing what we might have seen, and
our Savior knows this all too well.

Who was present at the baptism of Jesus in these verses?

1 _____

2 _____

3 _____

4 _____

As a response to our collective humanity's unbelief, God chose to have a
visual display far more unexplainable than anyone would expect, so that
there would be absolutely no doubt about what the bystanders had seen. In
this specific moment, we have four main characters: John, Jesus, God the
Father, and the Holy Spirit. This is the only time we see the three parts of
the Trinity in such a tangible way in the New Testament, showing their
individual characters while acting as one in perfect harmony.

📖 Taking one last look at Matthew 3:16–17, fill in the following spaces:

Jesus was in the _____.

God the Father spoke from _____.

The Holy Spirit descended as a _____.

### *Extra Mile*
## JESUS PRAYS

An interesting note—although all four Gospels mention the baptism of Jesus, only one mentions that Jesus was praying at the time that heaven was opened and the dove descended. Take a look at all four presentations if you dare—and find the one that mentions this fact! There is such a sweet moment here that we should reflect on. Even the Son of God, one third of the Trinity, communicated with the Father in prayer. At such a moment of spiritual connection, the response from the heavenlies was visible to all who saw the baptism.

### *Put Yourself In Their Shoes*
## FOLLOWING JESUS

Jesus receiving the Holy Spirit set the stage for *us* receiving the Holy Spirit—He was the model for what all believers would receive with the baptism of Jesus. Those who followed the teachings of John would now follow Jesus. The accounts after this moment in the New Testament often refer to being baptized in Jesus' name. Please don't be misled and see this as inconsistent with the baptism we practice today in the "Name of the Father and of the Son and of the Holy Spirit." Being baptized in Jesus' name meant being baptized with the acknowledgement of believing all He taught and following His ministry.

Again, we see that verses 16 and 17 together contain a clear image of the three distinct persons of the Trinity at work together—one in flesh displayed as a man, one in Spirit displayed as a dove, and one in a confirming voice from heaven! All three present. All three separate. All three functioning in perfect unity.

God wanted the believers watching this moment from the shore (as well as believers throughout the ages) to acknowledge Jesus Christ, as the Son of God—to acknowledge that Christ was charged by God to provide a more complete baptism to those who followed Him. This acquiring of the Spirit at the event of baptism is a confirmation of the promise that *we also* have access to the Holy Spirit. Through this amazing display, everyone could readily accept the change in allegiance that they had to make. No longer was John the focus, although he would continue to be used in Jesus' ministry. Now, the One who had been promised was in their midst, and all who believed in him could follow him personally. They now would shift from being followers, or disciples of John, to being disciples of Jesus.

We find references to the Trinity in other passages of Scripture as well. Look up Isaiah 61:1. In this verse, we see the Spirit of the Lord, God, and "me." Who is "me" in this verse?

_____

_____

Isn't it awesome to see the reference of the Trinity yet again? Father, Son, and Holy Spirit . . . Jesus functioning with the other two parts of the godhead—just as we see in our focus verse with His baptism.

The references to the Trinity aren't just for our fascination, believe it or not! There is such practical application for us as well. The model given by God to mark the beginning of Jesus' ministry on earth, the baptism and portrayal of the Trinity, continues even today with our charge to minister to the world. We know who our God is, so that we can tell others who our God is. God wants to be *their* God too. This is our mission as believers: to share the gospel with the world.

Read Matthew 28:18–20. This passage is referred to as "The Great Commission." What does it commission believers to do? What is the purpose of this charge?

_____

_____

_____

_____

_____

Look also at Acts 1:8. What do you see as the purpose for receiving the Holy Spirit in the context of this verse?

_____

_____

What does this mean for us today? We, who live in the generation of the Trinity revealed, with the Holy Spirit dwelling within us? This means that we have a baptism as Jesus described in Matthew 28; a complete baptism that reflects the perfect Trinity: Father, Son and Holy Spirit. This complete belief and baptism gives us power from God to preach the gospel to the "uttermost ends of the earth." If Jesus didn't want us to baptize others in acknowledgment of the Trinity, then He wouldn't have asked us to do so. The very scene with Jesus' own baptism confirms our perception of God and our method of baptism.

One of the most exciting things in this whole story is the fact that even Jesus, a part of our Holy Trinity, with all powers and abilities, had the Holy Spirit sent on his behalf to help and guide him. The same Holy Spirit is also sent to help and guide **us**!

📖 Read John 14:16–18, and verse 26. What is the purpose of the Holy Spirit in the lives of believers?

_____

_____

_____

According to these verses, do unbelievers (the world) have access to this Spirit?

_____

_____

The Holy Spirit was sent to believers to help guide us into all truth, leading us to the Father. Those who do not believe in Jesus are unable to receive the Holy Spirit, because they do not abide in God; Father, Son, and Holy Spirit.

Any time we feel that we can "do it" on our own, whatever "it" is, we need to focus completely on one thing: God wants us to function in His power, and in the abilities given us by the Holy Spirit. As Jesus was baptized, all were able to see the Holy Spirit (in the form of a dove) rest on Him—something they would not completely understand until the Day of Pentecost, when all believers received the Holy Spirit.

**APPLY** Do you see the Holy Spirit as a helper and comforter in your life? Can you think of a time when you knew that the Holy Spirit was with you, guiding you toward God's will? Journal your thoughts:

_____

_____

_____

_____

_____

_____

_____

_____

If anyone questioned the deity of Christ at that moment (at Jesus' baptism), they were probably very out of touch with reality. It is hard to comprehend how someone could deny such an act of God while witnessing it first hand. Isn't it great that John the Baptist had such a public confirmation to his ministry? He had been telling everyone that the Messiah was coming, and then

*Word Study*
## THE HOLY SPIRIT

John 14:26 describes the Holy Spirit as *"the helper,"* and this term is translated from the Greek *parakletos,* which can be defined as "an intercessor, counselor, advocate, or comforter." (Greek Dictionary of the New Testament in the *Key Word Study Bible,* AMG Publishers, p. 55). The Key Word Study Bible (NASB), adds in the cross-reference notes the following: "Paracletos, one called alongside to help; or, intercessor."

More verses to look up that identify this role of the Holy Spirit: John 7:39; 15:26; 16:7; Romans 8:26; and 1 John 2:1.

the Messiah finally arrived. God had unmistakably confirmed this. John's charge to service had been completed, and Jesus was now the focus of God's message to the people. What a wonderful moment for John the Baptist, to see the culmination of a vision given by God.

Do you realize how much Christ set aside to love us so deeply? Christ went from the ruling in the heavenlies to becoming an earthly vessel, and He chose to live like a human with human limitations. Christ never lost any of His divine qualities. Yet He was fully man on earth, functioning in the capacity that we do, so He would be able to experience all we are. Christ only used His powers to help others, to provide miracles that would show who He was, and to confirm His standing in God. To explain this, it's something like owning a sports car, but walking to work. Yet from the moment He descended to earth, Jesus focused on the goal He had, and lived in the exact manner necessary to fulfill the will of His Father, and the prophecies written about Him. With all that Jesus had experienced on earth to this point, we will see that this pivotal moment in time would dramatically change the culture of those who lived in the midst of Jesus, and had been accustomed to following the Jewish faith, religion and traditions of the day. Jesus was no longer simply the son of Mary and Joseph, according to their village. He was now the baptized, anointed, man of God that would do miraculous things both on earth and in our future in heaven!

Commit Matthew 3:16 verse to memory! We'll have a new focus verse for Day Three. Make it your goal to know both of this week's verses by heart.

> **Christ was fully man on earth, functioning in the capacity that we do, so He would be able to experience all we are.**

DAY THREE

# A Few "Sorta" Good Men
# 3:16 Verse: Mark

*"And He appointed the twelve: Simon (to whom He gave the name Peter)."*

Well, now that Jesus had been baptized, and brought into ministry, He needed to designate a staff, right? Great leadership always appoints people to help them accomplish the vision that God has given them. To provide an example for leadership and discipleship, Jesus had to establish that practice Himself. Who could better show us Christ-like living than Jesus Christ?

Jesus walked along, ministering to those in His path, and finding those whom He was going to bring alongside Him. This was no random selection; Jesus knew exactly whom He was calling and why. The men He used were busy tending to their family occupations, or were busy with a task at hand when Jesus asked them to drop all they were doing in order to follow Him.

> **If God could use twelve men in all their humanity, then He can use you and me today!**

The great thing about this scene is this: Jesus picked people just like you and me to do kingdom work. How exciting is that? Please remember from this day forward that if God could use those twelve men in all their humanity, then He can use you and me today!

Many people followed Jesus wherever He went, waiting to see a miracle or some amazing feat being accomplished by this man in their midst. The mass of people may not have realized that Jesus was gathering a group that would support Him in ministry as He traveled from place to place. He asked men who were actively working and busy with their own lives to drop everything they were doing to follow Him. *And they did.* When they became a part of His following, and when the timing was right, Jesus decided to bring structure to this plan. Jesus brought those He had chosen with Him on the mountainside, named them as His apostles, and these men were ready to go forth in a group, serving their Savior in unity.

📖 When John the Baptist had announced the baptism and arrival of Jesus, John's own disciples heard this proclamation. Look at John 1:35–40.

Who was one of the disciples who heard John? Where did he go with Jesus?

_____

_____

Andrew was one of John the Baptists' disciples. He was the first one Jesus called to be a disciple. He wasn't the only one in his family that would serve God, as we will see next.

📖 What did Andrew do in response, as seen in verses 41–42?

_____

_____

How did Jesus respond to Andrew and Simon?

_____

_____

Andrew told his brother about the amazing proclamation that John the Baptist had made, proclaiming that Jesus was the "Lamb of God," and took him to see Jesus. Jesus acknowledged Simon in a special way—giving him honor by changing his name to Peter, which means "rock." We will look into the significance of Simon Peter's name a little bit later. Right now, let's look at some more divine appointments.

📖 Read John 1:43–51. Who was appointed, and what was Nathaniel's initial response to Jesus? What changed his mind?

_____

_____

_____

_____

📖 Look up Mark 1:16–18. What happens in this passage?

_____

_____

_____

_____

Jesus sees Simon and his brother Andrew, casting a net, and calls them to be fishers of men. I imagine they had gone to work after meeting Him previ-

> Isn't it amazing that the disciples not only changed their occupation in a split second, but they left family and employees behind, not even finishing their work-day together? Now that is instant obedience!

ously, wondering when they would see Him again and this was the moment that they decided to leave their jobs and follow Jesus in ministry.

Now read Mark 1:19–20. Who were called, and what were they doing at the time?

_____

_____

Who did they specifically leave behind (in the boat)?

_____

Isn't it amazing that they not only changed their occupation in a split second, but they left family and employees behind, not even finishing their workday together? Now that is instant obedience!

In Mark 3:14, we see that Jesus ultimately appointed twelve men, designating them as apostles. He appointed them to follow Him and to preach the message He gave them. Why did He choose twelve disciples? Or a better question might be: why did he choose this motley assortment of leaders?

Most of the Twelve were not very noteworthy in society; a few were despised; and a few were even related to each other. Fishermen, tax collectors, and the like were not what that society would have considered being among the most respected professions!

It was not their impressive resumé or knowledge of Scripture that caused these men to be worthy in Christ's eyes—it was their potential dedication to the cause of spreading the gospel and the true intentions in their heart that won Him over. It was the simple fact that they would follow Him, and not try to take His spot as Savior. There was no great campaign with a controversial election. There was no "smear campaign" going on among these men discrediting others to elevate themselves. They did not ask to be selected. They were selected while focused on activities that were critical to their lives. They were selected because God wanted to mold them, use them, and walk with them. They were chosen because God called them.

These men who were chosen were already involved in activities they were dedicated to. They put their heart into their work and focused on the task at hand. Their hearts were set on the present and were not usually swayed by what others were doing.

Like the disciples, no matter what our words or actions may say about our intentions, our heart is what God sees, and God judges us based on our hearts. Their hearts are what God searched, and He found them to be useful vessels to serve Him. They were not necessarily perfect, but they were useful to God. Teachable. Loyal. Willing.

 Are you teachable? Would God consider you loyal and willing?

_____

Take a moment to ask God to shape you into a more teachable, loyal and willing servant, focusing on His will, and not just focused on pleasing man. So, who were the Twelve? What was their qualification for service? Let's do some research.

📖 Read Mark 3:16–18. Write down the names of the twelve apostles appointed by Jesus:

_____

_____

_____

_____

The first apostles were

"... *Simon (to whom he gave the name Peter), and James, the son of Zebedee, and John the brother of James (to them he gave the name Boanerges, which means, "Sons of Thunder"); and Andrew, and Philip, and Bartholomew, and Matthew, and Thomas, and James the son of Alphaeus, and Thaddeus, and Simon the Zealot; and Judas Iscariot.*" (Mark 3:16–19)

As we see the listing of apostles, and see how Jesus had a special plan for Peter, let's back up for a minute and search the Scriptures a little deeper. Notice the Scripture passages that come immediately before and after the one we are focused on. The passage directly before it deals with the crowds following Christ. Picture Jesus with many people following after Him, and He's attempting to separate Himself from the masses. Christ asked his helpers (disciples) to get a boat for Him to take him away from the multitudes, which they faithfully did. From this point, Jesus went up to the mountains, taking with him those He had chosen.

These followers were not just chosen men of Christ. He gave each of them the title of **apostle,** anointed them with power to preach the Word of God and authority to cast out demons. These were no longer just ordinary men who followed their Savior. They were separated for service, and given a task to complete.

📖 Remember the verse we looked at earlier this week from the end of the book of Matthew? Let's review for a moment the charge that Jesus would eventually give to all believers, found in Matthew 28:18–20. Record it here:

_____

_____

_____

Do you see the direction we are going here? That's right! The first disciples modeled the very charge for all believers. Again, Jesus gives us the example of how to fulfill what God asks. We bring others alongside us to help in the ministry of the gospel. Jesus showed us how to do this through His appointing of the disciples. Out of the multitude of believers, Jesus saw those with a call from the Father on their lives, and put them into positions of servant leadership. Jesus saw the ones whom the Father had brought alongside Him, and He asked them to serve with Him in ministry.

📖 Read Acts 6:1–7. Describe the scene:

_____

_____

> **The disciples were not just chosen men of Christ. He gave each of them the title of apostle, anointed them with power to preach the Word of God and authority to cast out demons. These were no longer just ordinary men who followed their Savior. They were separated for service, and given a task to complete.**

Here in the book of Acts, after Jesus had ascended to the heavens, we see the apostles carrying out the Great Commission. We see them appointing helpers. God had blessed them with a great following, and now these men needed to select other helpers to serve meals so that those chosen to preach could focus on preaching. The apostles were following the example of delegation given by Jesus.

**APPLY** Overload! Have you been involved with a task, project, or calling that was just way more than you could handle? Ever had a workload that seemed insurmountable? Explain how it felt to be so overloaded:

_____

_____

_____

_____

We have all experienced such a moment at some point in time. When overload hits, it is time to call in for backup. Today's lesson shows us how to scripturally call for backup—by asking others to serve alongside you, so that you can stay focused on your calling. The Lord *will* equip you to do what He has called you to do, and He will call others to come alongside you in service.

How does Jesus' example of appointing helpers compare with your way of asking for help? Do you look for the "right" person, or do you tag the person closest to you, whether that person is right for the job or not?

_____

_____

_____

_____

**APPLY** How can you change your method of asking for help so that it becomes more like Jesus' model?

_____

_____

_____

_____

Continue to memorize the verses for this week. Take a moment to pray, thanking God for His provision of servants to minister the gospel throughout the world. Praise God for your church leadership; pray for your pastors.

**Spend Some Time in Prayer.**

 *Lord,* I pray that as I go through this study, that I will see practical helps from Scripture for many aspects of my life. In this section specifically, I pray that the Lord will reveal those around me whom You have called to help me with the overwhelming aspects of ministry and/or daily life. I pray that You will supernaturally bring to mind those people that would be willing and able to assist me in meeting needs, and in keeping me focused on the task that You have for me.

# FOCUSING ON PETER
# 3:16 VERSE: MARK

*"And He appointed the twelve: Simon (to whom He gave the name Peter)."*

Please notice in our Mark 3:16 focus verse that Peter is not only mentioned first, but His name is separated in verse assignment from any others. It wasn't because he was the first one Jesus asked to follow Him, because that was Simon Peter's brother Andrew. In fact, Andrew brought Peter to meet Jesus! Whatever the reason, God had a plan. Peter's original name is Simon, but Christ decided to give him the surname of Peter. Jesus gave Peter a special new name, a name that means "rock." Let's take a few minutes and discover some unique moments in Scripture where God shows us a little bit more about Peter.

📖 Read Matthew 16:13–20. What does Jesus ask His disciples?

_____

_____

_____

Who answers Jesus? What does this person say?

_____

_____

📖 What is Jesus' response to this answer?

_____

_____

> *"And He appointed the twelve: Simon (to whom He gave the name Peter)."*
>
> *Mark 3:16*

Look closely at verse 18. This verse contains the first reference in Scripture to the church. Also key to this verse is Christ's statement concerning the "rock" upon which He would build His church. Controversies have ensued for centuries as to what Christ had in mind when he referred to this "rock." Many people believe that in this statement Jesus affirms Peter as the "rock" that the church is built on. Clearly, Christ praises Peter's bold response, and He uses it and the new name as a play on words that embodies the spirit of faithfulness and unswerving devotion that would often be exhibited within His church. In reality, Christ states in this verse that the body of believers collectively would be the "church," and that rock-solid faith first exhibited by Peter combined with Holy Spirit anointing would indelibly mark this institution. As for Peter himself, here he is only a follower who understands who Jesus is and who sent Him. No doubt Peter has a special role of prominence in church history—as apostle and foundational leader of the church—but the church is only built on the truth of the gospel. That truth is based on the fact that Jesus is the Son of God, and is the Christ, which is the very thing that Peter proclaims at this moment.

Looking closely at the original texts and words in Greek, we find that Peter's name may be indicative of a smaller stone (*petros*) or boulder, whereas the church type of rock mentioned in this verse (*petra*) likely refers to bedrock, or a much larger mass of rock formation. Therefore, the rock that the church is built on is a *petra* rock, and not a *petros* rock, and cannot refer specifically to Peter himself.

Remember that this discussion took place in Caesarea Philippi, where the gates of Hades were said to be; in a cave, in the cleft of a large rock formation. Picture the scene: Jesus is talking with His disciples; Peter confesses that Jesus is the Christ, and then Jesus says that He will free all believers from the fear of spending eternity in Hades. Jesus showed them right there in front of what was allegedly the entrance of hell that *He* was the path to heaven. There is no mistaking the intensity of the truth that as the little rocks (believers) proclaim that Jesus is the Christ and the Son of God, that the church will be formed through their belief in Him (the big Rock). Jesus is our rock! He is the foundation of our faith. We, as a collective body of believers, make up the church, and we worship Jesus Christ as our Lord and Savior.

Peter was just as human as you and me. In fact, he was so passionate about following Christ that he acted a little rash at times. One moment he is saying profound things in his zeal to follow his Savior, the next minute he is saying things that bring rebuke from his Savior.

📖 Read Matthew 16:20–23. What does Peter do, and what is Jesus' response to Peter's actions?

_____

_____

_____

Isn't this an amazing change in dialogue? The very disciple that Jesus renamed Peter is now the one who is rebuked by Jesus! Jesus even tells him to "Get behind me Satan," which is certainly not a gentle admonishment! Jesus' goal is to stay in the will of the Father, and this should also be our goal as believers. Peter's rebuke was based on this very concept. No matter how much we want to keep someone from suffering—and Peter obviously did not want to see his beloved Savior suffer—we cannot ask for anything less than God's will in the situation.

**Pay the Cost**
Read on through Matthew 16:24–28. What a wonderful passage this is for us, who, like the first disciples, want to follow Christ. This passage gives us a rundown of the cost of discipleship.

**List the costs outlined in the following verses:**

Verse 24:

_____

_____

Verse 25:

_____

_____

Not only do we lay down our lives, pick up our crosses, and follow Him daily, we also "lose our lives," or our focus on worldly gain, for Jesus. Verses

## HOSPITALITY OR BUSYNESS?

Could Peter have been following Abraham's example for hospitality toward those sent from God? In Genesis 18 we see a wonderful example of Abraham's hospitality. Surely, Peter would have known this passage, this story. The tents he was proposing to build were holy tents, or tabernacles, not just a camping shelter. Even so, it was no time to be building a tent; it was time to worship.

Whatever Peter's motive, Jesus used the situation as a teaching moment for Peter and for us all.

26–28 show us that these costs will be worth the sacrifice, as we receive our prize in the form of salvation.

**APPLY** In what areas do you feel you could change your daily routine that would better reflect a life of one who has "picked up their cross" and followed Him? Journal your thoughts here:

_____

_____

_____

_____

_____

_____

_____

_____

Read Matthew 17:1–9. This passage is right on the heels of the last moment with Peter and his wonderful confession of the deity of Jesus Christ, and his tragic missing of the point. What is the scene we read about here?

_____

_____

_____

What does Peter decide to do in response to what Jesus allows the group to see and experience on the mountaintop?

_____

_____

_____

What are God's words in response to Peter's actions, as shown in verse 5 of this passage in Matthew 17?

_____

_____

What is Jesus' response to the disciples after they have heard the voice of God (Matthew 17:7–9)?

_____

_____

Peter is the one who wanted to build tents for the figures seen at the Mount of Transfiguration. Maybe he was going on the example he knew from the Old Testament. Abraham saw three men one day, knew they were from God, and quickly made a meal for them. Abraham was focused on hospitality, so maybe Peter felt he had to do likewise. Or maybe, Peter wanted them to dwell on that mountain for awhile in those tents he wanted. Maybe Peter wanted to honor them with this action. Scripture tells us that Peter didn't even realize what he was saying. This was a knee-jerk reaction to being overwhelmed by the moment. Either way, Peter busied himself with his plans, and the Lord made a point of bringing him back to the reason they followed Jesus; to listen to Him! Peter clearly loved the Lord, and wanted to honor Jesus and the other two on that mountain.

📖 Now read John 18:1–10. What did Peter do in this passage, according to verse 10?

_____

_____

📖 Look at John 18:11, and also Luke 22:51. What is Jesus' response? What did He do to fix what Peter had impulsively done?

_____

_____

_____

_____

📖 List any further insight you gain of Jesus' response to Peter from Matthew 26:52–54.

_____

_____

_____

_____

### Did You Know?

### ? ELIJAH AND MOSES ON THE MOUNT

Why Elijah and Moses? These two men from the Old Testament were the only two recorded in the Old Testament that *specifically* asked to see God's glory. Elijah and Moses were the only two who God chose to pass in front of showing His presence in such a way. Both men were hidden in the rock, one in a cleft, and one in a cave, while the glory of the Lord passed in front of them. Both men were only able to see the back of God, for if they saw His face, they would have surely died. Both men were bold, and both men ached for God's presence.

Peter not only proclaimed Christ, and then tried to keep Him from His destiny; now Peter impulsively tries to protect an all-powerful deity. Peter is the one who impulsively cut off the ear of the slave of the priest, somehow trying to protect his beloved Savior. Jesus had a quick correction for Peter, and quickly healed the ear of the slave, restoring what Peter had done. Since Peter's actions were absolutely out of the will of God and outside of the prophetic words that Jesus was there to fulfill, Jesus corrected the impulsive action. The passage in Matthew holds such a wonderful quote, sharing with us a glimpse of just what the Lord could do in protecting Jesus if it were His will for a rescue to occur. Think about it. More than twelve legions of angels, and one legion alone equals six thousand troops.

This isn't the last weak moment we will see Peter experience during the final days of Jesus' ministry on earth. Unfortunately, Peter continues to make decisions that we all find ourselves making . . . impulsive, protective, well meaning, sometimes self-seeking, and occasionally even wrong.

📖 Read Luke 22:54–62. What happens in this scene? What did Peter do that Jesus predicted would happen? What was Peter's reaction when Jesus' prediction came to pass? (Another great account of this scene is found in John 18:15–27 if you would like to read it and compare).

_____

_____

_____

_____

The very follower of Jesus who proclaimed the Messiah's deity was now warming himself by the fire, denying that he knew the Savior. Even in Peter's zeal, Jesus saw his frailty. Even in his excitement to follow Jesus, Peter thought he was protecting himself from danger by denying he knew Jesus. The details that are the most riveting in this scene all point to the fact that those asking the questions already knew that Peter had been with Jesus. The slave girl by the gate was told to let Peter in by another disciple who had said they were together. The slaves of the officers who were warming their hands by the fire knew who Peter was, and the relative of the slave who got his ear cut off by Peter (this person actually witnessed the ear-chopping scene) was the third to ask him his identity. Their repeated questioning is all a clear indication to him that they knew he was lying, making his offense to God that much more glaring.

This was a strong man with strong beliefs who was caught in his own humanity. No doubt, Peter was a true follower of God. Peter's meltdown provides hope for us today as we struggle with weak moments as we follow God. I believe that we are given these examples in Scripture not to discourage us, but to encourage us. I believe we see Peter go through all these situations so that we will remain focused on God even when we mess up. I believe that God will never leave us nor forsake us—*this is a promise from His Word*. I believe that He will always allow us to repent and return to Him, no matter how impulsive or wrong we may be. God wants us to follow Him, even when our humanity rears its ugly head. I believe an example of this is found in the following scene with Peter.

📖 Read John 21:15–17. What did Jesus ask Peter, and what was Peter's response? What was Jesus' ultimate point here?

_____

_____

_____

_____

This moment in Scripture occurs after Jesus died on the cross and is resurrected. This development comes at a moment in time when the resurrected Jesus walked the earth, before He had ascended to heaven to sit at the right hand of God.

The interesting thing to note with this passage is the subtle difference in the two Greek words translated "love" here. Jesus begins by asking Peter if his love is of an *agape* nature—or that of such a deep love that sacrifice would be offered. After asking Peter twice if he had this sort of love for Him, with Peter's response only holding the *phileo* form of love (a friendship level love), Jesus changes His question. The third time, Jesus asks if Peter has a *phileo* love for Him, and in return, Peter in sadness replies that he in fact has *phileo* love for His Savior.

There is only one Savior, and only He could provide the sacrifice necessary to redeem mankind from the pit of hell. Even still, even with Peter's zeal, he could serve God with a type of love that Jesus would accept; a type of love that would be shown by spiritually feeding (teaching) others to follow Christ. Perhaps this was the moment that the rooster's crow finally stopped echoing through Peter's mind. Jesus made a point to personally allow Peter to reclaim himself from his previous denial. At this moment, Jesus also reiterates the reason we follow Him today—to share His gospel with others, to feed His sheep.

*In this touching moment between Peter and Jesus, our Lord reiterates the reason we follow Him today—to share His gospel with others, to feed His sheep.*

Hence, we see that while Jesus was proud to have Peter as an apostle, He also spent much time shaping Peter into a more worthy vessel—one who would think before he reacted. Praise God that Jesus took the time to teach Peter, and that He sent His Holy Spirit who also takes the time to correct us and direct us into a more Christ-like path.

*A Call to Ministry* | DAY FIVE

# FOR ME TO FOLLOW GOD

What a journey we have been on together this week! From John and Jesus standing in the Jordan River, to the appointing of the apostles—we have seen how Jesus began His ministry among us, and how He appointed those who would serve closely with Him. Isn't it amazing to see the details of God's plan? God's timing is always right, and His plan has always been perfect.

Isn't it great that God will take the time to shape us into what He needs for His service? If we look at our own lives, we can see that we are each very special to Christ, and each have things about our character that He constantly fine-tunes. Once we become better in one area, the Holy Spirit will begin the cleansing and changing process in another area—continuing to form us into more Christ-like people.

📖 Read 2 Corinthians 4:5–10. What type of object describes us in verse 7? How does this passage encourage you as you live your life for Jesus Christ?

_____

_____

_____

_____

_____

_____

> **If we look at our own lives, we can see that we are each very special to Christ, and each have things about our character that He constantly fine-tunes.**

The hope we hold inside of us is Jesus. The hope we have in Jesus is that He will sustain us, no matter what we go through. We have the power in us because God placed it there through His Holy Spirit. We are walking, talking, breathing, preaching, representations of the gospel as we share the message that Jesus is Lord with the world around us.

We will steadily continue to reflect more and more of Christ in us as we allow ourselves to be molded by the Master Potter! The lump of clay that we are is nothing without His hand on our lives. Why waste life being a "cracked pot" when God can make us into a beautiful sculpture reflecting His love and goodness?

The thing we can never lose sight of as modern day disciples is that *all* of us have the opportunity to believe, and we *all* have the opportunity to be saved; if we repent, and believe that Jesus is our Savior. At the time of the Twelve, the Holy Spirit had not made Himself available to the human race and had not equipped all believers for ministry. Those who followed Christ were equipped by Him to do the tasks He desired them to do. Now that we serve a risen Christ, a Savior we have dwelling inside us through His Holy Spirit, all believers are members of His church; we are His bride, and we are all equipped by God to do the work He has for us.

Just as John the Baptist proclaimed, we must decrease so Jesus can increase in our lives. We are all able to follow God and be used by God; but as mere humans, we must always realize who we are in relation to the God we serve. He is God, and we are not.

Take a moment to journal your thoughts about this week's lesson, and how it has changed your outlook on following God:

_____

_____

_____

_____

_____

_____

_____

_____

_____

_____

_____

 *Wonderful Savior,* oh what a week this has been. Lord, I pray that the concepts I have studied would be so much more than some intellectual concept that sounds good to itching ears. Lord, I pray that the concepts that I learned this week would be life-changing. I pray that I would continue to gain insight to the passages that I have studied in this lesson. I pray that as I continue studying, that each lesson would build on the previous one, just as the relationships between John and Jesus, and Jesus and Peter continued to grow and build. I pray that the goal of living a life that reflects Christ would be attained in a larger measure in my life and my fellow brothers and sisters in Christ. May I always hunger after You, follow Your lead, and lead others to Your truth. May the Name of Jesus be etched on my heart, my mind, and my actions. In Jesus' name I pray. Amen.

# Notes

# SIX

# The Point of It All

## THE LOVE OF GOD'S ONLY BEGOTTEN SON

## 3:16 VERSES: JOHN, 1 JOHN, 1 TIMOTHY

I am so excited about our lesson for this week. After spending the past few weeks examining some background information, this week we will focus on the point of this whole study and our walk as a believer, which is this: Jesus came; Jesus died; Jesus rose again. He died for *all*, and those who believe in Him enjoy fellowship with God for eternity in heaven. Learning about Jesus and all He is to us should lead us to living a life that reflects Him. What an honor to have a Savior that loves us so much.

After we grasp the idea of the free gift of salvation, we will learn more about how it applies to our life. We will dig deeper to see how to respond to others as we live in relationship with God. Our goal should be to live our lives in a way that will reflect Christ brighter and bolder each day as we run after Him.

*Our goal should be to live our lives in a way that will reflect Christ brighter and bolder each day as we run after Him.*

# A Man Named Nicodemus
# 3:16 Verse: John

*"For God so loved the world, that He gave His only begotten Son, that whoever believes in Him should not perish, but have eternal life."*

The beginning of Jesus' ministry brought forth the fulfilling of the prophecies about the coming Messiah and included the introduction of what some thought were new beliefs. Jesus traveled through the area proclaiming the truth of the gospel, all the while fulfilling the Scriptures that spoke of the Messiah. Some of the teachings of Jesus seemed to go against the teachings of the religious rulers of that day. Jesus claimed to be the Messiah that the Jews had been anticipating, yet He was a simple man of a simple heritage! He was Jesus of Nazareth; the carpenter's kid. How could this man be the one they had been waiting for so many years to see? The Sanhedrin (religious rulers) wanted nothing to do with the new teachings of Jesus; after all, in their minds they were the authority on such things, and to them, Jesus was the horse that upset the apple cart.

In John's Gospel account, there is a wonderful account of a man named Nicodemus, who went privately to visit Jesus and talk with Him awhile. Even though the body of Governors was unhappy with the teachings of Jesus, Nicodemus wanted to hear for himself. So he searched Jesus out, and expected an explanation. Not just the "sermon-ette of the day," but hard answers—proof—the sort of thing the Sanhedrin expected of all who crossed their path. He sought after Jesus under the cover of darkness, wanting to make sure that no one would realize what he was doing.

📖 Look at John 3:1. What type of man was Nicodemus? What was his position in society?

_____

_____

_____

> **Nicodemus was at the height of his career, and it must have seemed like he was sitting on top of the world. That is, until Jesus showed up.**

Nicodemus was a Pharisee, and a member of the Jewish ruling council. That term, *ruler,* is so much more than it seems. Nicodemus was a man in a powerful position, especially in the religious circles of their day. He was a man that was surely given much honor. Nicodemus must have been quite proud of how well he obeyed the laws put in place by God along with those added by man. He was not just any Pharisee, but a member of the Sanhedrin, a high-ranking leadership council similar to our Supreme Court or Congress in scope of power. He was at the height of his career at this point, and it must have seemed like he was sitting on top of the world. That is, until Jesus showed up. Nicodemus had a few questions for Jesus.

📖 Read John 3:2–3. Where does Nicodemus say Jesus has come from in verse 2? Why?

_____

_____

What is Jesus' response in verse 3 to Nicodemus' statement?

_____

_____

_____

Looking just at these two verses, it seems like we are watching two separate conversations. Nicodemus says that Jesus came from God to teach, and Jesus says that no one can see God's kingdom without being born again. Even though there is no clear question in this statement, the tone implies that there is so much that is left unsaid. This Scripture passage is such a clear example of Jesus looking at the heart of a person. There must have been so many questions running through Nicodemus' head at that moment, and Jesus, as always, sought to get to the bottom line as He brought up the issue of salvation.

The concept of salvation and being "born again" was totally foreign to Nicodemus. Looking at the Greek dictionary for the words **born** (*gennao*) and **again** (*anothen*), we see references like *bring forth*, or *be born*, *anew,* or *from above*. Such references would leave anyone in Nicodemus' situation confused, hearing about a concept as complex as salvation, especially if they were trying to simply understand what was said in an intellectual manner. This was the first time such a concept was introduced. How could someone be "born anew," or "brought forth from above"? Nicodemus just had to find out more.

📖 John 3:4–8 shows us the dialogue that explains the term *born again*. Pay particular attention to Jesus' distinction of the terms: flesh, water, and Spirit. Record they key points of this passage:

_____

_____

_____

_____

_____

What a magnificent passage of dialogue this is! How wonderful it is to have such a clear explanation of who we are as followers of Jesus Christ. Do you see how Nicodemus, in verse 4, responds to Jesus with the natural answer anyone would have to the thought of being born a second time? After all, here is Jesus, trying to convince one of the top religious rulers that those who want to enter the kingdom of heaven must go through some sort of new birth! Nicodemus wanted to know exactly what it means to be "born again." He must have thought to himself, *How could this be? Could a person go through the birth canal twice?* How can you explain heavenly things to an earthly mind?

As Jesus mercifully took the time to explain the way of salvation to this leader of the people, Nicodemus struggled not to trip over his own intellect. In this passage, Jesus teaches Nicodemus, and all who read this scripture, that we must believe when it makes no sense and be willing to follow God in faith when the situation or godly explanation defies our logic. Haven't we all met our own Nicodemus types in our lifetime?

**Nicodemus Syndrome:**

 Have you ever found yourself in the middle of a Nicodemus moment? Maybe you had heard the name of Jesus, the gospel mes-

> *"Jesus answered and said to him, 'Truly, truly, I say to you, unless one is born again he cannot see the kingdom of God.'"*
>
> *John 3:3*

sage, or even accepted Jesus as Savior, but something kept you from falling head over heels in love with Jesus. There was still a wall built between you and God for some reason. You may have had questions, doubts, or issues that you were not willing to let go of until God answered your concerns. Take a moment to think about those times in your past when you found yourself questioning God, what He does, and who He is. What brought the doubts into mind, and how did you get past those doubts? Journal your thoughts here:

_____

_____

_____

_____

_____

_____

Are there any parts of those concerns that still puzzle you today? Commit this time to the Lord in prayer, and ask Him to answer the questions of your heart. Be open to looking in Scripture for the answers to your questions, and listen closely for the still small voice of God as He speaks to you. Believe as Nicodemus believed, even when it may not make perfect intellectual sense. Have faith in God, and let God be God. Trust in His Word.

Nicodemus presents an intellectual response, which surely seemed sound to him. Jesus, in His amazing way of cutting to the chase, explains to the ruler that it is not an actual trip through the birth canal; but rather, a transformation of sorts, from being a person born of the **flesh** to a person born of the **Spirit**.

Please note that the reference Jesus gives in verse 5 of the word "**Spirit**" is the Greek word *pneuma*, which clearly refers to the Holy Spirit. This brings to mind our earlier discussion concerning the baptism of Jesus and the confirmation of the Holy Spirit descending on Him. Let's focus on the fact that here Jesus Himself states how important it is to be born of the water and the Spirit. Here Jesus not only refers to baptism, but He also focuses on a spiritual cleansing and purification through relationship with Jesus. The word "Spirit" again refers to the Holy Spirit one receives once a relationship with Jesus Christ is established. Jesus had just given this visual example in the Jordan River, and I'm sure that people were still talking about what they saw that day. Jesus' visual example was now being confirmed theologically through Jesus' teaching.

## TITUS 3:5–6

*"He saved us, not on the basis of deeds which we have done in righteousness, but according to His mercy, by the washing of regeneration and renewing by the Holy Spirit, whom He poured out upon us richly through Jesus Christ our Savior."*

Titus 3:5–6 has a great way of restating Jesus' words. Record why and how God saved us, according to these verses:

_____

_____

_____

In his letter to Titus, Paul shows that God saves us through His mercy. Paul also points out the importance of the water (spiritual washing that brings forth regeneration) and the Spirit, confirming the concept we studied in John yet again.

📖 Look up 1 John 5:4–8. What does John list in these verses? There are three components listed as witnesses to the fact that a believer has overcome the world:

_____

_____

_____

In these verses, we see mention of the water, the Holy Spirit, and the blood of Jesus Christ, which was shed when He became the sacrifice for our sins. We will talk more about this sacrifice in future lessons.

Also, we see in John 3:6 that Jesus makes a distinction between the Spirit and the flesh. The word **flesh** is translated from the Greek word *sarx*, which literally refers to "the body (as opposed to the soul [or spirit], or as the symbol of what is external)" and can also refer to "human nature," or "human being" (Key Word Study Bible NASB, Reference Section - Greek Dictionary of the New Testament, #4561, p. 64).

📖 Read Romans 6:6–11. What happens to our "old self"?

_____

_____

What effect does the death of Christ Jesus have over the believer?

_____

_____

Here we see how as people who have chosen to accept Jesus as Savior; we are no longer people who are ruled by the flesh, or the sin nature. Through the sacrifice of God's only Son, we have been given the gift of salvation; we now live free from sin, and alive in Christ! Through His death, we have life. When we have a relationship with the Savior, He will give us access to heaven, and eternal life.

📖 Before we leave Paul's epistle to the Romans, take a look at Romans 6:23. Record the verse here:

_____

_____

_____

What a gift indeed! Take a moment to reflect on this verse before you move further into the lesson.

**New Creation:**
📖 Look up 2 Corinthians 5:14–21. What a powerful passage this is.

🛑 APPLY What does 2 Corinthians 5:15 reveal to you as a believer? For whom should we live? Why?

_____

_____

_____

*"For the wages of sin is death, but the free gift of God is eternal life in Christ Jesus our Lord."*

*Romans 6:23*

> *"Therefore, if any man is in Christ, he is a new creature, the old things passed away; behold, new things have come."*
>
> *2 Corinthians 5:17*

_____

_____

According to verse 17, what changes take place in the life of a new believer?

_____

_____

Do you notice that you now live a different lifestyle than the life you led before you accepted Jesus Christ as Savior? Do you make different choices now that you are a Christian? Can you see a change in your life as a result of following Jesus? Journal your thoughts:

_____

_____

_____

_____

_____

When we become followers of Jesus, we no longer think like those who are bound to the system of the world (fleshly nature) around us. We are new creations in Christ Jesus, and we have the promise and the hope of a heavenly dwelling, and of life eternal. This is exactly why Jesus goes on to explain to Nicodemus in John 3:7–8 that it is not the term "born again" that should make him amazed; for those who are born of the Spirit will come and go, just like the wind. We are no longer of this world; we are of the heavens; we are waiting on our heavenly dwelling; *we are just passing through*. Through our acceptance of Jesus as Savior, we are truly new creatures!

Even with the Messiah Himself giving the explanation, Nicodemus, much like other doubters we have read about in Scripture, is mindful of how things normally happen in the world, and questions how Jesus' statement can be true.

📖 Read John 3:9–10. What is Nicodemus' question here, and how does Jesus respond?

_____

_____

_____

_____

_____

Once again, Nicodemus had a question of intellectual practicality, and Jesus corrects him. Jesus calls Nicodemus "the teacher", referring to his status in religious circles as a man who should know all there is to know about God.

There is an interesting shift that takes place in their conversation from this point on; we see the conversation change from what God has done for believers, to what believers should be doing if they follow God.

📖 Look at John 3:11–15. Observe the tone that Jesus takes.

**Verse 12:**
Jesus says that Nicodemus is focusing on _____
things, while he should believe what Jesus says about _____
things.

📖 In verse 15, what does Jesus say a person needs to do to have eternal life?

_____

_____

Between verses 12 and 19, Jesus makes a point to mention the word "believe" seven times. This is not a coincidence! Just as Abraham's faith was credited to him as righteousness, so does our faith. We must believe in Jesus and what He did for us as He went to the cross and rose again in order to receive eternal life. By doing this, we will be heavenly minded instead of remaining focused on the things on earth.

To gain access to eternal life, we need to believe. We need to have faith. And our focus verse, John 3:16, explains what we have to have faith in:

> *"For God so loved the world, that He gave His only begotten Son, that whoever believes in Him should not perish, but have eternal life."*

Memorize today's focus verse, and take some time to thank the Lord for His gift of salvation.

# HE LOVES YOU AND ME . . . THIS MUCH! 3:16 VERSE: JOHN

*Word Study*
## BELIEVE

The Greek word *pisteuo* is translated as "believe" in our English translations of the New Testament. It speaks of having faith in someone or something, and it implies that there is implicit trust in that person or thing. When we believe in the Lord, we put our trust in Him and His Word, believing that He did what He said He did and will continue to do what He says He will do. We walk through every day of our lives knowing that our time is in God's hands and that He has the best things in mind for us, even when circumstances do not make sense. This is the faith, or the level of belief, that Abraham exhibited when he left all that he knew and went where God told him to go.

*The Point of It All* **DAY TWO**

> *"For God so loved the world, that He gave His only begotten Son, that whoever believes in Him should not perish, but have eternal life."*

Ahh . . . John 3:16 . . . we are going to spend a day simply diving into this verse. This is a thrilling verse to study! Don't you just love to read God's Word? There is not a dull moment in the Book of truth He has given to us; if we are open to see what He has for us. Here is the very verse that encapsulates the crux of our entire belief system as Christians.

This has got to be the most memorized verse in every Sunday School program across the globe. (You might even remember, as I do, getting one of those shiny little foil gold stars placed by your name on the memorization chart posted on the wall for memorizing this verse as a kid.) Thank you to all those Sunday School teachers who challenged us to memorize God's wonderful Word. It is so sweet to have His word hidden in our hearts. God protects His truth, and He wants us to hide it in our hearts! Not a verse we learn will return void—God promises that every portion of Scripture we remember will be useful and life giving.

When was the first time you read or heard the verse found in John 3:16?

**APPLY** What did it mean to you then, and have your thoughts on the meaning of this verse in regards to your life changed since then?

_____

_____

_____

_____

_____

_____

Once a person grasps the magnitude of the essence of John 3:16 and begins to dwell on the richness of the verse, her whole outlook on Christianity will deepen. Perhaps the best way to study a verse or passage is to first read it in its entirety and then evaluate it section by section or even word by word. Let's take a moment to do the same. Let's look at the verse in sections. Read John 3:16, and fill in the blanks from each section:

*"For _____ so _____ the _____"*

*"For God so loved the world. . . ."* God Himself loved! He loved from the beginning and did it with passion. He loved the world! He loved all sinners, all the saints, all the world—without distinction of race, creed, or how deserving they were to receive His love.

When God loved the world, He loved with an *agape* love. Remember the conversation with Peter and Jesus? At one point Christ refers to *agape* love—that unconditional, limitless love. God loves us with a pure and unconditional love.

*"that He gave His _____ _____*
*Son"*

*"That He gave His only begotten Son."* He gave Him! He didn't charge us, expect any type of compensation, or even wait until He was asked for it. He was freely given to all mankind as a gift of love. All He asks is that we lay down our sins, and accept His Son's sacrifice that was made on our behalf. His only begotten Son—*God's Son!* Not Abraham's, not anyone else's, but His own—part of His majestic being. He only had one Son to give, and He gave Him to us, His family. Jesus is the Messiah that had been promised to the people of Israel for generations. Praise God!

*"that _____ _____ in Him*
*should not _____"*

*"That whoever believes in Him should not perish. . . ."* Who-so-ever! God sent the Messiah to all people; to all who believe in Him. No one is excluded from this pack. No one is left off the team. Unless we choose to turn away from the offer given us, we are His at the moment we believe in Him. Hallelujah! No one is turned away that believes, and those that believe should not perish. We will all die someday, but the perishing without a spiritual eternity is not the issue here, because of that final portion of the verse.

*"but have _____ _____."*

*"But have eternal life."* Eternal. Much longer than a decade, much longer than a century, much longer than a millennium; this is *eternity*. For those who believe, this is guaranteed. Not debatable. Fact. We will have everlasting life in Christ Jesus.

Observing your years (or perhaps days) as a follower of Jesus Christ, take time to dwell on this verse, and allow God to speak to you more about the depth of this gift He gives us, and the hope we have in eternal salvation.

God gave His Son as a sacrifice for us. There is no other way to get to heaven but through the shed blood of Jesus Christ. This concept is so simple, yet extremely complex. When we come to Him as a child, as Jesus desires us to, we read John 3:16 and are filled with assurance of salvation and a feeling of being loved. As our brain mulls this statement over in our minds, we may find ourselves asking at different points of time: "Why would He do that? If He knew we were sinners, why didn't He just make us pure, and save us without Jesus' sacrifice? If a good person doesn't know Christ, that person surely won't be going to hell, will he? What about other faiths? Are they wrong? Couldn't an all-powerful God get the "right message" to everyone?" Then there is the classic question that asks whether God created Jesus just because He messed up in the Old Testament. First of all, God is incapable of messing up! God is perfect in every way. Beyond that, as we have begun to discover over the past few lessons together, everything in Scripture sets the stage for, points to, or includes the life of Christ and the redemption that His sacrifice brings.

We need to set some goals in our minds as we field such questions from others: we should believe God's Word that tells us that Jesus is the only path to salvation. We should focus on the truths that are outlined in Scripture and not dwell obsessively on what questions are left unanswered. If God wants us to know something not outlined in Scripture, He will certainly reveal Himself to us through prayer and other ways. Any other topics are for Him to know and for us to trust Him as we walk in faith. Many times, in order to badger or "stump" a believer, skeptics pose unanswerable questions rather than thoughtful ones. As we saw with Nicodemus, God is faithful to answer if someone comes to Him with a question based on a pure desire to know. As we see over and over in Scripture, from the first page to the last, Christ is:

> *"the way, and the truth, and the life; no one comes to the Father, but through [Him]"* (John 14:6, emphasis added).

Christ was with God the Father from the beginning of time and came to earth as a man, fully God and fully human, to be the sacrifice we would need to receive the gift of salvation. Why a sacrifice? We studied the basics of this sacrificial system in Lessons 2 and 3, but let's look at more examples of sacrifice being instituted by God.

📖 Read Genesis 3:1–7. What was the sin, and who committed the sin? What was their best effort at covering up their sin (in verse 7)?

_____

_____

_____

What did God consider a better covering (in verse 21) for Adam and Eve's shame? What did He provide them to cover themselves with?

*Word Study*
## BEGOTTEN

The word **begotten** in John 3:16 is from the Greek word *monogenes*, which refers to being someone who is alone, the only one born, or a sole child. As believers, we are all children of God, but Jesus is the only Son of God who was born through the Holy Spirit. He was brought to earth in the form of a man, but was always fully God while He was fully man. The purpose for Jesus' arrival on earth in such a manner was for His sacrifice on the cross for our sins. He came to bring us back into a right relationship with the Father. He is the only one who can do this as the only begotten Son of God.

_____
_____
_____

In this very moment, God began to establish a system of blood sacrifice to atone for sin, starting with Adam and Eve. God gave them clothes made of skin, which were made thru the shedding of blood of animals.

&#x1F4D6; The next example of sacrifice is found in Genesis 4:2–5. Read this passage and describe the scene and the types of sacrifice:

_____
_____
_____
_____

Cain and Abel were required to sacrifice. One gave grain, and one gave an animal sacrifice that entailed the shedding of blood. The blood sacrifice, was the pleasing sacrifice to God. Once again, the system of performing sacrifices to atone for sin was confirmed.

Why was the blood of the sacrifice so important? And why did Jesus' blood examined in Day One in 1 John 5:6–8 matter so much? Look back at Leviticus 17:11, and describe the purpose for the shedding of blood as mentioned in that verse:

_____
_____
_____

*Just like the song states, there is truly power in the shed blood of the Lamb.*

Just like that song states, there is truly power in the blood! It is through the shedding of blood in the sacrificial way that provides atonement for, or cancels out, our sins. There has to be sacrifice that included the shedding of blood to set man right with God.

Think back to our lesson on Abraham, where the sacrificial system was strong (even without Abraham's having a written set of instructions from God yet), and then the lessons with Moses, where we learned about him receiving the written system for worship that included the details of the sacrificial system.

We have countless examples of people observing the sacrificial requirement. Even when Solomon's Temple was dedicated at a much later time, there was an incredibly large sacrificial ceremony that took place. Over and over, those who followed Him followed the system set up by God. Every generation's example of sacrifice blends together, and it all confirms God's overall purpose for atonement of sin.

With Christ, our Messiah, we were given the ultimate gift of sacrifice, *once for all*. Christ is our sacrifice for all generations, a covenant that will last for eternity. Because of the complete sacrifice of Christ, you and I have access to the God of Creation. When we accept Christ as Savior, repent of our sins and believe in Him, and confess that He is Lord of our lives, then we are children of the living God forever more. This is the gift from Romans 6:23

that we talked about yesterday. Praise Him for His wonderful, merciful gift to our lost and undeserving generation!

📖 John 3:17–21 gives us insight to the other aspects of believing in Jesus. What are some of the details mentioned?

_____

_____

_____

In this passage we see that God sent Jesus not to judge the world but to save it. We also see that judgment comes to those who do not believe because they reject the name of Jesus, and spend their time in darkness, away from the light—and Jesus is the Light of the World.

What magnitude there is in the gift given by God! That He would send a Savior for mankind; that we would share in eternal things, and that we would be free to believe in Him. It would take eternity to truly fathom the depth of such a gift. And it is ours! Our life on earth becomes but a tiny portion of our existence, as we will share eternity with all who believe.

There is an eternal promise of life everlasting for those who believe in God, His Son, and the Holy Spirit. We will dwell in the Heavenlies, bow down in praise, and lift our voices in sweet rejoicing to the King of Kings. Don't you just want to get a head start on that, and give a victory shout right now? I sure do. There is nothing better than sitting in awe of who our God is, and what He has done for us. He didn't have to, yet He did. Just because. And we are His. There is truly nothing better than to know that we are His!

# LOVING OTHERS
# 3:16 VERSE: 1 JOHN

_"We know love by this, that He laid down His life for us; and we ought to lay down our lives for the brethren." (1 John 3:16)_

I find it impossible to lose sight of the fact that Christ not only died for our sins, but He also endured everything we would have to endure, so that we could never say that He didn't understand our problems. In today's focus verse, we see how Jesus shows His unconditional, undeserved love through His willingness to die for us in order to give us life. With this action on His part, He has every right to request that we offer the littlest portion of such a gesture for someone else. This verse doesn't only talk about showing love by losing your physical life; but also about setting aside your own agenda in order to help, reach out to, and love others.

 Think of a time when you took time to help someone who was in a difficult situation. Did you feel blessed to be able to help them, and were they comforted by the love you showed them? Journal your thoughts:

_____
_____
_____
_____
_____
_____

**Almost daily, we see news reports of people putting their own lives on the line for others. How much more should we be willing to lay down our lives for others since we have the example of Christ being sacrificed once for all men!**

If you think there are no people on earth today that are willing to die for their fellow man, look again! All you have to do is take a look around your community—from the policemen, firemen, and emergency crews to members of the military. We see that such a love for others is all around us. It doesn't have to be as glamorous as the secret service in their dapper suits and earpiece communications to be a life-saving profession. We all witnessed countless heroes on 9/11 and during other tragedies who did their all to save the lives of others. We see accounts of heroism on some level just about every night on the evening news. People are seen laying their own lives on the line for someone else. *How much more* should we be willing to lay down our lives for others since we have the example of Christ being sacrificed once for all men!

If you ask any of these people (servicemen and women, firemen, policemen, etc.) "why" they do what they do, they may not be able to tell you, it's just something in them—a sense of duty that makes them willing. It's the same with our faith! With the Holy Spirit in us, we will just be walking as the Spirit leads, willing to do what we should as we love each other.

After reading all that John expressed in John 3, it is so good to link that passage with this one that deals with the application of Christ-like principles to our lives. John, the disciple referred to as the "beloved" disciple, had a deep and abiding love for the Lord, and the Lord loved him as well. John sought after God, and God entrusted him with godly wisdom and insight.

Read 1 John 3:1–2. What are believers called in these verses?

_____

Whom will we be like when Jesus returns?

_____
_____

How wonderful! We are children of God, and we will be like Him, in His image, when we are taken up in glory. Like we talked about before, we truly are no longer of this world. What a hope we have in Jesus!

📖 With that hope, what is our goal, according to verse 3?

_____
_____
_____

As we focus on the Lord, our goal in living a Christ-like life is to be pure; to live a life that reflects the purity of God.

📖 Reading on through verses 4 through 15, we see John writes more in depth about sinning. Record your thoughts about this passage:

_____

_____

_____

_____

_____

Though our sin nature does not disappear this side of heaven, our habitual sinning should disappear. We all stumble daily, but with a life focused on God, the stumbling should be less frequent and quickly dealt with. The Holy Spirit dwelling within us convicts us of our sin and brings us to repentance. Those who run after God will run away from the sins of the flesh. Just because Jesus died on the cross for us and bore our sins, doesn't give us free reign to sin all the time and consider ourselves Christians. Those who have truly repented and accepted the Lord and who are submissive to His Spirit's leading will be enabled to live in ways that are pleasing to the Lord. Such Holy-Spirit enablement increases as we fully submit to Him and allow Him to do through us what we could never do on our own.

📖 Reread verse 8. For what purpose did Jesus appear, according to this verse?

_____

_____

Jesus came to destroy the hold of sin that the devil has over us. Through Christ we are freed from a life of sin and death. How are we kept from habitually sinning the rest of our lives? Look at verse 9, and write what you discover:

_____

_____

Did you see the reference to the seed in verse 9? Again, we see that the Seed of God, which is Christ, is impacting the Christian life. With a relationship with Christ comes another promise of a seed and the life that should reflect Him. Jesus has deposited His seed or a transplant of His life within us, and as we follow Him, this seed will grow. As it grows, we will bloom and bear fruit and grow in faith.

📖 Read 1 John 4:9–10. How is God's love manifested in us? Why?

_____

_____

_____

As John continues to plead with the reader to live a life that reflects Jesus, our focus verse is written:

*"We know love by this, that He laid down His life for us; and we ought to lay down our lives for the brethren."*

We are not to imitate Cain who killed his own brother out of jealousy, but we are to imitate one who follows the command to love one another. We should be willing to support those around us no matter what. Our sacrifices and offerings will mean nothing if our heart attitude and actions are based on sin and jealousy, just as Cain's were.

📖 Compare this with 1 John 4:19–20. What does John say about the person who hates his brother?

_____

_____

The person who hates his brother and says he loves God really doesn't understand the meaning of loving God. By loving God, we will love all God's creatures, great and small, and will provide for their needs when we are able.

📖 Returning to 1 John 3:17–18, we see this thought spelled out in more detail. We learn more about how to apply this principle to our lives.

In these two verses, what are we charged to do with our resources? What should we do for those around us who have needs?

_____

_____

_____

_____

> "Dear Children, let us not love with words or tongue but with actions and in truth."
>
> 1 John 3:18 (NIV)

In this, we can see that loving one another Jesus' way is more than "mushy gushy love talk" and a quick hug. It's the real, lay down your life, pull together and help someone where they need you (even when it's not easy) type gesture backed up by genuine, hard-working action. Love is the best when it is being "worked out" and actions are involved. Love is an action. It is not just a passing emotion that requires little more than brainpower and some smooth talk!

Jesus showed love to those He came into contact with during His earthly ministry by improving their situation. He impacted their lives in positive ways. He cast out demons, making the possessed emotionally whole. He healed physical conditions; He helped out at a wedding to bring honor to those hosting it. He changed lives. Jesus helped us all by giving us the hope of salvation.

📖 We know about so many of the miraculous things that Jesus did while He walked the earth, but what does John 21:25 say about how many miracles Jesus performed?

_____

Imagine that! The thought of Him doing so much more than we read about in Scripture overwhelms me. Because of this verse in John, I tend to think of Jesus as someone in continual motion—someone who was constantly working out His love for others. Jesus wasn't the "Mr. Popular" guy wandering down the street blowing kisses, giving empty promises and false hopes. He was out *doing* His acts of love; even when it didn't appear to be penciled in on His calendar.

Jesus actually did most of the miracles mentioned while He was on His way somewhere, almost as a side note, and not the reason for the written account. He was focused on bringing them the message of salvation through Jesus Christ (His own message), and the rest happened on the way. Our works do not save us, nor does Jesus imply that we are required to earn our salvation. The balance to this concept does lie, however, in the fact that as believers, we show love and servant examples to others as a "working out" of our faith. The action of love is an outgrowth of our belief in and relationship with Christ. It just naturally happens when we are filled with the Holy Spirit, and are walking in the love of Christ.

📖 Read John 14:15. What does this verse say we will do *if* we love Jesus?

_____

_____

The picture of love that Christ showed us is perfect. Love in its simplest form according to Christ is obedience. Christ was obedient to the Father and became the ultimate sacrifice, a greater example of love does not exist! In John 14:15, we see Jesus give guidance on our relationship with Him, where He says, "If you love Me, you will keep My commandments." Obedience is a result of love and respect. When we love Jesus, we obey His requests. Jesus loved the Father and obeyed His commands. We love God and others and one way we show our love is through obeying God's commands. Jesus clearly tells His people,

> *"A new commandment I give to you, that you love one another, even as I have loved you, that you also love one another. By this all men will know that you are My disciples, if you have love for one another."* (John 13:34–35)

📖 In 1 John 3:23–24 John explains how we can abide in Jesus. Write down what John mentions in this passage:

_____

_____

We see John mention again that we must keep God's commandments if we are to follow Jesus. Even humans, as weak as we are, can choose NOT to love and help others. We can walk around full of hate and disgust if we choose. It is critical to understand the magnitude of God's love, and how easy it would have been for Jesus to turn the other cheek and take the easy road. Since Jesus didn't take the easy way out, I pray that you also would take the road less traveled, and love others in spite of the circumstances—at all times, and in all ways. We were created in His image, and we should act like it!

# THE MYSTERY IS SOLVED
# 3:16 VERSE: 1 TIMOTHY

> *"And by common confession great is the mystery of godliness: He who was revealed in the flesh, Was vindicated in the Spirit, Beheld by angels, Proclaimed among the nations, Believed on in the world, Taken up in glory."*

### *Put Yourself In Their Shoes*
## CHRISTIAN "DOWN TIME"

There are many instances in the Gospels that mention Jesus seeking to be alone to pray and rest. To me this confirms that we should find time to be alone with the Father. Jesus was continually pouring out His life in helping others, and in meeting needs. When He took time to rest, it was really needed. Our Savior always knew when He needed peaceful time to Himself, but never forgot the blessing in loving and helping others.

### *Extra Mile*
## MARY AND MARTHA

For extra study, look at the passages regarding Mary and Martha in Luke 10:38–42 and John 11:1–46. Observe the responses of these two women in the first passage and the change in the way they interact with Jesus in the second. Focus on the different priorities of each person and what that means to you in your walk with the Lord.

*The Point of It All*  DAY FOUR

If Christ becomes our example of a life dedicated to love, service, and obedience, and we surrender ourselves to the Holy Spirit's enabling power, we will become godlier or more like Christ over time. What is godliness? What is the *mystery* of godliness? Paul points out this "mystery" to Timothy; and for those who believe in Christ, the mystery is really no mystery at all. To the same extent that there is no "code" to the 3:16 concept, there is also no "secret code" to the gospel message of Christ. There are all sorts of code theories out there, digging into the Scriptures, twisting them to fit other information, or making predictions based on some obscure search-type of game. The only code there is to Scripture is the fact that everything in the Bible, from the first word in Genesis, to the last word in Revelation points to the overall message of the hope we have in Christ. Christ is our code. Christ is the mystery. If we want to be godlier, we must first repent of our sins and follow the model of Jesus Christ.

In the environment Timothy and Paul lived in, mysterious religions were commonplace. They were exposed to cultures and false doctrines that adapted popular thought and attitudes into religious teaching. Pagan religions permeated the culture around these men of God. Worshiping is part of a human's core being, but *what* we worship as humans is completely up to us. God created us to worship Him, but if we choose to turn from Him, we will inadvertently make something else our "god." Whether that god is our success, wealth, other images, or some other item or being, it doesn't really matter. Anything that takes precedence in our life over Jehovah God can become a "god" or idol to us.

&#x1F4D6; What does God say about following other gods, according to Exodus 20:3, and Deuteronomy 6:4–5?

_____

_____

_____

_____

Clearly, we are to serve one god, the God of the Bible, and we are to love Him with everything in us.

In Paul's day, the attitude of what we today identify as "political correctness" was rampant. The inclusion of any and all gods in one place of worship was common. The attitude of "you have your god, and I'll have my god, and we'll all live happily ever after" was the focus of the culture. Unfortunately for those who worship false gods, their "ever after" will forever be different than that of a believer in the one true God of the Bible! People could go into one place of worship in Timothy's lifetime, and see people bowing down to a multitude of different images and idols at the same time. In pagan society, the more *mysterious* it seemed, the more *spiritual* it was regarded.

This passage pertaining to the "mystery of godliness" is profound in that era of our history. This passage not only showed the wonder of Christ, but the frailty of the mystery religions of the day. Paul essentially states that there is no mystery at all to what the "formula" for godliness is! It all points back to Christ. Christ is the one and only path to God, not just the one that Paul urged them to pick over a multitude of choices. Christians in that age took this road more than once with people who listened to their preaching.

**God created us to worship Him, but if we choose to turn from Him, we will inadvertently make something else our "god."**

📖 Read Acts 17:16–21. What compelled Paul to preach the gospel in Athens?

_____

_____

_____

📖 Now read on through Acts 17:22–31.

What is our God referred to in verse 23?

_____

What did Paul say about God in verses 24–27?

_____

_____

Because of who God is, how does Paul say we should respond, as shown in verses 28–31?

_____

_____

_____

Paul is also very clear, as he makes his speech to the people of Athens concerning their monument to the "unknown god." Paul very quickly makes the "unknown" known, and the gospel was preached. Our God is not unknown! He is only unknown to those who are looking to false religions for answers to the problems in their life.

Our God is THE God—the eternal, all powerful God of Creation who is over all, in all, and through all—for all times. The very image of Christ that Timothy was to encourage the people to follow is the exact portrayal that we ourselves strive to reflect. Our God is timeless.

Knowing God—who He is, and who we are in Him—is critical if we are going to serve in ministry. Paul writes this third chapter to Timothy in order to give him some guidelines and requirements for appointing deacons and elders (overseers) in the church. It was important that those selected as leaders reflect the principles that Jesus taught. Those who served in the church needed to be sure of the God they served and committed to His service—not easily persuaded into following false teachings. Being an overseer meant more than just laying down your life for your friends; it meant living your life in a way that reflected Christ.

📖 Read 1 Timothy 3:1–12. What sorts of things were required of a deacon? What requirements are given for overseer (offices of elder, bishop, pastor)?

_____

_____

_____

_____

_____

In verse 9, we read that the gospel must be tied into our actions. If we, just as the leadership referred to in this section, *"hold to the mystery of our faith,"* what will the condition of our conscience be as a result?

_____

_____

_____

📖 1 Timothy 3:13–15 show Paul's reasoning for sending such requirements to Timothy in regards to overseers. Why did Paul write to Timothy about these leadership issues?

_____

_____

_____

The entire third chapter of 1 Timothy deals with how deacons and overseers are to conduct themselves. The discussion of gentleness, sobriety, and self-control is key. As Paul outlines the "dos and don'ts" of a deacon's lifestyle, the point is clear. Live a life that honors the principles that God has put forth in His Word, and make decisions that will bring forth a lifestyle that reflects the teachings and choices that Jesus exhibited while He walked on the earth. The people of that time had the teaching of Jesus and those who walked with Christ, and the time period focused on laying a lasting foundation for the church. We are still using this blueprint for leadership that Paul gave to Timothy so many years ago. We still refer to this section and others in Scripture as our model for requirements in church leadership roles.

### Another Look at Role Models

📖 Read Titus 2:1–8. This scripture passage deals with older women mentoring younger women, but the principles are applicable to all who are mature in their faith. Using a gender neutral focus, what does it say are the requirements for overseeing others? What are the older believers supposed to teach those who are younger?

_____

_____

_____

Is there someone in your life that is younger than you, that you take time to nurture or mentor? Do you see aspects of this passage that can relate to your interaction with them?

_____

_____

_____

In this passage, we see guidelines that are used in ministry, where we utilize the principles of godly women mentoring others. God has wonderfully provided ample examples for us on how we should conduct ourselves in a godly way.

📖 Paul doesn't stop with instruction; he has more to share with Titus! He goes back to the reason we instruct others in Titus 2:11–15. What does Paul credit as our reason for teaching those younger than us? Can we only mentor those literally younger than us, or can this principle apply to those less mature spiritually?

_____

_____

_____

_____

Don't you just love how Paul continually brings the focus back to Christ? Whether or not Paul was able to come visit Titus and Timothy and the churches they ministered to, and help advise them immediately, was not an issue. There would be no issue, that is, if these two men and their respective churches were basing their actions and expectations on Christ. When we look at Christ, we see God; when we know God, we also know Christ. The same is true with the Holy Spirit; all three entities reflect each other, and draw the believer into a complete relationship with all parts of God.

📖 Please take another moment and read Titus 3:1–7. On the heels of instruction, Paul links to our need for being Christ-like and the hope that we have in Jesus Christ. What new insight do you gain from this passage? Journal your thoughts:

_____

_____

_____

_____

As the passage in 1 Timothy encourages leaders to set an example that presents them as blameless, we see Paul in Titus 3 bringing our focus back to the point of the instruction. Why is it that we are so concerned with being upright and honorable? Why is being blameless and godly of benefit to us? As we read the "mystery of godliness" from 1 Timothy 3:16, imagine once again the magnitude of our Savior:

**"And by common confession great is the mystery of godliness:**
**He who was revealed in the flesh,**
**Was vindicated in the Spirit,**
**Beheld by angels,**
**Proclaimed among the nations,**
**Believed on in the world,**
**Taken up in glory."**

This is why we do all we do, believe all we believe, and preach all we preach. This is the point—the message of Christ and the reason for His coming to earth for us, and this is the reason we live a life that reflects Him.

📖 In Romans 16:25–27, Paul remarks again about the mystery of the gospel. What does he say in this passage about the message of Jesus that is preached? How and why is it preached?

_____

_____

_____

_____

*"To the only wise God, through Jesus Christ, be the glory forever. Amen."*

**Romans 16:27**

Our God took the time and loved us enough to appear in flesh-form on earth. He was vindicated and justified by the Spirit Himself. Angels saw Him; they knew who He was! He was and still is preached among the nations. By the way, He is also the main character of the bestseller of all time—no one has sold more books! Unfortunately, even with that status, there are still people who reject His message. It should grieve us all deeply when we come in contact with those who do not have the hope of Christ. Finally, Jesus was taken up into Heaven, where He sits at the right hand of God, petitioning on our behalf. Jesus Christ is there, waiting for us to join Him, waiting for us to reign with Him in the future. All this is our example, and all this is our foundation to why we are who we are—and why we believe what we believe.

Memorize today's verse, and thank God for revealing the mystery of godliness to you in increasing measure with each passing day.

*The Point of It All* **DAY FIVE**

# FOR ME TO FOLLOW GOD

What a week! Simply going through the magnitude of Jesus' sacrifice for all of our sins and learning how to live a life that is modeled after His gospel; it is all so very overwhelming. As believers, we could spend a lifetime simply basking in the truth of the gospel. The thankfulness that should be in our hearts and the measure to which we could never repay our Savior, should remind us that living for Him is so much more beneficial to us.

Look at the concepts covered this week in our focus verses and how they are interwoven. God loved us so much He sent Jesus, who laid down His life for us. We should lay down our lives for our fellow believers and live godly lives, by living lives modeled after Jesus Christ—lives that are a continual witness of Christ's gospel. How wonderful it is to see the concepts that the Lord longingly wants us to understand and see them in such consistency.

So many application points to our lives are found in these concepts we have examined this week! One such application point is that we must know Jesus, know why He came, and that we should live lives that reflect His message. We have to be ready for His second coming, when Jesus will come down and rule and reign as King of Kings and Lord of lords.

📖 Let's take a look at a parable that speaks of our necessity of being ready. Read Matthew 25:1–13. Journal your thoughts about this parable, and what it means to you in your walk with the Lord.

_____

_____

_____

_____

_____

We see Jesus picturing in this passage a theme of preparedness. In this parable, the ten virgins went to meet a bridegroom with their lamps in hand.

Some were prepared with oil; others were not. Whether our time on earth is a long time or not very long at all (since Christ will come back unexpectedly), the servants are to be prepared and not ashamed when they meet their bridegroom. In the same way, we, as believers should be ready and prepared when Jesus comes for us. Jesus is the bridegroom, and we are His bride. This parable refers to how we are to be prepared for the coming of the Lord, but also gives us another example of living a godly life. A godly life is a life that will be ready for Him when He comes again.

What does 2 Timothy 2:15 say we are to be?

_____

_____

_____

If we are living godly lives, we will not be ashamed or caught off guard in a time when others see who we truly are. Since we have no idea when Christ will return, this is a good lesson to keep in mind. And whether Christ returns in our lifetime or not, He still knows everything about us, good or bad. We must always be mindful that God see us for who we are; that is a sobering thought, one that hopefully leads us to repentance and surrender to the Holy Spirit. Jesus was never ashamed of who He was, and what He stood for—no matter what the persecution or problem He encountered.

Building our faith is a process. From the time we come to know Christ as our Savior, we take baby steps toward spiritual maturity. As we grow in our faith and relationship with our Savior, we begin to transform into a more Christ-like example. The only true spiritual development we can have in our lives is growth that is based on Christ. *He* is our model for true spirituality. Anything claiming to be "spiritual" that leaves Christ out of the equation or focuses ultimately on self or anything other than Christ, may be "spiritual," but we must be wary as to what spirit it is based! The mystery of godliness is Christ. Without Christ, there can be no godliness!

Take some time to go over the memory verses today. If you are studying this in a group, discuss the verses and the topics of the week, focusing on how your studies have impacted your thoughts and impressions of Jesus.

 *Merciful and Loving God,* how I thank You for Your gift of salvation! Though I can never fully comprehend the magnitude of such a gift, I pray that You would give me a deeper glimpse of Your vast mercies each day. I lay my sins at Your feet, and I yearn to dwell on Your Word day after day. Reveal Your truths to me Lord as I seek You. Lord I pray for everyone in our world who has not yet accepted Jesus as their Savior and Lord. May they hear Your message, and may they come to You with eagerness and love, and may they dwell in heaven for eternity. Just as John led the way for Jesus, I pray that You would use me in unique ways to lead others to You. May all I do bring glory to Your Name, and may the world know that Jesus is Lord. In Jesus' holy name, Amen.

> **We must always be mindful that God see us for who we are.**

# Notes

# Clear Message

## UNDERSTANDING ASPECTS OF OUR SPIRITUAL GROWTH

## 3:16 VERSES: PHILIPPIANS, 1 PETER, 2 PETER

In this lesson, we will have a chance to take a deeper look into concepts that we as Christians can apply to our daily lives. We can't just accept Jesus as our Savior and stop there. We have to press on each day with Jesus in mind. Also, just because Jesus paid for our sins on the cross does not mean that our Christian lives will be picture-perfect. Paul spoke numerous times about the afflictions and hardships he faced for the sake of Christ; yet he persevered through it all. Peter also instructed believers about persevering through suffering. It is a certainty that all believers will face hard times at some point; therefore, we all have to learn how to depend on God to carry us through those moments without compromising our beliefs or losing sight of our goal.

No matter what life throws our way, we have to pick ourselves up, dust ourselves off, and keep moving towards our goal: eternal life in heaven. The hope of salvation and the hope of the second coming of Jesus Christ is our motivation for getting through the hardest of times. Even with this hope, we must increase our level of faith through daily encouragement from the Word of God and the Holy Spirit, so that when we come against any adversity, we stand firm.

Our focus verses will take us through the process of humbling ourselves in our faith, standing blameless in our walk with the Lord, and clearly understanding and awaiting the return of Jesus Christ. Let's jump right in and learn all we can about building our faith.

*This week's 3:16 verses will take us through the process of humbling ourselves in our faith, standing blameless in our walk with the Lord, and clearly understanding and awaiting the return of Jesus Christ.*

# MAKE IT A LIFESTYLE
# 3:16 VERSE: PHILIPPIANS

*"However, let us keep living by the same standard to which we have attained."*

The book of Philippians is so wonderful! Whenever you are having a rotten day or feel like you have it all together because of *your own merits alone*, please take time to read the entire third and fourth chapters of Philippians. Once you dwell on the Word of God, either way, your attitude should always improve. In the previous lesson we talked about the mystery of godliness. Now that we know that the only mystery is that Christ is everything to a Christian, we need to look at the next step: application of Christ-like principles.

When we grasp a new concept in school, learn something new in life, or begin to take a deeper look at our faith, there is new information to process. Whenever we have new thoughts, one of two things happens. The thoughts are retained, or they are forgotten. With our faith, we must actively seek to retain the teaching that we have had concerning Christ. We must be passionately pursuing a more intimate relationship with our Lord. Part of this pursuit comes from the bonds we forge with other believers as we actively participate and worship the Lord in our local churches. Passionate pursuit of an intimate relationship moves us forward in becoming more Christ-like.

As our focus verse from Philippians 3:16 says, *"however, let us keep living by the same standard to which we have attained."* The word *standard* is used in this verse to refer to someone staying on track, or on the same path that he or she has been traveling.

Remember John the Baptist? What was his role, according to Matthew 3:3? What does that verse say about John and the path?

_____

_____

John's role was to pave the way for Jesus, and to make the path straight. This straight path would provide a clear introduction to the earthly ministry of Jesus. In the same way, Jesus has set a path for all who believe, and when we submit our lives to Him, we walk in His path and in His ways.

📖 Also, in Proverbs 15:19 we see a comparison of two paths. What are the two paths that are being compared?

_____

_____

The one who does not live in an upright manner has many obstacles; yet the one who is living an upright life has a clear highway ahead of them. They know the path they are on, and when they know their standard, it makes it that much easier to carry on.

**Passionate pursuit of an intimate relationship moves us forward in becoming more Christ-like.**

📖 Now read Psalm 119:10. What does the psalmist say?

_____

_____

We see here that with a life of seeking God comes the desire to stay in His will. As we follow clearly after Him, we will not wander far from his precepts.

David spoke often in the psalms of his passionate pursuit of God. Read Psalm 143:8–10. What was David's desire? Where did he ask God to lead him?

_____

_____

_____

David yearned for God to teach him. He wanted to follow God's guidance and commands, and he knew that only God could keep him on level ground. David had seen the consequences of making his own decisions and knew the safety net of living a life based on God's will. David was a man after God's heart in the fact that He desired the things that God desired. He wanted to follow God's will and God's ways. In many ways, David reminds us of Christ, as Christ's earthly ministry was marked by a willingness to do the will of the Father.

**APPLY** Does your path seem clearer, or more level, as you walk in the ways of the Lord?

_____

_____

_____

Have there been times when you seem to have grown in your faith more significantly than at other times?

_____

_____

_____

What was the difference with your interaction with the Bible and with other believers during that time?

_____

_____

_____

Were you seeking the Lord more, or studying more during times of growth than you were during the times when you seemed **not** to be growing in faith as much?

_____

_____

_____

_____

**"With all my heart I have sought Thee; Do not let me wander from Thy commandments."**

**Psalms 119:10**

### *Word Study*
### WANDER

The term *wander* in Psalm 119:10 is translated from the Hebrew *shagah*. *Shagah* speaks of a mistake, or an error, going the wrong way. It is a move in the wrong direction, whether out of ignorance or intentionally, and one that obviously calls for correction. As we see God referred to as our Shepherd, can't we just picture the wanderer mentioned in this verse as a lost sheep, wandering away from the flock in search of a blade of grass?

### *Extra Mile*
### PSALM 119

Study Psalm 119, the longest chapter of the Bible. Note how many times the psalmist refers to "Thy word." What is the goal of the psalmist in this chapter? What is his heart's desire? Notice the desire to obey, follow, understand, and live for God. Take some time to journal your thoughts and observations, and keep that journal at hand for other times of reflection on Scripture passages.

When we are actively pursuing God, He will actively meet us and reveal more of His truths to us. During those times, we will be growing in our relationship and knowledge of Jesus at a faster rate than during the times we are not seeking Him as intently. We will be sticking to the path that God has put in front of us. There is a distinct correlation between seeking God and becoming Christ-like—the two concepts are "joined at the hip" so to speak; one is never without the other. As we seek Him, we grow, and begin to walk the life of a Christian with some spring in our steps.

The surrendered walk is not about learning every Scripture and every Christian catch-phrase. *We must make our faith a lifestyle based on submission.* Dying daily to self allows us to maintain, perhaps even enhance a level of intimacy with Christ. As we maintain intimacy, our faith, our beliefs, and our convictions will permeate much of what we do and consume our daily existence. Then, our walk, or our daily interaction with others, will match our talk or our confession of faith. Evidence of this will be shown through gradual changes in our character, our approach with others, and the choices we make in our daily lives.

## Following Christ is a lifestyle!

**APPLY** How do you consider your "lifestyle of faith"? Is your daily routine and your interaction with others reflective of your relationship with Jesus?

_____

_____

Do you set aside time in your daily schedule to study God's Word, pray, or have fellowship with other believers? If not, how could you incorporate these things into your life?

_____

_____

_____

_____

That said; there is nothing we can "do" to *earn* our salvation. Just as Paul explains in this chapter of Philippians, there are no credentials, degrees, titles, or positions that make you a better Christian than someone else. There is no magic formula to having the perfect Christian life. There is no mantra, no ritual, and no activity we can do to gain a sense of peace **outside** of Christ. There is no way to manipulate God into giving you what you want just because you ask Him for it. God grants the free gift of salvation because He loves us enough to give it to us. None of us deserve it, or have earned it. We **all** fall short, but God has graced us with forgiveness anyway, out of His mercy and His love for us. Salvation is free for those who accept Christ. Those who reject Jesus Christ face eternal separation from their creator.

We must be careful not to put too much stock into our Christian resume, or the list of what we "do" as Christians. A busy Christian is not necessarily a mature Christian. Some will spend their lives being really busy to show others how spiritual they are, only to stand before the Lord and have to answer for why they neglected the most important relationship in their lives; the one with Him! Doing a lot may make people feel important or needed. Some may even think thoughts like, *"How will the church run without me? How will the ministry survive if I'm not there?"* Such thoughts discount the presence and power of God, and puff up the person doing all the work. The truth of the matter is this: God was doing fine accomplishing His purposes before we were born, and He will continue to do fine long after we have gone home to be with Him—so "getting over ourselves" is the first priority to Christ-like living! The only types of things we should "do for God" are the things He calls us to do.

📖 Proverbs 3:34 and James 4:6 give insight to being humble. What do you learn in these two verses?

_____

_____

_____

What does 1 Peter 5:5–7 add to this concept?

_____

_____

God does not need us to walk around proudly, looking down on those who do not believe. He calls us to be humble and to honor Him as we serve Him. God will exalt the humble. As we serve others out of love—in the church, in our neighborhoods, in our workplaces, and other venues—we must remain humble. Christ is everything, and we are nothing without Him—even on our best day!

As we seek God's path for us and walk in humility, Jesus must be our focus. In 2 Corinthians 10:5, Paul describes vividly how we can remain steadily gazing on Christ. What does Paul say we should do with our thoughts?

_____

_____

Even our thought life must be obedient to Christ!

Memorize today's verse. Take some quiet time and reflect on what God means to you and how your life exhibits that effect. Surrender your whole being to Him and ask Him to be the Lord of everything—even your thought life.

# PRESS ON!
# 3:16 VERSE: PHILIPPIANS

*Clear Message* **DAY TWO**

*"However, let us keep living by the same standard to which we have attained."*

We begin today reminded of yesterday's lesson and Paul's encouragement to remain committed to Christ in every aspect of our lives, including our thought life. As Paul taught about living a Christ-like life he was thorough in his description of challenges that a daily walk with God would encounter. Paul's epistles candidly discussed topics such as credentials, works, goals, humility, and so much more. He wanted

> "Getting over ourselves" is the first priority to Christ-like living!

nothing more than to have others see the necessity for loving Jesus, accepting Him as Savior, and leaving all other thoughts captive to Christ. Nothing is greater than Jesus.

📖 Read Philippians 3:1–6. What did Paul say about his past and his credentials and his standing in society?

_____

_____

Paul pointed out that he had all the credentials that the Law required. He had enjoyed all the status afforded to him as a member of the most elite religious order in Jewish society. Now, there is a big difference between him and the others who defend the Law: he followed Christ. All of the sudden, all of the credentials recognized by Jewish society and the religious elite were meaningless in light of the good news of Jesus and the power of God.

📖 Read verses 7–10. What was Paul's gain? What was it worth to him?

_____

_____

_____

Take another look at verse 8. How magnificent to see a man who, by the standards of the Jewish culture, was a highly esteemed man in society, yet at this point in his life, all that he had achieved meant nothing to him in light of his new found faith. All that had value to him was the *"surpassing value of knowing Christ Jesus* [his] *Lord."* May we all reach that point in our faith in God that He truly holds all value in our life, and that everything else would *"be as rubbish"* in our eyes. Paul acknowledges that it is not his observance of the law that makes him righteous, but it is his faith in Christ.

Paul states in Philippians 3:7–9,

> *"But whatever things were gain to me, those things I have counted as loss for the sake of Christ. More than that, I count all things to be loss in view of the surpassing value of knowing Christ Jesus my Lord, for whom I have suffered the loss of all things, and count them but rubbish in order that I may gain Christ, and may be found in Him, not having a righteousness of my own derived from the Law, but that which is through faith in Christ, the righteousness with comes from God on the basis of faith."*

This is a far cry from the guy Paul once was! Do you remember the account of how Saul of Tarsus became Paul the Evangelist? This role of evangelist was not something Paul had been striving for his whole life, was it? Let's take a closer examination at Saul's conversion. Saul was very good at what he did, and who he was. He was a man of the Law. He persecuted and sought the death of many Christians because of Jesus' message. Then one day, Jesus Christ met Saul on the Damascus road.

📖 Read the account of the transformation of Saul in Acts 9:1–9. Describe the scene of Saul's conversion:

_____

_____

_____

Looking at verse 15, who was Jesus calling Saul/Paul to preach to?

_____

What was Jesus going to show Paul, according to verse 16?

_____

Saul/Paul instantly had to answer for his actions. Jesus blinded him, told him of God's plan for his life, and three days later restored his sight. Paul was baptized, filled with the Holy Spirit, and sent to proclaim Christ to the Gentiles!

Paul literally laid his life at the feet of Jesus, and walked away with none of the credentials, status, and possessions of the past; but he walked with Jesus into the eternal path that God created just for him. Just imagine—here is a guy that had it all, yet "all" of it meant nothing compared to Christ! Paul had his eyes set on spending eternity with Jesus, and with receiving his resurrection from the dead, as promised through salvation.

The process of our faith is much like Paul's. We accept Jesus. We surrender to Jesus. We leave our past life behind (and all the things of the world that do not line up with God's plan for our lives). We now have to move forward! Paul called this "pressing on to the goal." As we go further into the passage in Philippians, we see the next step.

📖 Look at Philippians 3:12. What does the term "press on" mean to you, or what do you think Paul was trying to convey with such a term?

_____

_____

_____

_____

> *"For he is a chosen instrument of Mine, to bear My name before the Gentiles and kings and the sons of Israel."*
>
> **Acts 9:15**

This image of "pressing on" is a vivid one that gives reference to a runner, or a race that is being run. This is an action term that brings to mind intense movement, or determination. Imagine you were in the final lap of a long race and the finish line was in sight; wouldn't everything else fade away as you focused on being the first to cross that finish line? I believe this is what Paul wants readers to feel as they read those words.

Philippians 3:12 shows Paul in all his humanity and gratitude to Christ for this new life, as he exclaims, *"Not that I have already obtained all this, or have already been made perfect, but I press on to take hold of that for which Christ Jesus took hold of me"* (NIV, emphasis added).

Isn't that a wonderful comment? Paul "pressed on," because he was neither perfect nor finished with his race. Paul admitted that he wasn't perfect, and that his goal was still unachieved. Thank God we don't have to have our act together the moment we are converted! We are *all* in constant states of change as God continues to work on us, making us into the vessels He truly wants us to be! No one will ever be "done" until they are in heaven. The only perfect person to walk the earth was Christ. That puts you and me out of the running for that top spot. Praise God for His mercy toward us on that one!

Do you notice the second half of verse 12? Paul transitions into another portion of the equation. He makes the distinction that what he is pressing to

## PRESSING ON

This image of pressing on and running a race is a scene that Paul used to give relevance to his teachings by equating them with the times in which he lived. Paul knew of the races that took place in arenas such as the Circus Maximus in Rome, even though he may have never attended one. In such a race, there were horse drawn chariots that would circle a track, and the drivers had to be extremely focused; otherwise, his chariot would topple going around the curves, and injuries would almost be guaranteed, if not death. While holding the reins, if the drivers looked back, they might change the tension on the reins, which could cause a wreck. Thousands of people would come to watch the races, so the driver's skill and focus, or lack thereof, were seen by all who attended. The precision of holding the reins, the focused gaze, and the intention to win were all qualities that Paul associated with a dedicated faith. Those around us are watching, and they *will* see if we are focused on the Lord or on the world. For more information about how Paul used his culture as a frame of reference for teaching God's Word, consult the book *Paul's Metaphors* by David J. Williams (Peabody, MA: Hendrickson, 1999).

take hold of is a goal for which Jesus *took hold of him*! In the New American Standard Bible, that portion of the verse reads, *"in order that I may lay hold of that for which also I was laid hold of by Christ Jesus"* (Philippians 3:12, emphasis added). Jesus took hold of Paul in order to give him eternal life, and to use him to minister to nations, and *that* is why Paul pressed on.

According to the conversion story of Paul that we read about earlier in today's lesson, what was the physical condition that Jesus used to "grab hold" of Paul?

_____

_____

Jesus had such a purpose for Paul. The moment on that dusty road ushered in great changes in Paul. Christ blinded Paul and three days later restored that sight. Just as Paul learned what it meant to lose his eyesight, he also discovered what it meant to be without Jesus as well as what it meant to live for Him. Figuratively speaking, he had been blind for much of his life, yet now he could see. Paul finally knew how to follow Jesus.

In the same respect, God has such a purpose for you and me! Whatever God has purposed for us to do with our lives, this is the reason why He "takes hold of us." Paul was quick to show others that his goals were God's goals for him. Paul was obedient to go in the direction that God placed him and to run in that direction with all his strength. What a wonderful example this is for us today!

📖 Read Philippians 3:13–14. Paul expands his thought on running the race in these two verses. On what does Paul focus in verse 13?

_____

_____

What is the prize, as shown in verse 14?

_____

Here Paul focuses on the future, not the past, and had his eyes on the riches in glory that await all believers. He focuses on the goal of spending eternity with Jesus. Now, as we move on to verses 15 and 16, Paul shares how we should live as we focus on this same goal. In verse 15, he uses the term "perfect," which is used here to describe someone who is mature in faith instead of someone without defect. What did he say believers should do in light of this teaching?

Verse 15: *"have this _____"*

Verse 16: *"keep living by that _____ _____"*

Paul wants to make sure that those who heard his teaching would follow his teaching, and in turn, would be following Christ more accurately. This is reflected in verse 17, as Paul urges readers the following way:

> *"Brethren, join in following my example, and observe those who walk according to the pattern you have in us."* (Philippians 3:17)

Read the rest of the chapter (Philippians 3:18–21). Paul wonderfully proclaims the magnitude of the prize that awaits those who are focused on heaven. Praise God for His provision of an eternal life where we will become conformed *"with the body of His glory"* (verse 21)!

In the world that we are in, there will be many temptations that could make us stray from that narrow road. We must be on our guard against such schemes from the devil. We must understand that to keep moving in the direction of the goal of eternal life with Christ, we must continue to move closer to God.

**Some ways of pressing toward this goal:**
- staying focused on Scripture
- staying connected in a congregation
- staying delighted with our fellowship with our Savior
- spending quality time focused on God in prayer

All these things will better equip us to maintain current levels of faith and perhaps move beyond that point. We certainly don't want a "one step forward, two steps back" kind of faith, do we?

What does 2 Corinthians 13:5 tell us that believers are to do?

_____

_____

In order to stay on track with our goal, we must make sure we are checking our progress from time to time. We need to test ourselves to make sure our faith is still strong and that our focus is on Jesus Christ. Evaluation of our focus is essential. A check on our priorities and our true foundation may be eye opening. Our goal is ultimately to maintain a lifestyle that is consistent with the teachings of Jesus. The people in Corinth wanted proof of Christ, and Paul told them to test themselves to see if the knowledge of Jesus was in them. If they did not know Jesus, Paul said they would fail the test.

Beware of the moment a person forgets or moves on from the teachings of Christ to a faith or a supplement to their faith that is based on something else, something "new," or something "better." What may appear *new* may be inconsistent with what Jesus taught us to be and do. All that is based on the good news of Jesus will be consistent with this good news.

What does 1 John 2:23 say about denying Jesus?

_____

_____

First John 2:23 tells us that, *"whoever denies the Son does not have the Father."* Ladies and gentlemen, this is not a good thing. There is nothing new under the sun, and there is nothing better than salvation through Jesus Christ. Whenever we have learned something new or grown in our faith, it is critical that we retain what we have learned and continue to build on this foundation. There is no better goal than Christ!

# SUFFERING SAINTS
# 3:16 VERSE: 1 PETER

*"and keep a good conscience so that in the thing in which you are slandered, those who revile your good behavior in Christ may be put to shame."*

**A**re you a closet Christian, hiding who you are and who you believe in, or does everyone around you know that you are a "Jesus Freak"? Are you living out the Great Commission, or are you making a "great omission" of God's Word from your daily life? Do people not only *hear* your faith, but *see* your walk of faith? Take a moment to think of these different descriptions, and which ones would apply to your life.

Today's challenge for believers is to have a relationship with God that surpasses the once-a-week service and a few obligatory Amens. The challenge also includes reaching out to those around us with the love that Christ gives, and teaching them through our lifestyle and our genuine testimony. The times that we share the Bible and the truths of God through our own lives will make so much more of an impact in the lives of others. When we live our Christian life "out loud" (in obvious and consistent ways), we show others the strength we have in God *without even saying a word*.

When you have a stronger walk with the Lord, you have an extra layer of "holy protection" in times of trouble. Sunday mornings, while we are unified in Christ, we have little fear of harm. Sunday morning may be the easiest time to be a Christian, second only to times of fellowship with other believers, when we are huddled together in our little bubble of Christianity. But when we leave the security of the sanctuary and go back out into the world, things can change.

When we reach out to a lost world, things become a little different don't they? Reactions are not always positive, and we might even come under emotional, slanderous, or even physical attack. We cannot estimate the time the next lie will be spoken or predict when a hurtful remark will be made against us; just like we cannot accurately forecast the next tornado until it is swirling in the air and coming our way. Because of this uncertainty, we must maintain a lifestyle that is without compromise or question. We must be above reproach. Such a lifestyle can never be obtained in our own power, but through daily surrender to the Holy Spirit's enablement. We can't! God never said we could. He can; He always said He would.

When our Christian walk is above reproach, those who may falsely accuse us will be put to shame in their own foolishness. It's like the kid's phrase, *"I'm like rubber, and you're like glue—bounces off me and sticks to you."* People who intentionally cause harm to those who live lives above reproach will watch their own maliciousness exposed as an unfounded attack with the final result being their own conscience filled with guilt. When we are walking with the Lord and following His ways and living a Christ–like life, we are able to rest in the knowledge that God will fight our battles and that He will deal with those who cause us harm.

*Are you living out the Great Commission, or are you making a "great omission" of God's Word from your daily life?*

📖 Psalm 140 gives us a wonderful look at some of David's prayers for protection. Read verses 1–13 of this Psalm, and take note of the situation. Describe David's situation.

_____

_____

_____

What types of things were the enemies doing?

_____

_____

_____

How did David respond? Who came to his rescue?

_____

_____

_____

Looking at verses 12 and 13, in what was David confident?

_____

_____

_____

It seemed like David had enemies coming at him from all sides. No matter whether physical or verbal harm was thrown his way, David knew that only God would be able to give him victory. Through God, the situation would be resolved. David knew that he needed to seek the Lord and allow the Lord to bring judgment.

📖 Read Luke 6:27–28. What does Jesus tell us to do when someone curses us?

_____

_____

_____

📖 Now write down what Paul says in Romans 12:14:

_____

_____

📖 Proverbs 25:21–22 gives more direction on how to treat your enemies. What does it say will happen if we bless our enemies?

_____

_____

_____

*"Bless those who persecute you; bless and curse not."*

**Romans 12:14**

What an image! Heaping burning coals on our enemies' heads by blessing them? This verse is confirmed and quoted in Romans 12:20. Look back a verse, to Romans 12:19, and record why we should not be the one to take revenge:

_____

_____

## Vengeance is His, and the victory is ours.

We are to leave any battles to God and remain focused on Him. In so doing, we allow God to be God and allow Him to fight our battles for us. Vengeance is His, and the victory is ours. God will bless us as we bless others and stand firm in the knowledge that He is our Mighty Warrior!

It is a shame that we have to discuss situations of suffering: occasions where others mistreat us in spite of our goodness or kindness to them. Unfortunately, any thing we do, even if it is for the kingdom of God, has the potential to be misunderstood, twisted, or rejected by those around us who don't understand or find themselves filled with emotions of the flesh. With this realization, 1 Peter 3 reinforces the fact that we must remain blameless or above reproach in spite of our sufferings or persecutions. Once again, when we keep our focus on God, the rest will ultimately fall into place.

In this passage, and throughout 1 Peter 3 and 4, we see Peter remind us that even Jesus had to suffer; and if we are becoming more Christ-like in our lives, we should be aware of the fact that trials will come against us at some point as well. No matter how bad we think we have it, we must always remember that our Savior had it worst—yet He was victorious. Remember—our victory is in Christ! He has *already* paved the way for a glorious eternity for each believer, and this should outweigh even the worst of days. God's grace and mercy is always prevalent in Scripture. As we see in 1 Peter 3:21–22, we have the assurance that Christ is ultimately victorious and sits at the right hand of God. Likewise, we (who stand firm in our faith) will also claim victory as we live out our eternal life in the heavenlies with our Creator.

In comparison, the apostle Paul lists some of his own sufferings in 2 Corinthians 11:23–28. List them here:

_____

_____

_____

## "Jesus Christ, who is at the right hand of God, having gone into heaven, after angels and authorities and powers had been subjected to Him."

## 1 Peter 3:21–22

As we sit in our comfortable churches, can we even fathom all that Paul experienced as he proclaimed the good news of Jesus Christ throughout many strange and inhospitable lands? His listing here is long, and we are compelled by his dedication. What physical suffering he endured!

Though we can certainly admire Paul's steadfastness in physical measures, we must acknowledge that there is more to suffering than mere physical oppression. Paul also mentioned another type of suffering he experienced, as written in 2 Corinthians 12:7–10. What was the suffering, and what did Paul ask God to do? What was God's response?

_____

_____

_____

_____

_____

The exact details about the type of thorn Paul refers to are unclear. Scholars have speculated for centuries concerning the nature of the thorn that Paul talked about in 2 Corinthians 12:7–10. The reference to the thorn in this passage has been most prominently viewed as a physical ailment, while other scholars such as John MacArthur have presented a view that the thorn in Paul's flesh was more of a spiritual struggle. In light of MacArthur's view (as conveyed in the *MacArthur Bible Commentary,* pages 1649–1650), it involved a deeper ache; the ache of his heart over false teaching in the church that caused him distress. There may have been something or someone who was coming in trying to cause those who followed Jesus Christ to fall away and follow false gods or false doctrine.

Second Corinthians 12:7 calls this "thorn in the flesh" a *"messenger of Satan."* Here is a situation attributed to something much deeper than a superficial wound; this is spiritual warfare. According to the *Complete Word Study Dictionary*, the word "messenger" in this verse is translated from the Greek word *aggelos,* which, in this specific usage, refers to "the angels of the devil or Satan." Whether a physical ailment or false messenger the source of such grief is clearly pointed out as Satan in this passage in 2 Corinthians.

Paul shared some of his sufferings with the people of Corinth, as well as some of his blessings. He rejoiced in his weaknesses and readily admitted when he had difficulty or had suffered for the sake of Jesus Christ. Paul focused on Jesus and understood that by doing so, while there would be difficult times, God would sustain him through them all. Paul stayed the course, and remained blameless.

You may find yourself in a trial of which no one else is aware. Maybe someone personally attacked you where there were no witnesses. Maybe you suffer an illness no one can "see" or understand, and your cries of pain are constantly dismissed. Maybe the hurts in your family are just too deep to talk about to others. Maybe someone has wronged you terribly, and accused you of being the one at fault. Whatever the case may be, God is always there for you and *will* deliver you from that trouble. Especially when we are being persecuted falsely, we have a tendency to forget that "God has our back"— but by remaining upright in character, not stooping to the level of those coming against us, and relying on God for support and strength, we *will* prevail!

The more above reproach we are, the less blame others can put on us; very easy to comprehend, but a challenge to live out. What does it mean to be blameless? Let's look at some scriptural passages that identify different characters considered blameless.

Read Psalm 119:1–3. What is a blameless person like?

_____

_____

_____

Psalm 119:1–3 paints a very vivid picture of the blameless person:

> *"Blessed are they whose ways are blameless, who walk according to the law of the LORD. Blessed are they who keep his statutes and seek him with all their heart. They do nothing wrong; they walk in his ways."* (NIV)

Isn't that wonderful? It doesn't say that blameless equals perfect, but that the blameless person can stand before God *unafraid*. The blameless person has emptied out his or her "closet of shame" at the foot of the cross and can stand before God knowing that they have confessed their sins. The blameless person walks with the Lord and keeps His laws. The blameless person seeks, obeys, and honors God.

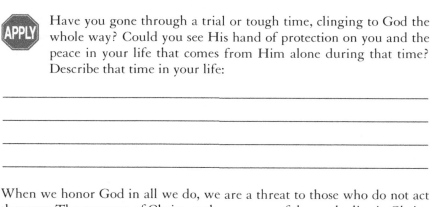 Have you gone through a trial or tough time, clinging to God the whole way? Could you see His hand of protection on you and the peace in your life that comes from Him alone during that time? Describe that time in your life:

_____

_____

_____

_____

When we honor God in all we do, we are a threat to those who do not act that way. The presence of Christ, or the presence of those who live in Christ, evokes a response in any situation; you either are drawn to Jesus, or you reject Him. Those who are unbelievers or follow false gods are naturally threatened by the presence of truth in their midst. This brings persecution and strife to us who are above reproach, which is actually an indicator that we are seen as the light that shines for Christ! Rejoice in those times, knowing that you are standing in truth against a dark enemy and that you are the victor. No matter the situation, your victory is in Christ.

📖 In 1 Peter 3:8–12, we have quite a summary of how to live a life that honors God. What types of things does Peter call us to do?

_____

_____

_____

*Extra Mile*
**PSALM 34**

Take time to read Psalm 34 and thank God for His provision in your life.

Peter urges the reader to live in harmony, to only speak kind words, to stay away from sin, and to *"seek peace and pursue it"* (v. 11). In these verses, Peter alludes to Psalm 34, which was written by David while he was acting in a way that would drive an adversary away. I simply love that image of "pursuing peace." It is an action, and it is intentional.

In the Old Testament accounts, we see that David dealt with much persecution. Here's a guy who went from being a shepherd to a king. He lived a long life of dedication to the Lord. Did he make mistakes? Absolutely. Did God deal with him about these mistakes? Absolutely. So why was he referred to as the "man after God's own heart"? David sought after His God, seeking to please and honor Him.

**A Portrait of David**
When Saul, who David replaced in leadership, continually came after David, seeking to kill him, David responded with blessing. Saul was threatened by David's success and anointing, especially because Saul had lost the Lord's favor. I couldn't imagine being in the blessings of God and then walking away. But Saul did. Many times, David had the opportunity to kill Saul, or totally destroy all he was, yet he didn't. David may have taken Saul's sword, and he may have played tricks on him, but ultimate revenge of death was not in his plan. David knew what it was to be blameless in that situation. He could honestly stand before his God and testify that he had not touched a hair on his enemy's head.

Once Saul was dead (at the hands of someone else), David continued to seek out family members in Saul's family line—to bless them. Who would go that far? It would be hard to find such a man. David, who had every right to go after this man and his family, decided to take the high ground, and bless them in spite of their unjust persecution to him and his family. Think of the magnitude of this! Not only blessing our #1 enemy, but his family line! David went as far as blessing the last relative he could find, a young man named Mephibosheth, and making him a part of David's own household and dining table guest list. What an example for us all.

David was willing to show the example of God's love to others with his experiences. Our conscience drives our moral reputation. David's reputation was based on how he carried himself, and what he acted like in his life. He told others about God in his extensive writings in the Psalms. David was willing to share God with others.

In 1 Peter 3:15 we are encouraged to have a constant willingness to share the gospel. No matter what our situation or schedule looks like, Peter urges us to be ready to witness to others. Observe how he states it: *"always being ready to make a defense to everyone who asks you to give an account for the hope that is in you."*

 We should always be ready with an answer for the hope within us. Do you readily tell others about your faith? Do you share the message of salvation with those around you?

_____

_____

This is an awesome challenge for us all. When we are willing to share His good news of salvation, we are most likely walking a path of life that is pleasing to God. Who among us wants to tell others about God's Word when we are in the middle of doing something we know we shouldn't be doing? Our sin would keep us from readily sharing. Yet in a blameless lifestyle, we are fulfilling verse 16's recipe for a clear conscience. A godly life is a clean life.

Memorize our focus verse for today and review all that we have learned as we sum up with this verse in 1 Peter 3:16: *"and keep a good conscience so that in the thing in which you are slandered, those who revile your good behavior in Christ may be put to shame."*

# DON'T MISUNDERSTAND ME!
# 3:16 VERSE: 2 PETER

*Clear Message* DAY FOUR

*"as also in all his letters, speaking in them of these things, in which are some things hard to understand, which the untaught and unstable distort, as they do also the rest of Scriptures, to their own destruction."*

Scripture is understood through the leading of the Holy Spirit—not merely through natural interpretation. The power of the Bible as our living Word involves the fact that every teaching God has placed in there has a confirmation somewhere else in Scripture. Every concept in Scripture has something else written in the Bible that backs it up. There is truth in the context and consistency of God's promises to us. He will give us His message as we read the Bible with the leading of the Holy Spirit. It is by His Spirit that we are able to interpret the Bible. There is not one person on earth that can interpret it without the Spirit's help, and there is not one person on earth incapable of interpreting Scripture if the Holy Spirit indwells him or her.

📖 Read John 16:13. Who will guide you into the truth?

_____

The Holy Spirit, as promised by Jesus, will guide us into all truth. He will speak to us the very message of God and will reveal all that the Lord wants us to know. As a genuine believer seeks the Lord, He will meet them in the same measure. And when *"the Spirit of truth, comes, he will guide you into all truth. He will not speak on his own; he will speak only what he hears, and he will tell you what is yet to come"* (John 16:13, NIV).

Paul himself is a wonderful example of just how the Holy Spirit can lead someone to the truth regardless of what kind of life that person led before divine revelation. Keep in mind that Paul, while still Saul, knew the Scriptures, but he still denied that Jesus was the Messiah. His heart was hardened, and the truth was not revealed to Him while he read. Saul delighted in persecuting Christians, until one day he was touched by Christ in such a real way on the Damascus road. He was totally transformed in life, belief, and influence on others. He was very versed in the law, and was very eloquent and educated before his conversion. He brought those qualities with him into his new life as a follower of Jesus Christ. Paul was misunderstood at times, and there were false teachers that took the teachings of Paul and twisted them, leading seekers away from the truth. Peter was concerned with making sure that no matter what someone heard from a teacher, he or she would remember what they knew was truth and rely on that.

Second Peter 3:1–2 reveals Peter's reason for this letter. What does he want for them to remember?

_____

_____

_____

The entire third chapter of 2 Peter deals with Peter's concern for those he has taught; specifically that they would be sure of the second coming of Christ. Peter is making sure that the foundation of faith that has been made in new believers is not neglected. He wants to ensure that we all realize that Jesus *is* coming again, and that this earth as we know it *will* pass away; it will be destroyed in fire and destruction. This is a certainty for all mankind.

He reminds the reader of the critical purpose for the faith we have in Christ; salvation and the promise of Christ's second coming. This concept is not easy, even for the life-long Christian. We know that Christ promised that He would come again. We know we will ultimately live and reign with Him in heaven. We know our bodies will be raised and we will have new, glorified bodies. We know all these things, but can we truly grasp the magnitude of these events? It seems so far off, so huge, and we may be easily persuaded to dismiss it as science fiction—something to worry about another day. Our nature is to worry about the moment, to live in the *carpe diem* mindset, and to leave the future to those who study prophecy for a living. Why do we so easily discount the future?

In our natural state, we as humans tend to be very impatient, especially in today's convenience-focused, self-seeking culture. Peter warns about becoming complacent or doubting that Christ will ever return.

📖 Read Isaiah 22:13 and Isaiah 56:11–12. What were the people doing in these passages, instead of focusing on God?

_____

_____

_____

📖 Now compare with the parable in Luke 12. First read verses 13–19, and describe the scene:

_____

_____

_____

What is the connection between the verses in Isaiah, and the scene in verse 19?

_____

_____

_____

The person described in this parable hoards his wealth, and becomes complacent about the future. In his eyes, he has made a great future for himself, and planned it out perfectly. Rather than sharing his wealth, or using it to impact more lives than his own, he is consumed with building his own "kingdom" so to speak. His nest egg has been built, and in verse 19, we see that he is prepared to spend years squandering all he has saved.

God has a very strong response to this mentality, as seen in Luke 12:20–21. How does God rebuke these actions?

_____

_____

_____

God clearly shows the rich man the error of his ways. All he saved up for, he will not enjoy, because he was selfish in his stewardship. In all of his "kingdom building," he never thought to help build *God's kingdom*. None of his wealth was ever shared with God. Whether monetarily or with talents and gifts, we are to be "rich toward God"—and share what we have with others, thereby making an impact around us.

Have you observed folks spending their whole lives hoarding money for personal gain and a grand retirement, only to *never enjoy it*? How did it make you feel to see their dreams go unfulfilled?

_____

_____

📖 Reading Matthew 24:44, in light of our last question, how should you now prepare for the coming of the Lord?

_____

_____

_____

We don't know when Jesus is coming again, but we do know He's coming. He may not come in our lifetimes, meaning we will meet Him upon our deaths. Knowing that we can't take a moving truck with us to heaven should inspire us to be ready and focused on Him in everything—even with regards to resources and finances.

📖 Read 2 Peter 3:3–4. Peter's concern for readers isn't just that they remember, but that they will be protected from those who would lead them astray. How does Peter describe these false teachers?

_____

_____

In this passage, we discover that "mockers" who have no interest in the Lord or His return to earth will be following their own lusts in the last days. Peter says that these people will say, _Where is this 'coming' He promised? Ever since our father's died, everything goes on as it has since the beginning of creation_ (2 Peter 3:4, NIV).

📖 The Book of Jude also confirms this teaching about "mockers" in verses 17–18. Read those verses, and write any new observations:

_____

_____

_____

📖 Peter continues to warn the followers about these mockers. Read 2 Peter 3:5–8. What proof of God's power and sovereignty does Peter point out?

_____

_____

_____

Through Peter's persistent reminder that the same God who created all things has already "reserved" the end of the earth, we can be assured that our promise of Christ's return is true. It will happen, and only if we stay true to the faith we profess will we be saved.

📖 Verse 9 gives us such a glimpse at the mercy of God! In this verse, we see why God seems to be slow in coming again for His people. What is the reason, according to this verse?

_____

_____

_____

With the end of the world looming and death a guarantee for all people, the question we all ask at some time is simply "when?" At times, it feels like Jesus will come back to take us to heaven any minute—especially when we watch the evening news and see the disturbing current events continually unfolding before our very eyes.

God doesn't want anyone to be denied His mercy, and He is patiently waiting for all of us to come to Him before our fate is sealed. Whether the Second Coming is a thousand years away or two minutes away, only the Lord knows. What we do know is that God will keep His promise and that we have a merciful God who *"is patient toward you, not wishing for any to perish but all to come to repentance"* (verse 9).

If God wants **all** to come to repentance, how do they get the message? Someone must share with them the message of Jesus. Therefore, we should be challenged to accurately convey the message of Jesus to the world around us, correcting in love those who are misguided, and explaining the hope we have. We are accountable for sharing the message of Christ with others. We are accountable for those we teach and those to whom we minister.

 Have you shared the good news of Jesus Christ with others? Were you able to lead them to repentance or help them see the need for Jesus as their Savior? Did you use a Bible, showing them the verses that support what was said?

_____

_____

_____

So often, people will hear something from another person, take it as truth, and use it as a basis to teach others that very concept. This is great if it lines up with Scripture, and it is *every believer's responsibility* to read and study Scripture to make sure it does. It is our duty to check our teaching out to make sure it in fact reflects the message Christ has given us. If a teaching sounds too good to be true or is not something you have heard before, please take the time to verify it with Scripture.

📖 Peter, with evident concern for those who might have been misinformed, reiterates the correct information about the coming of Jesus. Second Peter 3:10–13 outlines the certainty of the future. What does Peter say will happen?

_____

_____

In response to this, what is the believer to do, according to verses 14–15?

_____

_____

📖 Verse 15 mentions Paul, and the conclusion of that thought is found in verses 16 and 17. Read 15–17, and explain why Peter mentions Paul here:

_____

_____

_____

Peter clearly points out that Jesus *will* come again; the heavens *will* be destroyed; we *will* enjoy a new heaven and earth, and those who are righteous *will* dwell in the new creation.

Because of this, Peter urges believers to live a life that reflects Christ-like principles, even if others may come and try to dissuade believers from living such a life. Peter mentions Paul and his teaching to show that Paul agrees with what Peter is telling them here. Unfortunately, some people had taken what Paul wrote and said, and twisted it to fit their false theology, which is why our focus verse serves as a warning.

Peter mentions Paul and his agreement of this whole message of the Second Coming and validates Paul's message as coming *"with the wisdom that God gave him"* (v.15, NIV). The two men may have disagreed from time to time, and they may have had a different approach to evangelism—but the message of salvation they both had was the same. The message of Christ is from *Christ*, not man, as many unbelievers may argue.

God's Word tells us that in the Last Days, there will be those who attempt to lead believers from the truth, and they will distort Scripture to do their dirty work. People can take any passage of Scripture, and turn it around to say whatever they want. One phrase or thought can mean many different things. This is why we are to have confirmation from other believers and the Scriptures themselves. I believe this is another reason why Peter mentions Paul—to provide credibility and affirmation that what is said has been "double-checked" by those who are guided by the Holy Spirit. Thankfully, by reading such passages as this, we are alerted to such schemes and are able to take the timeless advice of God to *"be on your guard lest, being carried away by the error of unprincipled men, you fall from your own steadfastness,"* (2 Peter 3:17).

📖 Read 2 Corinthians 11:14. What does it say that Satan may look like?

_____

_____

_____

Sometimes, the devil will present concepts that sound very similar to God's Word. There may be such a fine line between truth and what we are told through deception that it takes prayer and seeking God's guidance to realize the error. Satan is not always going to appear like the ugly monster-like red creature with a long spiked tail and the pitchfork in his hand who roams the earth looking for sweet church going folk to devour that we are used to seeing depicted. Scripture tells us *"Satan disguises himself as an angel of light"* (2 Corinthians 11:14).

Satan is Lucifer, formerly one of God's own angels, who knows what it is like to be serving God, and knows how hard he fell when he betrayed his Creator God. He fell from God's grace because he thought he could be as good as God and could be like Him. There is no one like our God! No one can compare. Even Jesus was in submission to God while on the earth, and He is fully God.

Needless to say, the devil is mad that he is banished to the pits of hell for all eternity, and he wants revenge on all who follow God. Satan wants nothing more than to carry us with him into the depths of hell, and he will use God's own Word to work against us. As a person with a deep relationship with

**Jesus is the only defense you need from the schemes of the enemy.**

Christ, you should easily see the masquerade around you. Jesus is the only defense you need from the schemes of the enemy.

John 10:10 tells us what the devil's purpose is. What does it say about him? On the other hand, what is Jesus' purpose?

_____

_____

_____

These days it is easy to find books and tapes to teach us how to "fight Spiritual warfare," to defend ourselves against the things of the devil through rebuking this and claiming that. While I absolutely believe that Satan's purpose is to "steal, and kill, and destroy" (John 10:10), and that he focuses his attack on those who are strong in the Lord, we must be very careful to not give the enemy more credit than he is due. We especially don't want to give Satan more of our time and attention than we give God! If we spend all of our time speaking to the devil, even if it is with the intention of telling him to go away, then we may be wasting time that could be used for glorifying God.

We already have victory over the devil through Christ. Why would we spend the majority of our time trying to convince the enemy and ourselves of this fact? Jesus is our example for all things. When He encountered the devil and demons, Jesus very quickly dealt with it by responding with Scripture, or demanding that the demon leave the place wherein it dwelt. There was no great discussion. There was no deliberation. Jesus spoke the word with authority, and *knew* He had dominion over the darkness. If Christ is in us, we can walk in the authority Christ gives us.

Jesus has already claimed victory! He is already in heaven at God's right hand. He already has angels, powers and authorities in submission to Him. Through His victories and authority, we have already won the spiritual war—in spite of Satan's best efforts to convince us otherwise. Stand firm in what you know—as a victorious, righteous person in Christ, so that your battle is over before it has begun.

*If Christ is in us, we can walk in the authority Christ gives us.*

# FOR ME TO FOLLOW GOD

Clear Message    DAY FIVE

In this lesson, our focus has been on retaining the foundation of Christ in our faith, remaining blameless even during suffering, and being ready for the return of Jesus. In our key verses, we examined the importance of being rooted in the Word of God, which means we have to dedicate time to the reading and understanding of Scripture. We also discussed how important it is to clearly and accurately present the gospel to others.

 Let's do some brainstorming together. On the next page are some questions that you can answer to gauge your reaction and goals for sharing Christ with others. Take time to think about your answers, and journal your responses in the "now" area listed below. When you have completed all twelve lessons of this study, come back to this section and fill in the "later" area.

At some point in the future, maybe six months or a year from now, go over the questions again, journaling on a separate paper, or even in the side margins here, and compare the difference in your responses again. If you review these questions periodically for the rest of life, I imagine you would be able to see measurable growth in your spiritual walk over the course of time. Some answers may stay the same, yet others may change considerably.

If you were talking to a person, and he says that he does not believe in Jesus and asks you if you do, what would you tell him? What if you only had ten seconds?

Now:

_____

_____

_____

Later:

_____

_____

_____

If you could share only one passage of Scripture with a non-Christian, which verse or verses would you choose to share, and why?

Now:

_____

_____

_____

_____

Later:

_____

_____

_____

_____

If you could only spend ten minutes a day focusing on your personal relationship with Jesus, what would you spend those minutes doing? Why?

Now:

_____

_____

_____

_____

Later:

_____

_____

_____

What is the best way you could bless your worst enemy?

Now:

_____

_____

_____

_____

Later:

_____

_____

_____

_____

If your life on earth ended today, would you be ready for eternity? What would you wish you had more time to finish or fix?

Now:

_____

_____

_____

_____

Later:

_____

_____

_____

_____

Do you trust Jesus to get you through the hardest trials? Even when your reputation is on the line?

Now:

_____

_____

_____

_____

Later:

_____

_____

_____

_____

As we desire to live a Christ-like life, we need to challenge ourselves to live accordingly, and be ready to share the hope of salvation with others. I do hope that you will come back and ponder these questions again. In fact, make up some other goals or thought provoking questions for yourself and track your responses on those over time as well. May our walk with the Lord remain fresh, focused, and fully devoted.

 *Lord Jesus,* I praise you for all that You are, Jesus, and all that You have made me to be. I thank You for the promise of eternity and the security of knowing that You will be coming again for your children. Lord, help me to walk blamelessly, even when I and my brothers and sisters are being slandered or are suffering in any way. Lord, I pray that my enemies would be blessed. I pray that You would lead them to Your truth, and that any vengeance would be Yours, releasing me from the burden of bitterness and hurt. Lord, may I forgive those who attempt to harm me in any way. Help me to press on to that goal of a life focused on You, and may I always be prepared to give an answer for the hope I have in You. Jesus, I need You. I want You. I desire to know You. Show me Your ways, and may Your Holy Spirit reveal Your truth to me. In Jesus' name, Amen.

## Works Cited

John MacArthur, *The MacArthur Bible Commentary* (Nashville, TN: Thomas Nelson Inc, 2005), 1649–1650.

Spiros Zodhiates, Warren Baker, eds., *The Complete Word Study Dictionary: New Testament* (Chattanooga, TN: AMG Publishers, 1992), #32, 68.

David J. Williams, *Paul's Metaphors: Their Context and Character* (Peabody, MA: Hendrickson Publishers, 1999), 261–262.

# EIGHT

# Strength and Peace

## FOLLOWING THE GOD OF ALL COMFORT

## 3:16 VERSES: EPHESIANS, 2 THESSALONIANS

How the Lord loves to lavish His love on us! God gave His Son for us, and Jesus gives us eternal life through our relationship with Him. God wants us to know His love and have the assurance that His Holy Spirit, the gift to all who believe, will guide us into fellowship with the Father if we follow His lead. Anything we may have to suffer through on earth pales in comparison to the suffering Jesus endured because of His love for us, and we need to stay focused on that love no matter what we face.

At the end of these five days (or however long you will study this lesson), I pray that you will continue to spot the references to believers praying to the God of peace, strength, grace and love. God's love for His children is shown throughout Scripture and is experienced by those who study and dwell on His Word and communicate with Him through prayer. Remember the verses that build you up during "good times" so that when bad times come, you can gain strength from the truth you have hidden in your heart.

God is honored when we come to Him, and He also gets the glory when we lean on Him for comfort. We gain such strength from God in our times of need, and there is such peace when we rest in Him. God hears us when we cry out in prayer and praise, and He is faithful to strengthen us and give us peace in the most

> **Anything we may have to suffer through on earth pales in comparison to the suffering Jesus endured because of His love for us.**

difficult of times. The apostle Paul knew the power of this strength, and, as we will see through our focus verses this week, it was his desire to share that knowledge with other believers. We could probably spend an entire twelve weeks simply going over the multitudes of verses that remind us of God's strength, power, and ability to carry us through the toughest storms—but alas, we only have five days in this lesson.

Throughout this lesson, we will be able to understand Paul and his passion for the Lord and fellow believers more and more. Paul prayed for those to whom he ministered. We will also continue learning more about applying the good news of Jesus Christ to our life and to our interaction with the world around us. We must build each other up in the love of the Lord, and convey the magnitude of the God we serve to all who will listen. May He always receive the glory for all that is done in His name!

DAY ONE

# LOVE FOR THE GENTILES 3:16 VERSE: EPHESIANS

*"That He would grant you, according to the riches of His glory, to be strengthened with power through His Spirit in the inner man."*

When Paul addressed the Gentiles in the book of Ephesians, he wanted them to understand the magnitude of God's love for them. Paul was intent on showing the Ephesians that God truly was interested in them, and they, who once were outcasts, were now becoming unified with the Jews. God used Paul to convey this truth, I believe, because he was the very man who would understand how impossible this merging would be to the natural mind! And just as God planned, Paul lovingly carried them through the concept of the unification of all believers through Jesus Christ with excitement and passion. Paul loved the fact that God loves the Gentiles, so much so that while this epistle to the believers at Ephesus was being written, Paul was literally wearing chains and was held as a prisoner (probably in Rome at this time) for *their* cause.

 Are you wrestling with the fact that the very people that once had no inclusion in his belief system (while he was a Pharisee) now were the very people he was willing to be put in chains for?

_____

_____

_____

**To those Paul once detested, God called him to minister.**

For those he formerly didn't respect, he was now praying. Paul's transformation included the transformation of much more than his ministry, it reached down to his very soul. He served the people of Ephesus with a true Christ-like love. His concern for their spiritual condition is clearly evident in his letters, as he was willing to die himself in order that they would not perish.

**APPLY** Has God ever challenged you to pray for someone you may have once called an enemy?

_____

_____

Do you yearn to help those you once avoided? If so, give an example, and how God changed your heart.

_____

_____

_____

_____

Don't you think God must love to watch us as we see the power of His love being manifested in the most unusual ways? God literally turned Paul's world upside down. Paul responded by rejoicing *even in chains*.

The environment in Ephesus was tough for Christians. Blatant sin and false religion were rampant, making temptation difficult to avoid. Even through these distractions, people were coming to faith in Jesus Christ. The church at Ephesus was strong. Paul showed unswerving dedication to the church and its people by ministering there for three years. He knew what trials they faced, yet He grew to love the people of Ephesus deeply.

📖 Read Acts 20:17–38. This passage gives such a clear picture of Paul's love for the people of Ephesus.

For whom did Paul send in verse 17?

_____

Verse 21 reveals the unifying nature of the call on Paul's life. What was his message, and to whom did he share it, as shown in this verse?

_____

_____

_____

Reading verses 20 and 27, what was Paul's greatest source of satisfaction during his time of ministry there?

_____

_____

_____

According to verse 24, what was Paul's goal?

_____

_____

Verses 36–38 show us an emotional farewell. After reading this passage, do you understand Paul's attachment to the people at Ephesus a little better? How has this passage affected you today? Write your thoughts:

*Did You Know?*

### THE WORLD OF EPHESUS

At the time that Paul served the church in Ephesus, the pagan culture made it difficult for Christians to function. Temples were devoted to the worship of pagan gods, and the general public was more interested in serving its own needs than adhering to the standards of Jehovah God. The main focus of false worship, the goddess Diana, emphasized fertility and sexual pleasure. Paul and his teachings of God were very out of step with the world in which the Ephesians lived.

_____

_____

_____

_____

_____

When Paul passed through the area near Ephesus while making his way to Jerusalem, he called on the elders to meet with him. I imagine it was hard enough to see them knowing that it was only for a moment; the thought of going into town and seeing the entire church might have just been too much for him. Paul shared his heart, and reminded them of his dedication during his time of service, and after a tearful good-bye, he was off again.

As Paul poured out his heart to the elders in this passage, the thing that has always struck me is the fact that his *source* of accomplishment was not the size of the church, the amount of money its people raised, or the number of bodies in the pews—*it was the fact that he never hesitated in proclaiming the good news of Jesus and God's will for their lives.* This is huge! What a tremendous example for us today. This is Christ-like behavior for sure and a concept that we would all do well to implement in our own lives.

Paul's goal was to continue to build up the believers in Ephesus in their faith, continuing to pray for them and care about them long after he left their area—even when he was miles upon miles away. It amazes me that Paul, a prisoner, who at this point was suffering in prison, was more interested in encouraging others than worrying about his own situation. That also is Christ-like living! May we all press on and lean on the Holy Spirit to carry us to that level of spiritual maturity.

**APPLY** Have you had a time when you encouraged someone who was having a tough time, while you were silently suffering at the same time?

_____

_____

What impact did your ministering have? Did it bless the life of that person or encourage him or her in any way?

_____

_____

_____

_____

Did encouraging that person in his or her need bring a sense of blessing to your life?

_____

_____

_____

I imagine that Paul rejoiced in the fact that he was still able to encourage and impact the church at Ephesus with the love of Christ long after his

> *Paul never hesitated in proclaiming the good news of Jesus and the will of God who sent Jesus.*

departure. It must have blessed his spirit to still feel connected to them. In the same way, we can receive peace and a sense of blessing by encouraging others in their need; whether they are able to reciprocate or not.

The time period when Paul ministered was so unique. Christianity was new. The Law was no longer the only driving force for those who believed in Christ. God's chosen people, the Jews, were no longer the only ones with access to God. Paul was given the charge of ministering to the Gentiles—the very people who were always told they were *not* the "chosen ones. " These Gentiles had lived for generations as a people without hope—until Christ that is! They had fashioned false gods; they worshipped whatever they had access to, and now, they would have access to a relationship with the Messiah.

By the third chapter of Paul's letter to the Ephesians, Paul has explained how the body of believers in Christ was unified, and how *all* those who believed in Jesus were chosen. He told them they were united and were all chosen because of their *faith,* not their works or genealogical lines.

In Ephesians 4, Paul goes into more detail about their unity in faith. Read Ephesians 4:1–6. How do we find unity according to the passage?

_____

_____

_____

_____

## EPHESIANS 4:1-6

*"I therefore, the prisoner of the Lord, entreat you to walk in a manner worthy of the calling with which you have been called, with all humility and gentleness, with patience, showing forbearance to one another in love, being diligent to preserve the unity of the Spirit in the bond of peace. There is one body and one Spirit, just as also you were called in one hope of your calling; one Lord, one faith, one baptism, one God and Father of all who is over all and through all and in all."*

Everything that Paul lists in this passage is based on God unifying us, not the other way around. We cannot purpose to be unified outside of God's will and still be considered Christian. The things that unify us are the standards and purposes of God's plan for us and our salvation: unity through His Spirit, calling, faith, baptism, and God Himself. Our unity must be God driven, or it will drive us right to destruction. If you think that sounds harsh, think back to the account of the Tower of Babel in Genesis 11—and remember what God thought of *that* type of unity!

Paul does not propose some "limited-time offer" profession of faith—nor faith built solely on a family tradition. He explains the phenomenon of being a transformed creature in Christ. Paul yearned for them to become people with outer images as changed as their inner personalities; Paul was concerned about their innermost being. He wanted their spirit to be in tune with God's Spirit.

 Is your whole life, your outward and inward person, committed to the transforming power of Jesus Christ? What areas of your life need to be surrendered, or re-committed to the Lord?

_____

_____

_____

Christ doesn't just want our outward expressions of faith; He wants the whole kit and caboodle! He wants a permanent takeover of our lives, a relationship that will continually grow and mature. As we strive to become more Christ-like, how are we to achieve this? We can't achieve it. It comes only through the power of God.

Paul knew that a total transformation of someone's spirit could not and would not occur by human efforts. So, Paul prayed in Ephesians 3 for the one who *could* perform such a transformation; namely the Holy Spirit, to assist us in the process. Throughout the third chapter, Paul explains the magnitude of what we can experience with the Holy Spirit. As the Spirit dwells within us, He brings us strength and guides us, giving us the power we need to get through our hardest struggles.

Think of a time when you felt the Holy Spirit's presence and knew that you were being guided through a difficult situation. Describe your emotions during that time and the effect that the Holy Spirit had on you:

_____

_____

_____

_____

_____

_____

Trying to explain the depth of God's power shown in Paul's letter to the Ephesians is kind of like trying to describe the magnitude of winning the biggest jackpot lottery in history to someone who has never seen or used money before. We serve a limitless God, and we have unlimited potential as we lean on Him. I am excited to tell you that in Day Two we will attempt to grasp the magnitude of God's love. Be prepared to sit in awe of our God!

# SAYING A PRAYER FOR YOU
# 3:16 VERSE: EPHESIANS

*"That He would grant you, according to the riches of His glory, to be strengthened with power through His Spirit in the inner man."*

**Paul changed the face of the earth forever—all for God's glory!**

The suffering he endured during his ministry did not sway Paul, nor did he want pity from others. He only wanted others to understand and accept the message of Christ. He eagerly ventured into new lands, converting anyone to Christianity who would accept the good news of Jesus Christ. Through divine enablement, Paul changed the face of the earth forever—*all for God's glory!* The Holy Spirit equipped Paul mightily to do all he did: to preach, to travel, to suffer, to write, to win the lost, and to love the sinner. Paul was a worthy vessel because of his obedience and his love for the Lord.

Paul saw a glimpse of the magnitude of God's love for us through many experiences. First, he was impacted by his conversion experience. Second, Paul's experiences ministering throughout the region gave him a sense of God's presence as well. In spite of continual hardships, Paul continued to see God's love for him, and the apostle continually praised the Lord. Finally, in 2 Corinthians 12:1-6 Paul also tells us of a moment when "a man in Christ" (scholars believe he was referring to himself) was carried away into the third heaven. "The third heaven" or "paradise" is the destination for believers after death. Paul explains that this man experienced unspeakable things while being carried up close to God's presence. Paul gives us the impression that "this man" was forever changed as he felt the warmth and love of God and *"heard inexpressible words, which a man is not permitted to speak"* (2 Corinthians 12:4). Paul was transformed by the magnitude of the power of the Almighty. These experiences obviously shaped Paul's faith and gave him a heightened sense of God's love and presence in a believer's life.

In the midst of all he endured, he knew God loved him. Paul wanted that same confidence to be manifested in the believers in Ephesus. Paul's love for to the Ephesians compelled him to include a prayer to the Father on their behalf.

📖 Read Ephesians 3:14–21. What was Paul's overall theme of this prayer?

_____

_____

Why do you think such a prayer was needed, and why do you think Paul wanted them to hear his prayer for them?

_____

_____

_____

_____

Not only does Paul pray for their spiritual condition and for the Holy Spirit to empower them in their lives, Paul encourages them in their faith. This prayer would show them that even though Paul was suffering, he knew that God was in control of his situation. In the same way, no matter what would happen in their lives, God would be with them as well.

Paul begins the prayer in verse 14, acknowledging that he's praying to God the Father, and explaining his humble posture shown in reverence. What was Paul's posture? Was he standing, sitting, or kneeling? Why?

_____

_____

_____

_____

Philippians 2:10 gives us an explanation as to why he might have bowed his knees. Look up that verse, and write down what you find there:

_____

_____

_____

📖 Now, back in Ephesians 3:15, we see reference yet again to the unification of the Jews and Gentiles in their access to the hope of salvation through Jesus Christ. We are all God's children, and all of us will be grafted into the family of God upon our repentance and acceptance.

📖 Because of this relationship with the Father, Paul was able to make the requests found in our focus verse, Ephesians 3:16. What does Paul ask for? For whom is he asking?

_____

_____

_____

_____

By what resources would God provide this request?

_____

_____

_____

What would be the result of this prayer when answered? How would the people be changed?

_____

_____

_____

📖 Verse 17 gives us the reason Paul prayed for such provision. What is shown as Paul's goal?

_____

_____

*"That He would grant you, according to the riches of His glory, to be strengthened with power through His Spirit in the inner man."*

*Ephesians 3:16*

As Paul prayed that the people of Ephesus would be strengthened by the Holy Spirit and that their inner being would experience strengthening, Paul also prayed that Christ's presence would indwell the hearts of those for whom he prayed.

Let's look deeper into these verses, focusing on the visual description of the endlessness of God's love. There are some specific parameters that Paul defines.

**Wide (breadth):**
First, there is the width of Christ's love. Width describes a horizontal measurement. Imagine arms stretched out and a gentle voice saying, "I love you this much." With regards to Jesus, what does that image make you think of?

_____

_____

_____

It instantly takes me to the scene of the crucifixion of Jesus. With His arms stretched wide, nailed to that old wood, Jesus proclaimed His love for us, and took our sins to the grave.

**Long (length):**
Now, think about the word "long." "Long" is usually descriptive of a measurement of length rather than height or direction. God's love has no end, and the length of His love goes I imagine on and on. Knowing that our Creator God has the whole world in the palm of His hand reminds us that the length of His love is unfathomable to our mere human minds.

**High (height):**
Have you ever seen a space shuttle launch? Have you watched it soar into the atmosphere, with the trail of smoke following behind it? This is what I think of with the vast height of God's love for us. Long after we can visibly see that trail, it is still extending to the heavens. This reminds me of God's love. We may see His touch on our lives at a specific moment and not see the lasting effects that easily. Have you seen the heights of God's love in your life? How much more do you think His love extends towards you?

_____

_____

_____

_____

_____

**Deep (depth):**
How deep is the love of the Lord? His love extends deeper than the deepest ocean—further than anyone has measured. God is with us in our highest highs, and he remains with us in our lowest lows. And He loves us the whole way. What has been your lowest moment? Did you reach out to God for help? Did you sense God reaching down to you, even then, and surrounding you with His love?

_____

_____

_____

_____

_____

Wow! For those of us who love to visually imagine things we read, this passage of Scripture is profound. Can you grasp it? Can you fathom the love that Christ has for you? Can you comprehend how wide? How long? How deep? God is there, and His love extends beyond our wildest imaginations.

In verse 19, we see that Paul's goal for the people of Ephesus was for them to be *"filled up to all the fullness of God"* (Ephesians 3:19). Paul wanted them to experience the biggest amount of God that they could. Do you feel that you have that kind of fullness in your life? What could you do to become more full? Will you commit today to seeking the Lord and His complete presence in your life?

_____

_____

_____

### EPHESIANS 3:17–19

*"And I pray that you, being rooted and established in love, may have power together with all the saints, to grasp how wide and long and high and deep is the love of Christ, and to know this love that surpasses knowledge – that you may be filled to the measure of all the fullness of God."*

As overwhelming as this passage may seem, there is one more facet to the truths taught here. More than God merely loving us, God is love. He embodies love. Love is one of His characteristics, but it is so much more than that. God *is* love. We serve an all-powerful God that exceeds all we can comprehend!

📖 Read Psalm 139:1–12. In verses 1–6, what touches your heart the most?

_____

_____

_____

_____

Read verse 7: *"Where can I go from Thy Spirit? Or where can I flee from Thy presence?"* This is one of those verses in Scripture that has come to my mind time and time again—especially in times of difficulty. I challenge you to commit this passage (specifically verses 7–10) to memory, and etch it on your heart. Remember it. Love the God to whom it was written. There will never be a location or a situation where God will be unable to meet us!

Verses 8–12 show some of the examples of the places we might be and where God is able to send His Spirit to comfort us. List those locations:

_____

_____

_____

_____

No matter what we face, God is there. Whether in the highest heights or the lowest of lows, we are never so far away that God can't be there. He is our Creator, and He is omnipresent, which means He is everywhere. We only need to ask for Him.

📖 Paul references God's omnipresence in his letter to the Romans. Read Romans 8:35–39. What situations and trials does Paul mention in verses 35, 38 and 39?

_____

_____

_____

_____

How do we conquer such things, as shown in verse 37?

_____

_____

_____

Our victory over every situation is the love of Jesus Christ—which is available to all who repent, believe in Him, and make Jesus Lord of their life. With Christ, nothing, not even death, will have a grip on us.

![walking figure icon] *Extra Mile*
**PSALM 139**

Read Psalm 139 in its entirety. What do verses 13–16 address? How does that change or impact your understanding of God's hand on new life and His idea of when that life begins? What is the overall theme of the psalm, and how can you incorporate that type of relationship with God to your own life?

As we look at an eternal God, whose purposes stand forever, what makes us think that His love has an end? God's love for each of us will stretch on through eternity. His love for us will last as long as the salvation he provides us—for eternity.

Remember our John 3:16 verse? "For God so . . ." what? Yes indeed! He *loved* the world enough to give us Christ. That's some amazing love He has for us, isn't it? And just as Christ is joined with the Father, we are joined with Him. Just as the Father loves us that mightily, the Son does as well. There is no way to measure that kind of love. It would take many lifetimes to really begin to understand just how much the God of all Creation loves us. Thanks be to God that we will have all eternity as believers to learn to understand His love. May we always give Him honor and praise.

Just when we think Paul couldn't possibly be more passionate about God, he surprises us once again with a final statement in his prayer that encourages all believers. I have heard many people quote Ephesians 3:20–21 in hopeful anticipation, in awe, and in praise.

📖 Read Ephesians 3:20–21. How does this expand your thought of the limitless qualities of God we have been describing today?

_____

_____

_____

_____

We can't put God in a box, and we can't limit the all-surpassing power He possesses. Just as we cannot fathom the extent of God's love, we cannot imagine how much He will show that love through blessing, provision, anointing and calling.

God *can* and *will* exceed our greatest expectations! Paul reminds the reader of God's limitless power, the limits of man's thinking, and the power that we have through the Holy Spirit dwelling in us. Paul ends by giving God the glory, reminding us of our standing in Christ, and acknowledging the time-lessness of Jesus' message. Amen indeed!

This whole passage is one of my favorites in the Bible; it is so exciting to see Paul so fired up about the God he served. May we become as excited as Paul when proclaiming the magnitude of the God we serve. I pray that this passage has spurred you on and encouraged you in your faith.

**Don't put God in a box! He can and will exceed our greatest expectations!**

# ACTING UP
# 3:16 VERSE: 2 THESSALONIANS

*Strength and Peace*  DAY THREE

*"Now may the Lord of peace Himself continually grant you peace in every circumstance. The Lord be with you all!"* (2 Thessalonians 3:16)

## PAUL'S MINISTRY

Although Paul had poured himself out in service to the church of Ephesus for three years, he had also ministered with passion in many other areas. Paul took multiple missionary journeys and planted numerous churches during his time as a believer. What we see in our study of Ephesians is not unlike the passion and dedication we see in his letters to the Philippians, Galatians, Corinthians, and others. The entire collection of Paul's epistles give light to his dedication to all he ministered to.

**Peace is found in Christ.**

**When we believe in Jesus and allow Him to rule our hearts we will live in peace with each other. It is our faith and our Savior that cause this to happen.**

Paul wasn't just concerned for the Ephesians. He wasn't only passionate about ministering to the people of Ephesus and training them up in righteousness. No. Paul was passionate about all who called on the name of the Lord and all whom the Lord was calling to Himself. As in the book of Ephesians, where we are blessed to be able to read his prayer for those he served, today's focus verse is also part of a prayer. In Days Three and Four we will focus on Paul's closing prayer in his second letter to the people of Thessalonica. Frequently Paul would share his prayers, and many times they would include the petition on their behalf for grace and peace.

Think of your friends and family, those close to you. What type of prayer would you pray for them? Take a moment, and write out a prayer that you would pray specifically for those who have a significant place in your life:

_____

_____

_____

_____

_____

_____

_____

_____

Now that you have thoughtfully prepared a prayer on behalf of these loved ones, take another moment to pray to the Lord in this way for them. You may want to commit to pray for them on a regular basis, if you are not already doing so!

Looking at today's focus verse, we are reminded that "Peace" in God's world means so much more than any political movement or social revolution. The inner peace talked about in this verse is the calm confidence in our faith and Savior that will overcome many hardships we may have to endure.

Peace is not an emotion, or something we can conjure up on our own. Peace is not something that we can talk others and ourselves into doing. Peace is found in Christ. Christ is the author of the peace we can have as Christians. After all, Jesus is the Prince of Peace, right? He is in charge of this thing called peace. And He freely gives it to those who rest in Him.

📖 Do you remember what Psalm 34:14 says? Take a moment to look it up, and write it down again:

_____

_____

_____

Psalm 34:14 tells us to "seek peace and pursue it." We have to purpose to go after our God with all we have, submitting to Him in all things, and obeying His commands. If you haven't figured it out by now, our relationship with Christ is based on a lot of action.

**We act when we accept Christ.**
**We act when we believe.**

**We act when we pray.**
**We act when we change.**
**We act when we obey, love, ask, seek, honor and serve our God.**
Do you see your faith as an active faith? What areas in your relationship with Jesus represent active faith, and which areas are more passive in nature?

_____

_____

_____

_____

_____

New believers may think that once they become Christians, they will instantly be perfect and live in a world of continual bliss. Maybe they think that they can sit back, look spiritual, and wait for Jesus to come back. Wrong! Unfortunately, these wonderful people tend to get their bubble burst pretty rapidly when something goes wrong. At some point they will read such Scriptures as 1 Peter 4:12 which states, *"Do not be surprised at the painful trial you are suffering."* As we journey through the Christian life, we are going to experience times of suffering. Sometimes, we will have to endure suffering simply because we believe in Jesus.

📖 Read Psalm 34:17–18 and Psalm 145:18. To whom is the Lord close?

_____

_____

_____

> *"The Lord is near to the brokenhearted and saves those who are crushed in spirit."*
>
> *Psalm 34:18*

The Lord hears those who cry out to Him. Prayer is the key. God hears the cry of the righteous. God is faithful to deliver those who cry out to Him.

Folks who have gone through trials with God can tell you that when situations were at their worst, when all hope appeared to be gone, deliverance suddenly arrived—signifying that only God was able to get them through.

**A Personal Moment**
When our son Owen was eighteen months old, we were told that his heart had significant structural defects. We were living in the country of Panama at the time and had to be flown on a military flight back to the U.S. for open-heart surgery. In the midst of such a crisis, God was tangibly with us. We were blessed with a Bible study friend that sent us Scriptures to lift our hopes during our stay. We had a family that prayed. We were in a constant stream of prayer.

My only prayer at times was "HELP," but God heard it even when it wasn't eloquent.

He truly is the God who delivers those who cry out to Him.

One unforgettable moment during this process was the morning after surgery in the PICU. They were about to take the IV out of Owen's neck (from his jugular vein I think), and fear overcame my thoughts because it was such a long tube. It now strikes me funny that after such a long, extensive, surgical procedure, of which I held up rather well, that I would suddenly become distraught about his IV. You wouldn't believe how gracious God was! As I

God answers all of our prayers. He will answer with a "yes," with a "no," or even a "not now." Sometimes God's response will be as we expected, and other times it will seem very unusual. No matter the case, God's answer to our prayer will always be within His will and will have our best in mind.

prayed that God would watch over him during this moment, I looked up and noticed that the TV directly over our son's bed was on. Keep in mind he was only 18 months old, and no one was sitting with him watching it. I know now that God was clearly providing strength and peace for us. At the very moment they were removing the tubing, Terry Meeuwsen from a daily Christian TV show was on the screen, with her head bowed and eyes closed, praying during the broadcast's daily prayer time. With the angle the TV screen was pointed, it looked like she was praying directly over Owen! The mute button was on, so there is no telling what she actually said, but honestly, it didn't matter, because I knew that she was praying. Through Terry's prayer, God gave me the comfort that was needed in that moment. I praise Him greatly for giving me that little boost of love. And God did it . . . because. Our son recovered well, is fine and healthy, and he loves the Lord. We got through that time and are stronger because of it. We give God all the glory for what He has done in our lives, and for all the times He gives us the comfort that we need.

📖 Read Matthew 18:20. What happens when we gather together in Jesus' name?

_____

_____

God hears our prayers, *"For where two or three have gathered together in [His] name, there [He is] in their midst"* (Matthew 18:20; emphasis added). God not only hears our corporate, or group prayers, but He is with us when we pray. He hears the cries of our hearts and longs for us to lean on each other and Him in a time of prayer.

📖 According to Galatians 6:2, how do we fulfill the law of Christ?

_____

_____

God loves it when we *"carry each other's burdens,"* and Galatians 6:2 (NIV) says that when we do this we *"fulfill the law of Christ."* Corporate prayer is a wonderful tool that we have at our disposal to bring our concerns to the feet of God and leave them there for *His* response. When we hand over all control to Him, we can walk away with the peace of knowing that God is in control of our situation.

God is pleased when we bring Christians together in worship and in prayer. He is honored when we pray to Him personally and collectively. Together, as we pray to God for our needs, God will be near us. He will hear, and we will find comfort as we lean on Him for peace and comfort. As we meet, pray, and worship, we are active in our faith.

*Strength and Peace* — DAY FOUR

# PARTING WORDS
# 3:16 VERSE: 2 THESSALONIANS

*"Now may the Lord of peace Himself continually grant you peace in every circumstance. The Lord be with you all!"*

Our focus verse comes out of a prayer that Paul has for the Thessalonians. He is petitioning God on their behalf with a deep desire that their lives would be filled with the peace that only God can bring. In this passage, Paul conducts a time of personal prayer for the corporate body of believers in Thessalonica. Just as with Paul's prayer, your prayers connect your concerns to Christ.

📖 Read 2 Thessalonians 3:1–5.

What was Paul's prayer request, as shown in verse 1 and 2?

_____

_____

_____

What does Paul say he is confident of in verse 3 and 4?

_____

_____

What does verse 5 reveal about Paul's feelings and concern for the people in Thessalonica?

_____

_____

*Your prayers connect your concerns to Christ.*

This passage contains the closing thoughts of Paul's second letter to the Thessalonians, in which he focuses on end-time events, and standing on what you have learned in your faith. Once again, Paul urges believers not to be swayed by false teachings and manipulations. Paul knew the societal ills of Thessalonica and how easily the temptations to worship other gods would infiltrate the lives of those in the church there. Paul was proud of the Thessalonian church for showing genuine faith and commitment to Christ, and he wanted to make sure he encouraged them even more to finish the race before them.

Paul knew the power of prayer and asked those receiving this letter to keep him in prayer as he continued to minister. Prayer is not just for pastors and leaders to speak, it is the primary mode of communication for those who have a relationship with our Father in heaven; all who are His should be praying and petitioning the Lord over any concerns they might have.

With Paul's prayer, notice that his request did not reflect any personal vanity in any way—this is a request for protection and for God's message to continue spreading. What an example of Christ-like living!

When the disciples asked Jesus how they were supposed to pray, He gave them an example that we still pray today. He gave them what we call the Lord's Prayer.

📖 Read Matthew 6:9–13. What is the first order of business in this model prayer (verse 9)?

_____

_____

_____

What is the request in verse 10?

_____

_____

What do we ask God to provide according to verse 11 of this prayer?

_____

_____

_____

What is the focus of verse 12, and is it just a request, or does it state action on our part? What kind of action are we to take?

_____

_____

_____

_____

Verse 13 prays for protection in what area?

_____

_____

The New International Version ends the prayer there. Looking at the New American Standard Bible or the King James Version, what is included at the end? What final statement is given about God?

_____

_____

_____

_____

*"And do not lead us into temptation, but deliver us from evil. For Thine is the kingdom, and the power, and the glory, forever. Amen."*

*Matthew 6:13*

The Lord's Prayer begins with acknowledging who God is, and it emphasizes the sovereignty of His position as Lord. Then, as we pray this prayer, we move on to acknowledging God about His will and his kingdom's establishment on heaven and earth. From there, we ask for provision of daily needs, forgiveness, and protection from temptation. Isn't it interesting that forgiveness is given as we forgive others? This is yet another aspect of our active faith. We must forgive. The final statement found in some translations of the prayer is so powerful to me. We begin by acknowledging God for who He is, and we finish the prayer by restating His sovereignty; giving Him the glory. To me, this is critical. With this prayer, may we always see the active faith that Jesus wanted us to have, even modeled in a simple, yet powerful prayer.

To Jesus, Christ-like prayer includes beginning with God the Father, seeking the Father's will, asking for provision, following Him in our forgiveness, being protected by God from the enemy, and ending the prayer with further praise and recognition of the Father. God the Father hems in our prayer, as our focus should begin and end with fearful adoration of God. God answers our prayers, and meets our need when it is all within His will.

How does your prayer life compare to this example of prayer? Do you incorporate the same concepts, and take time to begin and end your prayer by simply praising God for who He is?

Describe your prayer life and how you would like to bring it closer in line with Jesus' model:

_____

_____

_____

_____

Do you see the active nature of this type of prayer? Is your prayer life active in that you are willing to forgive others as you ask God to forgive you?

_____

_____

May we focus on how God is pleased with our prayers and not how the sounds of our words or the length of our oration pleases us. May God truly receive the glory, as we are willing to meet God in prayer, and confess our own shortcomings. May we always be willing to forgive those who have wronged us; just as God is faithful to forgive our sin.

In 2 Thessalonians 3:6–15, Paul takes time to warn the people about one more danger before he closes his letter. What does he discuss in these verses? Summarize:

_____

_____

_____

_____

Imagine! Paul having to constantly warn these people about complacency! Whether they were simply sitting in their spiritual bubbles, waiting for Jesus to return, or if they were simply sitting around thinking they were too good to do the work of the ministry—we will never know every detail or every motive. But we do know this: Paul gave great caution against those who were "busy bodies."

Those identified as "pew warmers" often come to Christ—yet forget to serve. They wait for others to do the work, while their own faith stands still. They have no desire to serve the Lord or others, nor do they desire growth in their relationship with Christ. Although Paul makes it clear that we are supposed to love such worshippers, we are obligated to warn them or correct them in love. They need to see that they are now called to be active in Jesus' ministry.

📖 Read John 15:19. What does it tell us about those who belong to God?

_____

_____

_____

Those who believe and serve God must be separate from those who do not—we are in the world but not of the world, as John 15:19 tells us, *"because you are not of the world, but I chose you out of the world."* Jesus has chosen us, and we are to serve Him through serving the world. We must

### Doctrine
## FALSE HOPES

At the time of the writing of this epistle, around AD 50, some of the people of Thessalonica were caught up in a false sense of the immediate return of Jesus. They thought He was going to come to take them to heaven at any moment, and because of this, they stopped working and keeping up with daily activities, in anticipation. Paul's correction was purposed to bring them back to lives filled with work, activity, and structure. While they were to be aware that the Lord could come back suddenly, they had to be careful not to become inactive while constantly looking to the sky for Christ's appearance. The same correction is valid for us today—though we may be in a season that seems to point to the imminent return of Christ, we must be careful not to leave all our duties and responsibilities while we stare at the clouds. There is much to do and many who need to hear the good news of Jesus.

remember that we are not to conform to the ways of the world, even if it is unpopular. We belong to Him, and our peace comes from Him, not the world. We cannot expect the world to provide something it is incapable of providing. Only in Jesus do we find perfect peace. The peace of the world, if it lacks Jesus, is a false peace.

Paul begins the third chapter of 2 Thessalonians with a prayer and ends it with a prayer. We see that after this discussion of busy bodies, Paul's warning is complete, and he closes the letter with a loving prayer. His transition from correction to petition is one that we would see a family member or loved one make. From concern to concern, their best interests were always in his mind. In verse 15 in particular, Paul reveals the truth that his correction of their complacency is not meant to be viewed as condemnation; it is for the purpose of bringing them closer to the Lord.

📖 Let's read that closing prayer. Look at 2 Thessalonians 3:16–18. Take notice of how he covers them in prayer, how he distinguishes that the letter is from him, and how he focuses his final words.

Paul's prayer in verse 16 refers to God as what?

_____

In that role, what is God's gift to believers?

_____

_____

Paul often had a word of encouragement before he closed a letter. We see this same sentiment spoken in Romans 15:33, where Paul states, *"Now the God of peace be with you all. Amen."* Take note of the similarity to this verse, and our focus verse from 2 Thessalonians. Paul wanted all believers to know the peace-giving power of his God.

Just as God is the God of peace, He is also the God who grants peace. With a limitless God, we have limitless provision and blessing that can only come from God. He is the God of peace, the God of comfort, the God of healing, the God of provision, the God of righteousness, and so on. God is not only able to do exceedingly abundantly more than we ever thought; He is also able to bestow anything upon us that He desires. God is the answer to all our needs and all our concerns.

Continue memorizing this week's verses. Take a moment to dwell on the magnitude of God's provision in your life—in all areas of your life. Give Him praise!

> ## We cannot expect the world to provide something it is incapable of providing.

> ## "Now may the Lord of peace Himself continually grant you peace in every circumstance. The Lord be with you all!"
>
> ## 2 Thessalonians 3:16

*Strength and Peace* | **DAY FIVE**

# FOR ME TO FOLLOW GOD

Believing in God means more than simply saying one prayer and stopping there. It means more than acting good one day a week. It means more than doing good things or being a good person. Believing in God and becoming Christ-like means that you sacrificially follow Jesus wherever He may lead. Believing means knowing that no matter what, God's got your back, and He will give you peace and strength for the journey!

God equips us and sustains us for the journey, but He also longs to have a real relationship with us that will go beyond our wish list and basic needs. God wants us to be engaged in communication with Him day in and day out, in times of peace, and in times of crisis. This, of course, is achieved through prayer and dwelling on the Word of God.

Purpose today to become a person with a strong prayer life! This is not a request for you to join a class where you learn breathing techniques and chanting skills or even a time to memorize a poem that is spoken over and over. This is a request for you to commit to regular communication with the Father. The basic items necessary for this activity are nothing more than time and a quiet place to sit. A Bible would be a wonderful addition to this as well.

Do you have a quiet spot in your home where you like to sit while praying and studying the Word of God? Describe the area where you usually sit while praying and studying:

_____

_____

_____

_____

Is there enough bright lighting for reading? Do you keep a notepad, journal, or other paper, as well as a pen and maybe even a highlighter? What supplies do you like to keep on hand?

_____

_____

_____

_____

Do you dedicate a certain amount of time each day to prayer and study, or do you just fit it in when you have a free moment?

_____

_____

From these questions, you might be able to gauge how to prepare your study space a little better and how to set aside more time in your day for prayer. We all have room for improvement in these areas, but prayer should be a lifetime, all day activity. Think about your prayer habits, and incorporate good lighting, comfortable seating, a quiet environment, and any needed supplies stored near the area where you will sit.

 Do you pray as you are doing other daily activities? What times do you find yourself praying while outside the home?

_____

_____

I find that beyond my quiet time at home with the Lord, I also pray alot while I am driving down the road, while walking through the day, and while doing errands or getting from "Point A" to "Point B." When we purpose to have a lifestyle of prayer, we can incorporate prayer into just about anything we are doing.

*Believing means knowing that no matter what, God's got your back, and He will give you peace and strength for the journey!*

*"Pray without ceasing."*

*I Thessalonians 5:17*

As we spend time praying to God, laying our hearts bare before Him, we enter into communication with God. This is quiet time, but the definition of "quiet" in this type of prayer was never intended by God to result in empty-headedness; but rather, a time of sharing our thoughts and waiting to hear that still, small voice from God. Our minds will be full of the goodness of God, His thumbprint in our lives, and the impact He has had on every step we have taken. We will be full of anticipation of what God has for us next. True worship is never empty; it is alive and full of awe and praise. We will be quiet as we wait for a response to our praises and petitions, but we should be full of the Spirit of the Lord while we wait. I promise you that as you spend more time simply communicating with the Lord, your life will change in amazing ways. God will give you the peace that passes all understanding, just as the Bible promises.

The Bible offers many examples of prayer. We have already discussed many parts of David's prayers in the psalms, and we have delved into the Lord's Prayer that Jesus gives us. The Bible is literally filled with prayers of many people, and all these prayers show honest, humble, eager, and reverent praise, questions, and petitions to their God. All contain dialogue, and all show the desires and intentions of the one who is praying.

Let's look at a tremendous example of effective prayer that Jesus has given us, in the book of John. Read John 17. We are shown a glimpse of the prayer life of Jesus, as he prays for Himself, His disciples, and all believers.

For whom does Jesus pray in John 17:1–5? What is His request?

_____

_____

_____

_____

Now, in verses 6–19, for whom is Jesus praying? Summarize His requests.

_____

_____

_____

_____

Verses 20–25 show another prayer focus. On whose behalf is Jesus praying in this section, and what is His request?

_____

_____

_____

_____

As we see throughout this passage, Jesus takes time to pray in three distinct ways. First, Jesus prays for Himself, asking for God's glory and for eternal life to be given to all believers. Next, He prays for His disciples, that they would be protected and that they would share in the blessings given to Jesus. Finally, Jesus prays for the unity of all believers and for all believers to be in fellowship with the Father.

*Extra Mile*
**PRAYER**

Look up the words "pray" and "prayer" in your Bible concordance. Take time to read the verses referenced and take note of the similarities and differences of the passages. Why are they praying? To whom are they praying, and what is the desired outcome of the one in prayer? What does God think of our prayers?

What part of John 17 stands out to you? What struck you as you were reading it?

_____

_____

_____

_____

Do you see a similarity between Jesus' prayer in the chapter of John and Paul's prayers for the believers in Ephesus and Thessalonica? Describe the similarities:

_____

_____

_____

_____

Paul models Jesus in his concern for believers and their desire to share the good news of eternal life with those in the world. The prayers of Paul and Jesus are not focused on temporary needs, nor do they speak of financial gain; rather, they are set on asking the Lord for His will to be done and for others to grow in their relationship with God. Their prayers are godly. Their prayers are Christ-like.

On what do most of your prayers focus? What types of requests do you offer to God?

_____

_____

_____

_____

How can you make your prayer life more Christ-like?

_____

_____

_____

Take time to honestly evaluate your prayer life. Plan out your schedule to fit in more time to sit and pray. Take more initiative in your reading of the Word and your memorization of Scripture. Praise God that He allows us to come before His throne in prayer and supplication! What an honor it is to be able to speak to the King.

 _Dear Lord,_ how I thank You for who You are! You know everything about me, and You love me anyway, and for that I am forever grateful. I thank You Lord for those in my family and circle of friends. May they live in safety and in health, and may they seek after You with their heart, mind, and soul. Lord, I thank You that You have given me examples of godly prayer throughout Scripture. I pray that my prayers would be pleasing to You and that they would not be hindered by unforgiveness and sin in my life. May You be glorified in all I do, all I say, and all I am. In Jesus' Holy name, Amen.

# Notes

# NINE

# *Powerful Name*

# POWER IN THE MIGHTY NAME OF JESUS

# 3:16 VERSE: ACTS

We closed Lesson 8 with a discussion on the prayers of Jesus. Jesus, who left a vivid example of His prayer life in John 17, shows us that He has a strong concern for His flock, and that His utmost concern is our standing in Christ and our adherence to the will of God. We have quite a "safety zone" in the will of God. No matter what comes against us or what we may face in our lives, it is in that standing with God that we find our protection, our comfort, and our strength.

In Lesson 8 we studied about the power of prayer and the peace and strength that Jesus will give us if we simply ask Him. Communication with God is essential, and encouraging fellow Christians, as Paul continuously did, is also key. We must share the hope we have with others, and we must take time to talk with our Heavenly Father, and listen for His voice.

In this week's lesson we will deal with an account of a man who has been healed from a life-long illness. We will focus specifically on that event and on the surrounding issues. There is so much more to focus on than the healing itself! We will discover the connection with our prayers and our faith and see what impact a strong and active faith can have on our lives and the outcome of our most difficult situations.

> *We have quite a "safety zone" in the will of God.*

As magnificent as the healed body's testimony is, the *greater fact* in every account of healing done in Jesus' name is the **source** of that healing: Jesus Christ our Lord. Those who were healed called on Him—they called on His mighty name. There is power in the name of Jesus. Let's get right into this lesson and find out more!

*Powerful Name*  DAY ONE

# A NEW DAY
# 3:16 VERSE: ACTS

*"And on the basis of faith in His name, it is the name of Jesus which has strengthened this man whom you see and know; and the faith which comes through Him has given him this perfect health in the presence of you all."*

The Book of Acts introduces us to the world as it was when the Holy Spirit became available to all believers. The Day of Pentecost, which occurred fifty days after Christ's resurrection, is a pivotal moment in the history of our Christian faith. Christ had been resurrected from the dead, and spent forty days continuing to teach the apostles.

📖 Read Acts 1:4–8. What is going on in this scene? What does Jesus command the apostles to do?

_____

_____

_____

_____

_____

What are the apostles concerned about in verse 6, and what is Jesus' response in verse 7?

_____

_____

_____

_____

What were the apostles going to receive, and from whom?

_____

_____

_____

What was the purpose of this gift? What were they supposed to do as a result?

_____

_____

_____

**"But you shall receive power when the Holy Spirit has come upon you; and you shall be My witnesses both in Jerusalem, and in all Judea and Samaria, and even to the remotest part of the earth."**

**Acts 1:8**

Jesus says farewell to His followers in this passage and tells them that the Holy Spirit will come to them, giving them power, and making them witnesses.

📖 Do you see the connection between Acts 1:8 and the Great Commission in Matthew 28:18–20?

_____

The Holy Spirit was being sent to the believers to empower them to fulfill the commission that Jesus had given them.

📖 Now read Acts 1:9–11. Where does Jesus go in verse 9, and how does He do this?

_____

_____

_____

In verses 10–11, what are the believers doing, and what happens as a result? Who speaks to the believers?

_____

_____

_____

_____

Jesus ascended to heaven, and as the believers stood staring at the clouds, two men appeared and told them that Jesus would return just as He had left them. When He ascended to heaven, the group of apostles dutifully returned to Jerusalem, to the room *"where they were staying"* (Acts 1:13). The believers were waiting in the Upper Room for the sign that Christ had promised to send. The apostles were not alone; there were 120 people gathered together there.

They were united together in faith and in prayer. They were one body, waiting for their Savior to give them a sign. Keep in mind that at this point, Judas, who betrayed Jesus for thirty silver coins, had already been cast away from the apostles and had died in the field he bought with his earnings. This left the group without one of its twelve. As a response to this absence, while waiting together, they cast lots to decide who would replace Judas Iscariot in the apostle's group, as they sought a return to the original number of twelve men. The lot fell on Matthias, and he was added to their group. Many others joined them in that room to wait. They stayed there and praised God, anticipating what was to come.

The apostles, who were the people who knew first hand the teachings of Christ, were pondering the warning of the end of the ages and the return of Christ. Would it be soon? Would it be in their lifetime? What did Jesus mean about them being *"clothed with power from on high"*? (Luke 24:49) They knew there was a promise of a helper, but when would this happen, and what would it mean? Christ was equipping them, but how? There were so many questions that must have been buzzing through their minds while they waited together.

*"These all with one mind were continually devoting themselves to prayer, along with the women, and Mary the mother of Jesus, and with His brothers."*

**Acts 1:14**

Picture the scene. In the Upper Room the apostles and the others are waiting. Outside, throughout Jerusalem, we read that *"God fearing Jews from every nation under heaven"* (Acts 2:5, NIV) are here. God has assembled everyone in one place, in one holy city, all to witness what He is about to do! God's plan is in place. The body of believers is united in praise and prayer, and was seeking God.

📖 Read Acts 2:1–13. Describe the passage:

_____

_____

_____

As we know from the account in Acts 2, the Day of Pentecost is amazing. The Holy Spirit came like a rushing wind, and rested on their heads like fiery tongues. The people spoke in languages they didn't know. Some thought the believers had been drinking, misunderstanding what they were witnessing.

Look again at verse 11. What was the purpose of the different languages, as shown by the message of the foreign words?

_____

_____

_____

When God's timing was perfect, He sent the Holy Spirit to witness to the believers through the speaking of foreign languages by the Galilean apostles. The people from other nationalities heard their own tongue with the wonders of God declared in their own language. The purpose of the gift of tongues in this scene was for the sharing of the Gospel. They were telling the "mighty deeds of God" (Acts 2:11).

While the crowd was still stunned at the display, Peter stood and gave a rousing speech, explaining what was happening and recited passages from Scripture that confirmed the scene. The crowd could not deny what they had just seen.

This passage in Acts makes me think of a big graduation ceremony. For years, we study under teachers who show us the correct way of doing things, and we learn so much. The things we learn and the new knowledge we possess are necessary for our future occupations. Once we have been given the resources and information needed to fulfill the job we have trained for, we graduate, and move out into the world, *doing* what we have learned to do.

Now, with the Great Commission in mind, think about this scenario. If the time Jesus spent on earth was the schooling or training ground for the apostles, then the Day of Pentecost becomes much like that graduation day. And Jesus is so much more than just a teacher; He is our Savior! The apostles had been commissioned by Jesus, had received the Holy Spirit, and were on their way out into the world to put what they had learned into practice. Possessing the Holy Spirit and having a relationship with Christ are the only credentials we need to fulfill the Great Commission. Peter didn't delay in stepping out into his new occupation, as seen in the following passage.

> *The purpose of the gift of tongues in this scene was for the sharing of the gospel. Through the gift of tongues, the apostles displayed the "mighty deeds of God" (Acts 2:11).*

📖 Read Peter's sermon in Acts 2:14–36. What is the topic of Peter's sermon? What is the message he wanted them to understand?

_____

_____

_____

_____

_____

Peter proclaimed the gospel of Christ and announced that it was the "new day" that had been prophesied by Joel. In order to understand what was going on, they had to understand Jesus. They had to know Him to know why He was sending the Holy Spirit and why the believers seemed to be acting in a way they didn't understand. Once Peter told them the "why" of the scene, they believed, and wanted to know "how" to proceed.

📖 Read Acts 2:37–41. What did they have to do, according to verse 38?

_____

_____

_____

How many people chose to believe in Jesus that day, according to verse 41?

_____

They asked how to proceed, and Peter told them to:

> *Repent and let each of you be baptized in the name of Jesus Christ for the forgiveness of your sins; and you shall receive the gift of the Holy Spirit. For the promise is for you and your children, and for all who are far off, as many as the Lord our God shall call to Himself.* (Acts 2:38–39)

Thank God for His provision of the Holy Spirit in the lives of the apostles and in the lives of all believers.

# THE SOURCE
# 3:16 VERSE: ACTS

*"And on the basis of faith in His name, it is the name of Jesus which has strengthened this man whom you see and know; and the faith which comes through Him has given him this perfect health in the presence of you all."* (Acts 3:16)

**W**hy all this background information? Yesterday's lesson is important to picture so we can conceptualize what a wonderful time this was for the apostles.

■ They had been hand chosen by Jesus.
■ They had walked with Jesus.

*"Jesus the Nazarene, a man attested to you by God with miracles and wonders and signs which God performed through Him in your midst."*

**Acts 2:22**

*Powerful Name* DAY TWO

- They had watched Jesus perform countless miracles.
- They had watched Him die on the cross.
- They knew He had risen from the grave.
- They had seen Him walk the earth after His resurrection.
- They had watched Him ascend to heaven.
- Now, they watched as the Holy Spirit came upon them.
- They had been commissioned to change the world forever.

**Christ's apostles were no ordinary group of men.**

This was no ordinary group of men.

The eleven original apostles (minus Judas Iscariot) had seen Jesus do so much! The miracles He performed in their midst were too numerous to count. Jesus had healed many. He had fed thousands and set captives free. *Jesus had brought salvation.*

**APPLY** Think of the miracles you have heard of or read about from the four Gospels. Write down some accounts of healings and miracles you remember from the Bible:

_____
_____
_____
_____
_____
_____

**APPLY** In your lifetime, have you seen or heard about miraculous events that have been attributed to Jesus, or as a result of praying to Jesus? Do you think God is still in the same business He was in when the apostles walked with Jesus? Is God still capable of healing those who pray to Him? Can God still provide for His children in miraculous ways? Write your thoughts:

_____
_____
_____
_____
_____
_____
_____
_____

No matter what our denominational background, our church affiliation, or what our fellowship of believers might have as a set guideline, God is still God. He will do what He wants to do, and He is able to do everything He has ever been able to do. God *is* all-powerful. God *is* all knowing. God *is* ever present. Yes, He can heal those He chooses to heal. Yes, He can provide for needs that seem impossible to fill. Yes, God can and will do miraculous things—just as in the days of Abraham and Moses and in the days of Jesus and the Apostles. All God does, is in *His will*, and *His timing*, just as it has always been. God is the same, and He is sovereign. He can. He will. He still does.

Imagine what it was like for the apostles! They were not watching Jesus from a distance; they were walking in His footsteps! They were in the front row, and behind the scenes. The apostles saw so much more than is even recorded, and they must have been overwhelmed by the continuous realization that Jesus was truly the Messiah. Jesus was their source of joy, their purpose for spreading the news of salvation, and their example for Christ-like living. Through the things Jesus did while He walked with them, the apostles were able to anticipate what they would be able to do in the name of Jesus now that they had received the Holy Spirit that Jesus had promised to send.

📖 Read John 14:26. What is the purpose of the Holy Spirit, according to Jesus in this verse?

_____

_____

_____

The apostles had gone through times of wonderful fellowship with the Lord, and had waited through times of quiet anticipation. They experienced periods of great confidence in the Lord, moments of doubt, and even a fleeting sense of disillusionment when they couldn't physically see Christ anymore. Now Pentecost had come, and they were energized for a new phase in their ministry. The apostles and all believers were now equipped through the Holy Spirit to do what God had called them to do. Yet they were still mere men. All power exhibited through them was still God's power. All power will *always* belong to God. God equips those through whom He wants to accomplish His purposes with His own strength.

*All power will always belong to God.*

An obvious shift in their approach to baptism must be pointed out again. In an earlier lesson we discussed the details of baptism and the shift to being baptized in Jesus' name. Do you remember why the distinction was made? Write it here if you remember:

_____

_____

_____

_____

When John baptized Jesus, it was John's ministry that was focused on baptism, and John was associated with the teaching of baptism. As soon as Jesus was baptized and came into the forefront, Jesus became the focus of the people, and many began following Him. As a result, there had to be a clarification that people would now be baptized in Jesus' name; to mark that they followed His teaching and through baptism identified Him as the influence in their lives.

In this charge shown in Acts 2:38–39, this distinction is repeated so that the apostles would have no question as to whom everyone should follow. Regardless of the stature or fame of an apostle, the people were never to be baptized in the name of "Peter," or "John," or "Paul," but *only* in the name of Jesus.

Why do you think this is the case? Why is it only in the name, or teaching, of Jesus (Father, Son, and Holy Spirit) that we are baptized today? What makes Jesus so different from the others (Paul, Peter, John, etc.)?

_____

_____

_____

_____

_____

## There is power in the name of Jesus, because He is God, and because His blood was shed for us.

### *Extra Mile*
### THE FIRST PASSOVER

Read in Exodus 12:1–30 about the first Passover. Why did the Hebrews in Egyptian bondage place blood on their doorposts? What did it protect them from? How is Jesus the fulfillment of that action? Journal your thoughts and observations, and research additional passages that deal with the Passover celebration, like Exodus 12:42,43; Leviticus 23:5; Numbers 9:2, 12, 14; Matthew 26:2, 18. John 19:4; Acts 12:4.

The name of Jesus is more than a name; it is how we identify ourselves with Him. Through Jesus we have salvation; we have instant access to the throne of God, and we have total remission of sins (if we repent and believe). There is power in the name of Jesus, because He is God, and because His blood was shed for us.

A visual picture of that covering we have with Jesus is simply this: just as His perfect sacrifice once for all covers our sins, His blood covers us and protects us, just like the blood on the doorposts protected the Israelites on that very first Passover. When anything comes against us, if we are under Jesus' name, we are essentially covered by Him, and He will protect us, and go to battle on our behalf. Our victory is in Jesus.

With that, the apostles are being told in this last part of Acts 2 that even though they were being empowered by the Holy Spirit, the power they would receive would be from Jesus, and *it was only God that would receive the glory*. They weren't in this for their own fame—it was and always will be—all about Jesus!

📖 Read Acts 2:42–47.

What was their new life with the Holy Spirit like?

_____

_____

_____

In verse 43, we see the response of everyone and the actions of the apostles. Describe what the verse illustrates.

_____

_____

What did all the believers share, and what was their daily routine like, according to verses 44–47?

_____

_____

_____

Can you imagine? The feeling of awe was overwhelming; the miracles and signs were plentiful, and the sense of community was tangible and real. They shared everything, witnessed to everyone, and helped all who had need. The Lord God received all the glory, and the number of believers continued to increase.

 Think about your Christian community—those you worship with, those you hang out with, those you study God's Word with. Do you feel the type of community shown in Acts among those in your fellowship?

_____

_____

_____

Does everyone in your group share at least some of their resources and help those in need in your community of faith?

_____

_____

Does everyone give God the glory? Do they stand in awe of the God they serve and believe?

_____

_____

_____

_____

📖 Do all of you sense the urgency to continue the commission given by Jesus in Matthew 28 and in Acts 1:8 to share the message of Jesus Christ with the world?

_____

As you look at your responses to these application questions, don't be too hard on your community of faith, or yourself. We would be hard-pressed to find a group as unified as the early church was in this passage. We all have areas where we can improve, and we all have things we do very well. Take a moment to pray to God for His help in focusing you and your fellow believers on the things you are to focus, especially as outlined in this passage in Acts. May we all be kingdom minded, loving to our Christian community, and willing to lend a hand where needed.

*Do you stand in awe of God?*

# THE GATE BEAUTIFUL 3:16 VERSE: ACTS

*Powerful Name*  DAY THREE

*"And on the basis of faith in His name, it is the name of Jesus which has strengthened this man whom you see and know; and the faith which comes through Him has given him this perfect health in the presence of you all."* (Acts 3:16)

The apostles were dedicated to worship and prayer, and were continually sharing all they had with the others. They were a true community of faith. Luke gives us a wonderful story tucked into this scene, and because it relates specifically to our focus verse, let's take some time to examine the details of the account.

📖 Read Acts 3:1–10. What happened?

_____

_____

_____

How long had the man been lame, according to verse 2?

_____

What did he ask Peter and John, and what was their response, according to verses 3 and 4?

_____

_____

_____

Look at verse 5. How did the beggar's attitude and expectation change in response to Peter and John's comment in verse 4?

_____

_____

_____

In verse 6, what did Peter deny the man, and what did he give instead? By what authority?

_____

_____

_____

_____

As the man began to walk, what else did he do?

_____

_____

How did the people around him react?

_____

_____

> "And he began to give them his attention, expecting to receive something from them."
>
> Acts 3:5

One day, on the way to temple for their time of afternoon prayer, Peter and John encountered a beggar who was asking for money. This beggar had been placed at the Gate Beautiful, a perfect spot for catching the attention of the religious people entering Herod's Temple to worship. The beggar had been crippled since birth, so this must have been a regular routine for him. Do you wonder why it was *this particular day* that the man had an encounter with Peter and John?

If he was begging every day, and they were there on a regular basis, they must have seen him before, but why did it take this long for them to react? It happened *that* day because the Holy Spirit led them to action. It was the day that *the Lord chose* to bring this miracle about.

Keep in mind, this man made his living begging for money from people entering the Temple. Understand this—he was not just a man with a physical defect—here was a person whose livelihood and identity was shaped by his appearance and limitations. The whole town knew him. They passed by him every time they went to worship. They sometimes felt sorry enough for him that they threw a little loose change in his cup.

**APPLY** What has shaped your identity? Do your physical abilities shape your existence? Have you been limited by a physical condition that left you immobile? How did it affect your daily life and daily activities?

_____

_____

_____

_____

_____

_____

He was not living *above* his affliction, but living *on* his affliction (financially). Someone had to physically carry this man on his mat to the place where he sat to beg. There was someone there to help him continue this pattern, but *who* would actually help him with healing?

Peter and John saw this man and heard his request, and instead of giving him enough money for a meal, they gave him the life-changing gift of healing. The two apostles looked at him at the same time, and demanded that the beggar look straight into their eyes. The man was eager for their response; he was *expecting results* of some kind. There is a very important clue here: the man was expectant—he was anticipating something; he had faith that they would provide for his needs.

The man was expectant, but what specifically do you think he was awaiting? Do you think he was surprised by Peter's response?

_____

_____

_____

_____

_____

Peter's response would change the man forever, as he said:

> "Silver or gold I do not have, but what I have I give you. In the name of Jesus Christ of Nazareth, walk." (Acts 3:6, NIV)

That man was healed *in the name of Jesus Christ*, not in the Apostle's own power or will. The onlookers were shocked as to how this could happen, and Peter told them that it was this man's belief in what had already been offered to them (and rejected), namely Christ, that gave the man a healed body. They rejected Jesus out of ignorance; Peter believed, and by doing so, Old Testament Scripture was fulfilled.

*Did You Know?*

**THE GATE BEAUTIFUL**

Herod's Temple, which was built in 20 BC, remained until about AD 70, when the Romans demolished it. The entire complex was complete in the mid 60's (AD), and therefore, the completed area was only in use for about five years. Surrounding the temple were outer courts, and the main entrance to the outer court was called the Beautiful Gate. This is where many people would enter, and this is the entrance where beggars positioned themselves, hoping that people would give them alms on their way to worship.

*There was someone there to help the beggar continue his routine, but who would really help him with healing?*

📖 Look at Mark 16:15–20. In this passage we see the last words of Jesus to the apostles before he ascended to heaven. What did Jesus say they would be able to do?

_____

_____

_____

The last part of verse 18 confirms their ability to heal others. Write that part of the verse here:

_____

_____

_____

Jesus tells them that they will be able to do many things, and healing the infirmities of others was one of them. Though the gift of healing was so hard to comprehend, Jesus promised that events triggering these special powers would come to pass.

**APPLY** Has anyone ever promised you something that seemed impossible? Did you expect it to happen, or were you anxious to see what they were going to do?

_____

_____

_____

_____

_____

_____

In the same way, have you read the promises of Jesus in Scripture? Do you expect them to be shown in your life as well, or are you anxious to see how God will fulfill those promises in your life?

_____

_____

_____

_____

_____

We can take this example as a modern-day lesson in faith. No matter what the community around you may believe, stand firm, "expecting something" (verse 5), paying attention, and focusing on the power of Christ. Realize that when the miraculous does occur, not everyone will understand where the blessing has come from.

Did unbelief keep the man from walking? No. The apostles knew what they could do, and the man also believed something was going to happen. In turn, he knew in his heart what had happened, and he praised God.

Keep memorizing this week's focus verse. Now that you know the context of the verse more clearly, what new insight do you have about the verse? How can this verse be applied to your life?

_____

_____

_____

_____

_____

# SAY THE NAME
# 3:16 VERSE: ACTS

*Powerful Name* | DAY FOUR

*"And on the basis of faith in His name, it is the name of Jesus which has strengthened this man whom you see and know; and the faith which comes through Him has given him this perfect health in the presence of you all."* (Acts 3:16)

There is great power in the name of Jesus! When we pray in Jesus' name, God listens to our prayers with the same interest level He would exhibit while listening to His Son. All God sees as He looks at us is the covering of the sacrificial blood of Jesus. And Jesus acts as an intercessor our behalf, literally pleading our case for us. What an amazing comfort this is! To have someone sitting at the right hand of God who hears our plea, and puts His hand in ours, guiding us in all things!

📖 Read Mark 16:19. After Jesus ascended to heaven, where did He sit?

_____

_____

📖 Look up Philippians 2:9–11. In this passage, we see the description of Jesus, exalted by God. With this exalted position, Jesus' name holds distinctive qualities. According to verses 9–11, what are the distinct qualities of the name of Jesus, and what is the unique position that Jesus holds as Lord?

_____

_____

_____

📖 Part of verse 10 references Isaiah 45:23. Look that verse up. What else does the verse in Isaiah say?

_____

_____

_____

Let's compare this additional detail from Isaiah, the fact that allegiance will be sworn to Jesus, with another passage. Go with me to Luke 4:38–41. Who was healed in this passage?

_____

In verse 41, who is talking, and what was the conversation about?

_____

_____

_____

I think it is very interesting that Jesus' first recorded healing, where Jesus healed Simon's mother-in-law, isn't the only thing going on in this passage. After she was healed, and many more came for healing, we see another type of healing taking place. Jesus also began to drive out demons from people, and while doing so, the demons cried out something very specific. In light of Isaiah 45:23, do you see the magnitude of the name of Jesus as you study this passage about Jesus and these demons? When the demons were removed, they acknowledged Jesus' deity. They announced His power as the Son of God. They knew that He was Lord. Even as they were driven from the people, they had to "confess" that Jesus Christ is Lord. There are other passages throughout the New Testament that mention demons acknowledging their fear of Jesus or demon-possessed people following Jesus, boldly proclaiming who He is. Just as the verse in Philippians says— whether in heaven, on earth, or under the earth—the response will be the same: every tongue, good, or evil, *will* confess that Jesus is Lord. Every knee *shall* bow. He *is* Lord!

Jesus is sovereign, and He is seated at the right hand of God. He is there, as God, and at the sound of His powerful name, every knee *will* bow down, and all *will* confess that He is Lord. Jesus' name commands worship. His name is exalted, just as He is. His spoken name, or calling on His name, calls not only on the name, but the power that it represents.

We live in a Christ-like manner when we give honor to Jesus and His name. We live in a Christ-like manner when we understand the power of His name and how we as believers can come boldly before His throne with our needs.

Read Hebrews 4:14–16. When we come to Jesus with our needs and concerns, what does verse 16 say we will receive?

_____

Now, once the discussion of healing and faith has begun, inevitably, there will be questions on the assurance of healing and whether healing is commensurate with the level of faith of the believer. Remember that only God knows why He heals some and not others. In Romans 9, Paul reminds us of something God told Moses in Exodus 33:19:

> *"I WILL HAVE MERCY ON WHOM I HAVE MERCY, AND I WILL HAVE COMPASSION ON WHOM I HAVE COMPASSION."* (Romans 9:15)

The meaning of this statement may expand far beyond physical healing, but my point is this: He is in control, and we are not. Never let anyone tell you

## PHILIPPIANS 2:9–11

*"Therefore also God highly exalted Him, and bestowed on Him the name which is above every name, that at the name of Jesus EVERY KNEE SHOULD BOW, of those who are in heaven, and on earth, and under the earth, and that every tongue should confess that Jesus Christ is Lord, to the glory of God the Father."*

that you were not healed (or that someone else was not healed) simply because you did not have enough faith. Yes, faith is essential, and I am in no way saying that it does not play a part in healing. Faith is critical. Faith mixed with our prayers brings forth results. But *God's will* is the ultimate determining factor in every case, not just how much we can convince ourselves that something will happen. We cannot manipulate our situation to fit *our will* or our needs only, no matter how godly we think we are in our actions.

Only God can heal, and our focus verse drives this point home. The man was healed *in Jesus' name*, and Jesus actually did the healing—not Peter, nor John. These men were merely instruments (vessels) used by God to bring glory to no one other than God and Christ himself. When Jesus' name is used, all resulting outcomes and glory belong to Him. He is the source of the miracles, signs, and wonders! Any prayers for healing should have the intention of furthering the work of Jesus. Our healing and our answered prayers are never to be used to further our own name; they are not for personal gain, but to show God's glory, power, and the wonder of Christ's love.

Back to our story in Acts, we return to the scene with the healing of the man completed and with the onlookers standing in amazement. At this moment, Peter is energized again and ready to preach.

📖 Read Acts 3:11. Where did Peter and John go with the healed man?

_____

Who met them there?

_____

What was Peter's response, according to verse 12–13?

_____

_____

What does Peter remind them of in verses 14 and 15?

_____

_____

_____

It is amazing to me that Peter reminded them of Jesus' deity in a place that was familiar to Christ's disciples. Look up John 10:22–33. Summarize the passage.

_____

_____

_____

_____

_____

John 10:22 shows Jesus teaching at the portico of Solomon, the same location as our story in Acts. During this scene, the Jewish leaders confront Jesus about His deity, and He boldly asserts that He is indeed God, but that they do not know this because they are not His. The knee-jerk reaction of the Jews is to stone Him, because they believe He has blasphemed God. And

> *"God's will is the ultimate determining factor in every case."*

here in Acts, with Peter's sermon, the Jews are reminded that it is the very same Jesus they threatened to stone at this spot that had healed the life-long beggar. Peter strongly and clearly taught that it was the power of Jesus that had made this man well.

📖 Now, take a closer look at our focus verse, Acts 3:16. What worked together with Jesus' name to bring forth the healing of the man?

_____

_____

It is not only the name of Jesus, but the faith of the man that brought the healing. Through the strength that comes from Jesus' name, and the faith in Him and His sovereignty, great things are bound to happen. In the same measure that we seek Him, He will meet us.

Peter reiterated to the skeptics that the Old Testament continually points to Christ and His redemptive work on the cross. Then Peter closed out his sermon. What a great occasion this moment in time was to lead others to Christ! Read through the rest of the third chapter if you have time. It will provide an awesome ending to today's study!

**The same Jesus the Jews had threatened to stone at this very same spot had healed the life-long beggar.**

*Powerful Name* DAY FIVE

# FOR ME TO FOLLOW GOD

Isn't God great? He took a normal journey to the temple, and turned it into a great evangelistic tool and gift of healing. God has a way of impacting lives, doesn't He? Peter and John were willing vessels, focused on God and used by God. The power they showed came from Christ alone. We shouldn't wonder when we will be able to share the gospel of Christ—there is no need to worry. God will provide the message, the people, and the power to do just that. We just need to make ourselves available.

Peter used this opportunity with the crowd to give them a second chance at salvation. He wanted them to see that they had missed their moment with the Savior once, but that they could accept Jesus the second time around. His approach with the crowd was exactly what they needed, and I'm sure the Holy Spirit was guiding Peter as he spoke.

We had a chance to look at the rest of Acts 3 at the end of Day Four, but let's go into it in a little more detail now.

📖 Based on your reading of Acts 3:17–26, how does Peter explain Jesus? What people or situations does he mention to help them understand Jesus?

_____

_____

Peter talks to the crowd in terms they understand. He mentions the Old Testament and people from those accounts that the people would surely know. Peter mentions Moses, Samuel, and the other prophets, and Abraham. He shows them that what they have known all along points to what they have yet to understand.

With most Christians today, it is the opposite situation from what Peter encountered with the crowd. Peter's sermon was tailored to showing them Christ by showing them Old Testament Scriptures and prophecies. Today, Christians know about Jesus in the New Testament, but many have no idea that the Old Testament has any relevance or significance in the role of Jesus and salvation.

**APPLY** Have you spent much time studying any of the Old Testament? Have you studied an even percentage of New and Old, or have you focused more on New Testament studies?

_____

_____

_____

Before taking this study, did you realize that Jesus was referred to, or foreshadowed, in the Old Testament?

_____

_____

_____

Have you learned more about the connection of Jesus and the Old Testament through this study? How has that helped you understand the role of Jesus in God's overall plan for mankind?

_____

_____

_____

_____

_____

_____

Since the New Testament had not been written and compiled, Peter was a walking, talking New Testament of sorts. He and the other apostles were the teachers who would tell people of Jesus and His promises. His mission was to tell the rest of the story to those who had only focused on one half of the story.

In the same way, it is our job as believers to share the full Gospel of Christ, which includes God's whole story, from beginning to end! What a shame it would be if generations went on without knowing that Jesus appears _throughout_ the Scriptures as is that His redemptive plan for mankind was for Him to die on the cross and rise again!

What new realizations have you made this week in regards to your faith and the power of Jesus?

_____

_____

_____

_____

_____

_____

**ACTS 3:19–21**

_"Repent therefore and return, that your sins may be wiped away, in order that times of refreshing may come from the presence of the Lord; and that He may send Jesus, the Christ appointed for you, whom heaven must receive until the period of restoration of all things about which God spoke by the mouth of His holy prophets from ancient time."_

*Jesus our Healer,* I praise You for being our Healer. I call out to You in faith and in praise, acknowledging who You are as God. Holy and righteous Father God, I thank You for Your Son. I thank You for providing strength and power in His name, and I stand in awe of the magnitude of the sovereignty of Jesus. I thank You for healing those who are sick, for healing lives that are broken, and for showing me through the many testimonies in the Bible that You can and will do the miraculous. Lord, I thank You for helping me build my faith moment by moment, situation by situation. May I never be like those in this lesson who rejected You and stoned You. May I be expectant, just as the beggar was; eagerly awaiting the move of Your Spirit.

Lord, may Your will be all I desire. In Jesus' name, amen.

# TEN

# Body Building

## BUILDING UP THE BODY OF CHRIST
## 3:16 VERSES: 1 CORINTHIANS, COLOSSIANS

In Lesson 9 we studied about a man with a mat who was changed forever by the power of Jesus Christ. We learned to connect our prayers with faith and discovered that there is power in Jesus' name. These concepts are so critical to our personal walk with the Lord! In this lesson we will cover the next step of relationship: *community*. Our goal as Christians should be to function as a wonderful body of believers, working together and worshipping, giving all honor and glory to the Father. As we function in the corporate unity that God calls us to live out, lifting up the name of Jesus and giving Him our praise, God is truly honored.

Just as Peter found every opportunity to share the good news of Jesus Christ with the crowds around him, we too should be ready to tell the world about Jesus. As we function in our Christian community inside *and* outside the church walls, we will have ample opportunity to work with other believers. Working with others "God's way" means that we will focus on doing things within His ways and His will. God's will is found in the passages of Scripture and through prayer. The Great Commission of Matthew 28, where Jesus calls all believers to spread the good news throughout the nations, is a wonderful example of how to live in community according to God's will.

*In this lesson we will cover the next step of relationship—community.*

When the body of Christ (the church) is functioning together collectively as God has ordained, isn't it a beautiful thing? It is incredible to witness a congregation or groups of congregations worshipping and serving together, everyone doing his or her part, everyone spurring one another on to spiritual growth and to Christian maturity, and everyone concerned with living a life like Christ lived. There is so much more to the concept of community than our small individual sections of the body of Christ, but we have to work within that body before we will ever experience true unity in faith throughout the nations.

How does this cohesive community happen? By staying true to Scripture, and staying focused on the will of God. This week we will find applicable insight into living as a Christ-like community.

## *Body Building*  DAY ONE

# THE DWELLING PLACE 3:16 VERSE: 1 CORINTHIANS

*"Do you not know that you are a temple of God, and that the Spirit of God dwells in you?"*

**The Holy Spirit leads us into all truth.**

When we accept Jesus Christ as our Savior we have the promise of the Holy Spirit, who is one third of the Trinity, and whose relationship with God is timeless. The Holy Spirit hovered over the waters in Genesis and will remain throughout eternity. He is living and active among us today. Through the events we read about in the first few chapters of Acts concerning the events surrounding the Day of Pentecost, we know that the Holy Spirit is given to all believers in order to guide and direct us into all truth. We have the Holy Spirit's presence in each of our lives as we invite Him to dwell in us and work through us. We become the Holy Spirit's dwelling place on earth both personally as individual believers and collectively as a community of faith. It is through the Holy Spirit's leading that we are able to interpret Scripture and that we are able to discern the right choices to make in order to live a Christ-like life.

What type of dwelling does the Holy Spirit have in you? There are many ways to describe your personal "temple" or tent:

- a wonderful mansion or a broken-down camping tent,
- a small peaceful retreat in the mountains or a large conference center,
- a subway station's graffiti-covered train or a fine automobile,
- a stock market building or a small-town bank,
- a fine dining establishment or a drive-thru restaurant,
- a modern studio in the city or a farmhouse in the country

Many things can give you a picture of what your life represents. Ideally we are to be vessels God can use, not merely ornaments of beauty that provide eye candy to on-lookers. God can use the most broken vessels for His glory. He desires an obedient heart and a surrendered will, not just a pretty façade.

📖 As we begin to study the concept of "being a temple," the first passage we will look at is 1 Corinthians 6:19–20. Read these verses and answer the questions below.

*Whose* are we?

_____

_____

What should we use to honor God?

_____

_____

In the personal "temple" comparison in 1 Corinthians 6:19–20, Paul asks,

*"Or do you not know that your body is a temple of the Holy Spirit who is in you, whom you have from God, and that you are not your own? For you have been bought with a price: therefore glorify God in your body."*

How much more straightforward can that be?

When I read that passage, the phrase that pops out to me most is *"you are not your own."* We don't own ourselves—God owns us! He is the creator and sustainer of all things. We are His and have been created to glorify Him and uphold the standards and principles that He has set for our lives. The price for our salvation was paid once for all through Jesus' sacrifice. He is the perfect sacrifice—the Lamb that was slain for all sinners—and, because of Jesus, we are able to fellowship with the Lord and to experience eternal life. Our relationship with God is based on our surrender to Him and our acceptance of His gift of salvation. We are called to glorify God in our bodies.

It's pretty easy to see what Paul is saying to the people in Corinth in this passage. Our bodies belong to the Lord, and our lives and our treatment of our vessels must remain holy. If we engage in sexual immorality or other sins that involve our actual flesh and bones, then we actually sin against ourselves as well as against God. Jesus didn't just redeem us in "theory." He redeemed every single facet of us—including our bodies.

Imagine we are on one of the many reality TV "home makeover" shows. In such a game, we would be challenged to make over our old "sinful selves" into new "Christ-like servants" in no time flat. Let's think of the parallel those types of shows can have to our lives and have some fun!

**APPLY** How would you restructure your life? Which walls would have to be torn out, and which structural improvements would have to be made before anything else could occur?

_____

_____

_____

_____

How would you decorate? What theme or décor focus would you like others to notice the minute their eyes opened to the room you showed them? Think about the values God wants to see instead of the actual colors, coverings, cabinetry, and so forth.

_____

_____

_____

_____

**Jesus didn't just redeem us in theory—He redeemed every single facet of us; to include our bodies.**

Would you use clashing, thrown-together items that really weren't meant to be together, or would you purposefully choose items and resources that were consistent and made to fit together?

_____

_____

_____

_____

What reaction would those who only knew your "old room" have about your "new room"? What reaction would you have in showing them the new you?

_____

_____

_____

_____

_____

*"Whatever you do, do your work heartily, as for the Lord rather than for men; knowing that from the Lord you will receive the reward of the inheritance. It is the Lord Christ whom you serve."*

**Colossians 3:23–24**

To be used by God, our "temples" must reflect a style that God would be comfortable sending His Spirit to inhabit. God expects our personal vessels to be free from grime, unpleasant situations, or things that would offend Him! Our temples must reflect the things of God that are consistent with His Word—His complete, unabridged Word—not just the portions that justify our lifestyle.

We must give God our best effort at living a holy life, and we've got to really mean it. We have to realize that we cannot simply decide to live holy lives and expect to accomplish this in our own strength. Living a truly holy life is something that is *only* obtained through the grace and strength Christ can provide. So, are we perfect the minute we accept Christ? Nope. Does He expect to see progress? Absolutely. As we put off our old selves and take on our new Christian nature, keeping sight of His presence is essential to continuing to grow in our faith.

📖 Read Romans 12:1–2. What should our lives be like as Christians?

_____

_____

In the first verse we see that presenting our bodies as living sacrifices to the Lord is our worship to God. What does that mean to you? How does that manifest in your life?

_____

_____

_____

_____

God is not just talking about the outer exterior. He wants each believer's body to be a temple that reflects the will of God and the principles, promises, and teachings that are found in the Bible. We are to live holy lives, pleasing and acceptable to our God.

📖 Luke 6:46–49 presents a powerful parable concerning daily life and how a relationship with Christ is built. Describe the scene in this passage:

_____

_____

_____

_____

On what is your house built? How strong is your foundation in Jesus Christ? Is your house built on Christ the Rock? Will your standing in God keep you from perishing? Our lives must be a reflection of our beliefs by putting what we hear into practice. This is the essence of Christ-like living!

One of my favorite verses along this line is found in 1 John 2:6. Write that verse out here:

_____

_____

_____

> "Whoever claims to live in Him must walk as Jesus did."
>
> 1 John 2:6, NIV

In order to come together in unity as a community that upholds the name of Jesus Christ as Lord, every believer must first make sure that his own life exhibits such beliefs. As an extension of that surrender to God, we are able to have a positive impact on the community tent.

We will all impact our community of faith one way or the other. We can either work together to uphold truth and godly principles, or we will work together within a false sense of community based on feel-good philosophy and compromise. Which type of community reflects Christ and honors God?

_____

_____

_____

Unfortunately, counterfeit communities of faith exist everywhere. They look really happy and cohesive on the surface. They all live, play, and worship together. But when investigated more deeply, on what are they based? What is their source of unity? What is their bottom line—*their foundation*—built on?

The community that honors God is the one that is based on a foundation of Jesus Christ as Savior and *Jesus Christ as the Son of God*. Followers of Jesus adhere to the consistent teachings of God, from Genesis to Revelation.

# BUILDING HIS KINGDOM
# 3:16 VERSE: 1 CORINTHIANS

*Body Building*    DAY TWO

*"Do you not know that you are a temple of God, and that the Spirit of God dwells in you?"*

All of us will set different kinds of goals for ourselves in various areas of life during our lifetime. Some goals are personal and for building our own character and abilities, while others are distinctly for the benefit of others around us. When we become a part of a large organization, as with our occupation or our church, we see the bigger vision of the organization and begin to move in that direction. Once we commit to being a part of that larger entity, we go forth supporting the vision of the leader of that organization and purpose to bring its goals to fruition.

As we dive into our focus verse, we'll see what the verse means to us as a body of believers. Fellowship with other Christians is such a wonderful gift of God. Godliness in our corporate fellowship should be held to the same standard as in our personal lives. Again, we will see that God is consistent.

> As Christians, our goals—no matter the area of our life—should be based on the Word of God.

📖 Looking at 1 Corinthians 3:16, we see that Paul takes the concept of a God-honoring temple one step further, with Paul referring to the temple as the entire church. Read the focus verse, and write down the similarities and differences between this verse and 1 Corinthians 6:19–20.

_____

_____

_____

_____

_____

So, this means that the individual requirements for us are also expected of us collectively in the church body! In other words, *play nice and don't make Dad mad.* I'm sure you remember the infamous phrase, "As long as you live in MY house, you'll do as I say!" Somehow, our fathers knew when we were up to something bad. In the same way, we must remember that God always knows what we're up to, too! We all "live under God's roof" as Christians, and that saying is just as applicable to us in our areas of fellowship in the church body. As we come together in communities of faith we have to play by "daddy's rules." We have to play by the standards that God the Father sets forth in Scripture.

> The church body consists of the redeemed: believers in Jesus Christ who are indwelt with the Holy Spirit, who are living transformed lives in Christ.

📖 Jesus gives us an example of how He felt when those in church were misusing their church time for personal financial (worldly) gain. Read Matthew 21:12–13. Describe this scene, and what Jesus said to those He corrected:

_____

_____

_____

_____

📖 Now compare to John 2:13–22. What new insight do you gain from this passage?

_____

_____

_____

_____

In these two accounts, we see Jesus clearing the temple of the moneychangers and anyone else who was there to make God's house a business opportunity. God's house is not a place for personal financial gain; it is a place of worship, and Jesus very clearly showed the moneychangers in the temple this point. Jesus showed the people and all generations after them that the House of God is His house, not the local marketplace. Beware of the commercialization of God's house!

Is the temple just the building (bricks and mortar) of God? Of course not. Does a group become a church body by agreeing on the color of the carpet, showing up and holding down favorite pews, making prayer requests during Sunday School while devouring yummy donuts? On the contrary! The church body consists of the *redeemed*: believers in Jesus Christ indwelt with the Holy Spirit who are living transformed lives in Christ. We are a body of believers whether we agree on every minute detail or not. In God's family, just like our earthly families, in God's family, we can be sure that we don't get to pick our Christian siblings, but we are expected to love and respect them anyway!

📖 Look at James 3:8–10. What does James warn us about in this passage?

_____

_____

_____

Unity in the body of Christ is essential, and one of the major pitfalls in our attempt to be unified stems from the very problem that concerned James. We cannot bless God in one moment and curse man in another and think that we are building up the temple of the living God, either personally or collectively. The cursing described here is the type of speech that does not edify God or bring others closer to Him. The cursing in James 3 refers to speech that is a reaction to our fleshly desires and based *outside of the will of God.*

Our unity must be focused on collective priorities of building on the foundation that Jesus made and building a community that is Christ-like. When Jesus corrects others, as he does in Matthew 21 and John 2, it is for the purpose of upholding God's standards and truths; not merely for His own edification or personal agenda. In the same way, when we are focused on blessing the Lord, there will be times when we may correct others, but it should not be delivered in a spiteful way as James describes.

📖 Psalm 133 gives us a beautiful picture of unity. Read the psalm, and picture the unity described. What according to the end of verse 3, is the result of godly unity?

_____

_____

The result of our Christ-like unity is the *blessing of eternal life.* That is our goal, and that is the source of the greatest blessing we will ever receive. For that, we should be excited to worship the King every minute of every day. We are united in Christ Jesus as we worship and dwell in His house of worship. The church body as a whole is the collective vessel of worship for the King. If we want to be effective in our community of worship, we must be of one mind and one spirit.

### Did You Know?
### TEMPLE DOVES

In the temple, sacrifices were an ongoing thing. Look again at the topic of cleansing the temple of moneychangers from the verses we just discussed in Matthew 21:12–13 and John 2:13–22. Did you notice what type of table Jesus turns over? It is the dove vendor! The doves were the acceptable sacrifice for the lowest income families who wanted to follow the temple customs. Accordng to Luke 2:21–24, Jesus Himself was dedicated in the temple with a sacrifice of doves. Maybe this is why He chose that particular table, in both of the passages we just read. Either way, with the sacrifice of Jesus it is no longer necessary to buy sacrificial animals; Jesus has become our perfect sacrifice.

*"For there the LORD commanded the blessing—life forever."*

*Psalm 133:3*

📖 Paul gives us more details on our source of godly unity in Ephesians 4:4–6. Read this passage. Where is our unity located?

_____

_____

As Ephesians 4:4–6 says,

*"There is one body and one Spirit—just as you were called to one hope when you were called—one Lord, one faith, one baptism; one God and Father of all, who is over all and through all and in all."* (NIV)

This passage says nothing about personality quirks or preferences in music selection. This passage reminds us of the more important items upon which we should be focused: our Savior, our faith, and our lives together. When focused on these three things, we will have unity in the body of Christ.

📖 In 1 Corinthians 3:3, we find Paul admonishing the people of Corinth about their actions. What does he describe as their barrier to unity?

_____

_____

📖 Now read verses 4–5. What is the struggle Paul points out?

_____

_____

_____

📖 What is Paul's response to this struggle, as shown in verses 1 Corinthians 3:6–9?

_____

_____

_____

No one is the "star" of the church but Jesus Christ. All glory *must* go to God. Christianity is a faith that is to be shared. We should build each other up in faith, not tear one another down in search of personal power or self-made righteousness. According to Paul's epistles, no one should have selfish ambition in the church. No congregation should place more honor on its human teacher than the God of the Bible they worship.

📖 First Corinthians 3:10 shares a powerful truth. What do you learn from this verse?

_____

_____

_____

Building God's kingdom means using God's truths and God's promises as the only building materials. We cannot take the world's materials, resources, and ideas and form them into bricks to build the kingdom of God. The world can only provide us with inferior building materials such as hay and straw. In God's kingdom we are able to build with godly resources that stand forever, such as gold and silver. Therefore, by staying with God's ways

**"I planted, Apollos watered, but God was causing the growth."**

**I Corinthians 3:6**

**"But let each man be careful how he builds."**

**I Corinthians 3:10**

and teaching God's Word, we build layers on the foundation that will last—and layers on the foundation that honors God.

The accumulated influence of many Christian believers affects the growth of each person's faith. The building of each person's faith is based on many different believers pouring into an individual's life throughout a lifetime.

- **We have parents that nurture us in faith.**
- **We have Sunday School teachers who mold us.**
- **We have youth group leaders who shape us.**
- **We have peers who grow and share along with us.**
- **We have mentors that continue to encourage us.**
- **We have pastors who shepherd us.**
- **We have choirs that sing praise with us.**
- **We have a multitude of other believers in the body that worship with us.**

Together, they all have helped us become who we are in Christ. At any and every point in this process, *only Christ* should get credit for this transformation in our lives. As workers and servants in the church, as well as teachers, we must be very careful how we build on another person's foundation. As each of the teachers, pastors, and mentors share Christ with others, the consistency of God's Word and God's will must permeate every layer for the building process to continue in a God-honoring way.

The third chapter of 1 Corinthians tells us a lot about how to function in a Christian community and how to build *God's* kingdom in a way that will last, brick by brick. Verses 11–15 show us a wonderful way to test the quality of the building that is finished.

📖 Read 1 Corinthians 3:11–15. What are the different kinds of building materials described?

_____

_____

_____

How is the worker's labor evaluated and tested?

_____

_____

_____

What is the sign of work that receives a reward?

_____

_____

_____

What happens to the work that doesn't pass the test?

_____

_____

_____

*As teachers, pastors, and mentors share Christ with others, the consistency of God's Word and God's will must permeate every layer.*

> **"Do you not know that you are a temple of God, and that the Spirit of God dwells in you?"**
>
> **1 Corinthians 3:16**

The image of the refiner's fire given here is powerful, isn't it? We are shown that our success in the building of God's kingdom depends on the quality of the layers we build on the godly foundation already laid. Anyone without a foundation in Christ is sure to burn up. Upon what foundation is your faith community built?

With this passage in mind, we come to our focus verse again, 1 Corinthians 3:16. What new insight do you have about this verse now that we have examined the context more fully?

_____

_____

_____

Another parallel to the concept of building God's kingdom is found in the second chapter of Ephesians.

📖 Look up Ephesians 2:19–22. How does Paul refer to Christ Jesus?

_____

_____

What are we forming through our relationships with Jesus, according to verse 21 and 22?

_____

_____

_____

### Word Study
### CORNERSTONE

The word "cornerstone" is used in Ephesians 2 as well as in 1 Peter 2:6. The cornerstone of the foundation of a building during that time was a large (sometimes as long as 4 yards) stone that held the foundation together, and provided extra strength for the building to rest on. With regards to the passage in Ephesians, we see a wonderful visual example of how the teachings of Christ are the pivotal foundational block on which all other teachers, prophets, and Christian beliefs rest. Without Jesus as the foundational cornerstone, our faith will buckle and crumble to the ground.

Picturing ourselves so intricately knit together, we can almost get a glimpse of how God sees us. We come together as a wonderfully built structure, with the *"foundation of the apostles and the prophets"* (verse 19) and the cornerstone of Jesus. The most essential piece of any building project is the corner stone—it supports the entire structure. Without that piece, the structure would fall. It is no different with a community of faith. Without Jesus, it ultimately cannot stand. It will not receive eternal life. There is no salvation for those who do not have Jesus as the cornerstone.

📖 Going back to 1 Corinthians, we read that Paul finished out the passage by warning the people in Corinth one last time about quarreling over teacher preferences. First Corinthians 3:17–20 reveals another concern that Paul had for them. What does he address here?

_____

_____

_____

The people thought they had it all figured out and that they were standing firm by following one teacher over another. But Paul warned the people in Corinth about thinking they were wiser than they really were.

📖 Read verses 21–23, Paul's ending statement. What is Paul's final point?

_____

_____

_____

Who does everything belong to, including Christ?

_____

We have to stay humble and focused on God. Paul belonged to God, and so did the rest of the teachers. For that matter, so did the world, everything in it, and every span of time. So do you, and so does Christ. We are all His. Our role in God's equation is to build the church using the supplies and resources He has given us, focusing on the truth of the good news of Jesus, so that the result will be a building that will stand the toughest trials and will come through the refiner's fire.

"Our ministry" is never really our ministry anyway. It all belongs to God. Think of it as God letting us borrow the ministry He owns. We are mere facilitators of His vision and His plan. It all belongs to God, and it all should bring Him the glory.

As we look at the collective temple in this verse, keep a few ideas in mind. We must keep Jesus as a foundation. The church will be strengthened through the focus on God (and His Word) instead of an overemphasis on the person preaching. And finally, when we avoid division based on our own egos and edification, and focus on building up *God*, our body of faith as a whole will honor God. I encourage you to fellowship and "build" with your local congregation. Help it to become a "temple" that is pleasing in the eyes of the Lord!

> *Our role in God's equation is to build the church using the supplies and resources He has given us, so that it will be a building that will stand the toughest trials, and so that we will come through the refiner's fire.*

# GODLY LOVE
# 3:16 VERSE: COLOSSIANS

*"Let the word of Christ richly dwell within you, with all wisdom teaching and admonishing one another with psalms and hymns and spiritual songs, singing with thankfulness in your hearts to God."*

We begin Day Three with Colossians 3:1–2, which states:

*"If then you have been raised up with Christ, keep seeking the things above, where Christ is, seated at the right hand of God. Set your mind on the things above, not on the things that are on earth."*

Those two verses adequately sum up what we have studied in Days One and Two. When our goal is heavenward, a temple that reflects God is sure to develop, both individually and collectively.

The third chapter of Colossians is dedicated to teaching believers how to live a life that is holy, or how to reflect holiness. Through this chapter, Paul teaches the people how to be Christ-like.

📖 Look at the Colossians 3:3. What could Paul mean by this statement?

_____

_____

We haven't died yet, but we have died to our sin. We are dead in Christ, which means that we are dead to our sins and alive in Christ due to His sacrifice for us. Our lives are now "hidden" with Christ. We are safe in His protection.

A wonderful image of God's protection is found in Psalm 91:4. How is God described in this verse?

_____

_____

Imagine! The God of the universe protecting you with wings as an eagle, with his arms stretched over you, giving warmth and security. Jesus is a protection, a refuge, and a shelter to all who rest in Him.

📖 What does Colossians 3:4 tell us about our standing in Christ? Is it temporary or eternal?

_____

_____

_____

This verse uses the term "revealed" which is the Greek word *phaneroo*, which in this context refers to an absolute arrival or appearing. This verse holds yet another confirmation that we will one day live with Christ in heaven, just as Jesus has promised. As the verse states, our life is in Christ. Let that sentence reside in your spirit for a moment. Our life is in Christ! Let's look at verse 5:

> "*Therefore consider the members of your earthly body as dead to immorality, impurity, passion, evil desire, and greed, which amounts to idolatry.*"

Ouch! Why did Paul have to go and ruin our cheerful moment? That statement sounds harsh, doesn't it? Well, it is true. It is consistent with the previous thought that our life is in Christ. Christ is without sin. Sin cannot dwell where God's presence is. Therefore, if we are in Him, we cannot also be engrossed in habitual sin. The concepts of being in Christ and being enslaved to sin just don't work together. Either we repent and stay in relationship with God, or we continue to sin and harden our hearts while our relationship with God suffers.

📖 What does Colossians 3:6–9 identify as the types of sinful nature? What will be the punishment for sin?

_____

_____

_____

_____

_____

All of the things we used to do, before we had Christ, we should no longer do. Anger, sins of speech, immorality, and all other sin should no longer be a response in our lives. Why? Read verse 10, and record what Paul says:

_____

_____

_____

*Sin cannot dwell where God's presence is.*

We are new creations! We are "being renewed" in the image of God. We are becoming more Christ-like. Personally and collectively, changes happen when a relationship with God is established and nurtured.

📖 The discussion in Colossians 3:11–14 dovetails with our discussion concerning unity. What does Paul teach within these three verses about unity in the body of Christ? Journal your thoughts:

_____

_____

_____

_____

_____

**APPLY** At this moment in your life, are there people that you need to forgive? Who and why?

_____

_____

_____

_____

To whom do you need to show more love?

_____

_____

_____

Are there fellow believers that you have a difficult time accepting? What makes it hard to accept them?

_____

_____

_____

Just as Paul points out, *"Christ is all, and in all"* (verse 11). No matter the origin, color, or denomination, all who call on the name of Jesus as Lord are Christians, and we are all in Him. We are already unified; we just need to match our actions with our standing in Christ.

*Putting on love*, as we see written in verse 14, is such a great visual for women. Think of the most luxuriously expensive outfit, piece of jewelry, or pair of shoes, and make sure it would be something that you would never have a chance at owning because of the high price tag. This has to be something so overwhelmingly out of your league that the thought of trying it on would be enough to make your year memorable.

What did you think of? Describe the item:

_____

_____

_____

*"Put on the new self who is being renewed to a true knowledge according to the image of the One who created him."*

**Colossians 3:10**

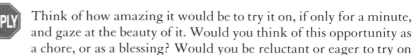 Think of how amazing it would be to try it on, if only for a minute, and gaze at the beauty of it. Would you think of this opportunity as a chore, or as a blessing? Would you be reluctant or eager to try on this item?

_____

_____

_____

Well, Colossians 3:14 tells us to put on **love**. Think of love as that beautiful garment you just imagined. Is putting on Christ's love a beautiful picture to you, or do you think of it as a chore?

_____

What if you had to put on love in a difficult situation? How would your eagerness change?

_____

_____

_____

God wants us to show the love of Christ to all we meet—even those we find hard to love. I don't know about you, but I have issues with this very thing, and more often than I'd like to admit. God knows that we, in our humanity, have a hard time loving the unlovable ones in our lives. But through countless passages of Scripture, God lovingly continues to call us to do just that—*love*. Can't you almost audibly hear God saying to us over and over through certain Scriptures, "what part of 'love one another' aren't you getting?"

We are His, and we are to love one another. Love manifests itself in many different ways.

- ■ **We show love by helping each other.**
- ■ **We show love by listening to each other.**
- ■ **We show love by just being there in whatever way needed for those around us.**
- ■ **We show love by encouraging others and improving their lives in some way.**
- ■ **We show love by "pouring ourselves" emotionally into their lives.**
- ■ **We invest time and energy into their needs, interests, and causes.**
- ■ **Our love is active. Showing love is an action.**

Loving others is an action, but it goes further. When we move in behalf of another, we are becoming unified with them in that purpose. When there is unity involved, there is a sense of peace.

📖 Colossians 3:15 goes one step further. After love, what does this verse say that we should allow to rule our hearts as well?

_____

_____

_____

"And beyond all these things put on love, which is the perfect bond of unity."

Colossians 3:14

Verse 15 also says that we are to be one _____, and that we should be _____.

**Love, peace, unity, and gratitude.**

These words make a great set of attributes in our quest for Christ-like living. These qualities are truly wonderful *if* they are built on the foundation of Jesus Christ and lived out through godly principles and motives.

God calls us to be united in peace. When we are all focused on *Christ first*, we will naturally find a peaceful union of minds because we are united in Christ. When we are all focused exclusively and completely on our own needs while sharing a path with others, there will most likely be a struggle. We cannot all be walking in the same direction with different motives and still be considered in peaceful unity. Unity comes through having a relationship with Jesus Christ first and those around us second. Jesus will bring us into unity as we seek Him and follow His steps in unison.

With a sense of unity established, we can move into the application of the godly principles we have obtained. Today's focus verse in Colossians is a wonderful example of how we can love others, be in unity as we are praising God, and pour ourselves into the lives of others.

Look at the focus verse again:

*"Let the word of Christ richly dwell within you, with all wisdom teaching and admonishing one another with psalms and hymns and spiritual songs, singing with thankfulness in your hearts to God."*

As we live a life that is set apart, and dwell on God's Word, we become transformed. The most amazing gift that we can give to another person is to spur that person on to that same process of transformation we experienced. As God's Word resides in our heart, it will naturally go forth from our mouths!

📖 Read Luke 6:45. What does the second part of that verse tell us about our speech?

_____

_____

Look at the two versions of this portion of Luke 6:45 below. How wonderful it is to see both ways of saying this profound truth. That which is in our hearts will be shown through our words. We reveal our heart in our speech.

"For his mouth speaks from **that which fills the heart**." (Luke 6:45b, NASB)

"For out of the **overflow of his heart** his mouth speaks." (Luke 6:45b, NIV)

As we know Scripture, we can use this knowledge of truth to help others by teaching and guiding them as well as even going as far as asking them to change their ways when those ways are inconsistent with a Christian lifestyle. Asking those we love to change a bad habit or sinful lifestyle isn't easy—but godly love is also exhibited when we bypass the easy road in order to remain focused on the right road. We love someone with a godly love when we care enough to help that individual be a better person, even when it is uncomfortable to say something. "Speaking the truth in love" is still giving the truth and is expressed in order to improve the other person's situa-

*When we are all focused on Christ first, we will naturally find a peaceful union of minds, because we are united in Christ.*

*Godly love is exhibited when we bypass the easy road for the right road.*

tion. This process is the "admonishment" part of our verse. We must be concerned with helping others find their way to Christ and to continue growing more in their relationship with Jesus.

Memorize today's verse, and pray for those you know who need to be delivered from sinful habits or lifestyles.

# KEEP YOUR CHIN UP!
# 3:16 VERSE: COLOSSIANS

*"Let the word of Christ richly dwell within you, with all wisdom teaching and admonishing one another with psalms and hymns and spiritual songs, singing with thankfulness in your hearts to God."*

The crux of our focus verse, Colossians 3:16, is found in the phrase *"Word of Christ."* The *Word of Christ* includes the Bible—the Scriptures given to us by God Himself to lead us to Himself. Through the Holy Spirit's leading we come to a fuller understanding of this Word.

**Without God, it is simply a book.**
**With God, Scripture brings life.**
**God's Word is life giving.**
**The Bible points to life, which is Christ Jesus!**

The Greek word used in our focus verse for "word" is *logos*, and it specifically relates to the revelation brought into the world through Jesus. The Bible should be the plumb line in our life—the very thing that we cannot get through a day without! We have to make ourselves at home in God's Word.

📖 Jesus is where we must keep our eyes fixed, as seen in Hebrews 12:2.

Write out Hebrews 12:2 here:

_____

_____

_____

*"Fixing our eyes on Jesus"* . . . what a goal indeed!

As we go through our daily lives helping others to grow in their faith, we must keep a good outlook ourselves. The second part of Colossians 3:16 confirms this.

■ **We are not only to teach others, but we are to praise God in the process.**
■ **We are to sing to Him and rejoice in the God we love.**
■ **We are to do all this with thankful hearts.**

As we reach out, we must never forget that God has given us this life, and He has given us other people in our lives to love.

**God is the one we praise:**

    **…not the teacher who brings the information**

    **…not the flashy evangelist that gets us all worked up**

    **…not the terrific praise team at our church.**

**God.**

**He is the focus of our praise!**

As soon as anything or anyone takes the place of God in the number one spot of importance in our lives, a little thing called *idolatry* occurs. This sense of idolatry simply means that another person or ministry has come between you and your relationship with God.

**APPLY**   Has this ever happened to you? Have you ever become more interested or dependent spiritually on a person and his or her teachings than God Himself? Or the Bible? Describe the situation.

_____

_____

_____

_____

_____

How is this problem fixed? Very easily. Listen intently, take notes, and learn from people used by God, but *always* spend time with God in prayer and Scripture study on your own. God will wonderfully confirm and/or test what you have been taught and show you in His word what He has promised and whom you are to serve! A rule of thumb I use in my own life is this: the amount of time spent listening and learning from outside sources (speakers, books, recordings, etc.,) should be equal to or optimally less than the amount of time spent directly reading and studying the Bible. In this way, I allow God to speak to me through His Word as much as I let others speak to me about God's Word. This goal keeps me rooted in the Word and searching the Scriptures as the Bereans referred to in the Book of Acts.

God has orchestrated every opportunity we have to share the gospel. For those who are in ministry, it is easy to get frustrated with the details of the work. We might get irritated with administrative processes, personality issues with others, and a myriad of other concerns. We may grow weary in serving those He brings into our ministry. God wants us to put those problems in the backs of our minds, and focus on the task at hand. We must remain set on serving Him and praising Him in all things!

📖 Read Galatians 6:9–10. What type of encouragement is Paul giving to those who serve others?

_____

_____

_____

In these two verses, Paul tells the workers in Galatia not to give up and to remain faithful in their focus of serving God. You may be thinking, "Well, that's great, but I'm not in ministry! I'm just taking this study!" None of us are immune from the needs of God's ministry. From the minute we accept Christ until the minute we go to be with Him, *we are all called* to share the message and hope of the gospel of Jesus Christ! Remember the Great Commission? That's the calling! That "go ye therefore" implies action and forward *motion*, doesn't it? Again, we are to be involved in our faith, and in the faith of others—no matter where the Lord tells us to go!

Don't be afraid of God calling you into ministry; not all of us will go to some far off village in the middle of nowhere to share with the natives. A lot of us are in "ministry" in our local churches. We are placed by God in the very place He needs us. He has the exact people in mind that need to hear our words of encouragement. Many times we are at church to build fellow Christians up in faith through our testimony and through our life experiences. Believe it or not, God will take the worst thing about your past and allow you to share it with others—all the while using it to be a testimony of the grace, love, and mercy of our God. There is not one of us that doesn't have "that story" of what a mess we were in some area of our lives before we committed our lives to Christ. We have all fallen short. Even still, while in that fallen state, there is not one person that is such a mess that God will not forgive him *if* he does not repent. There is not one thing you could have done in your lifetime that will keep you from the mighty power of Christ's forgiveness, *if* you lay your life down before Him.

**We all have access.**
**We are all invited.**
**We are all called to invite others.**

 Whether we tell a million people about Jesus Christ or just one, isn't the point. We are to go and share wherever God calls us—and if we have obeyed God's call for our lives, then we have done well in the sight of God.

What is God's calling for your life?

_____

_____

_____

_____

How have you been able to share the gospel with others?

_____

_____

_____

_____

_____

Have you been able to share your testimony with someone? Did you have a "messy story" before you accepted Christ of which others could relate?

_____

_____

_____

_____

## GREAT COMMISSION

Jesus charges us all to *"Go ye therefore, and teach all nations, baptizing them in the name of the Father, and of the Son and of the Holy Ghost: teaching them to observe all things whatsoever I have commanded you: and lo, I am with you always, even unto the end of the world. Amen"* (Matthew 28:19–20, KJV).

If you don't know what God's calling is on your life, ask Him! If you have never shared the gospel, share it! If you don't think you have a testimony, take some time right now to think about your life and how God has changed your outlook, your responses, and your eternal standing. Write your testimony out. You may be surprised to learn that you do in fact have a testimony! All a testimony is, and ever needs to be, is the simple story of how God has changed a life. It is a life story that points others to the foot of the cross and to the Savior.

While we are sharing our testimony and praising God with a thankful heart, we are also able to thank Him for putting other people in our path who enlighten us with a deeper understanding of the faith we share. It is a blessing to hear the life experiences and transformation of others. When we share our story we inspire the listener with our transparency and honesty about the way that Jesus has impacted our lives. Above all else, we are able to thank God and celebrate the fact that He has chosen us to be His own, and that eternal life is ours for the accepting.

### A Personal Moment

It is never too soon to share our faith, and to teach others. Our son at one time was involved with a youth group that was based on a fun nautical theme, and the kids had a great time listening to stories, memorizing verses, and singing songs of praise. The ministry's main memory verse was the very verse we are discussing. Watching the kids make it through the verse, reciting every word—in King James English—is encouraging to us all. If they can do it, anyone can! Verse memorization is possible—and modern translations are perfectly fine for this.

What fun it has been to see our child memorizing Scripture verses over the year, committing them to his heart, and understanding their impact in his life. When our son realizes yet another facet of God's promise and purpose for his life, there is a new freedom expressed on his face. The playground issues disappear. The struggles of childhood seem a little more tolerable. And knowing that God has guided his parents, his house, and his life, is huge. We have a child who has allowed God to strengthen him through His Word. He has the promises of God engraved on his heart, and to me, there is no better thing. All of us have the opportunity to memorize Scripture, but we have to practice and be faithful in learning God's Word.

While riding to church one morning, I mentioned to our son Owen that I was working on this chapter about "his verse." It was so awesome to see him perk up, and respond with the recitation of that verse from his heart. Once again, this confirms how powerful Scripture memorization can be. Once the verse is in your heart, it may be downright impossible to forget it—but then again, isn't that the point?

Even though Owen could rattle off his verse with ease in the back seat of our car that day, his recollection of that verse was a direct result of time spent in dedication to memorizing the Scripture. In the same way, he and the youth group kids he studied with had a tough time pronouncing the word "admonish" when they first learned the verse. The word just didn't roll off their tongues; they had to make an effort to get it right. After practicing, learning, and understanding the verse, the tough words got easier. "Admonish" was no longer a struggle, it was doable. It is still a fresh image on my mind—kids in their uniforms, practicing and re-practicing the verse, and happily learning not only the pronunciation of the word *admonish*, but the meaning as well.

*All a testimony is, and ever needs to be, is the simple story of how God has changed a life.*

Think of the parallel between the kids stumbling over the pronunciation of the word "admonish" and how we approach admonishing others. Again, the thought of guiding others away from a wrong path and advising them against error is something that is hard to do. To admonish someone simply means that we are going to call attention to something or guide and direct them gently in some way. In the sense of this verse, we will be guiding others toward godly principles, and away from sin.

We guide others into truth by teaching them the Word of God, and warning them against wrong paths with the warnings that we read in the Bible. Our hymns and spiritual songs also tell of God's majesty and lead us into a deeper knowledge of Him, conveying the concepts that we have in the Bible.

**We guide others into truth by teaching them the Word of God.**

**APPLY** Have you ever felt God leading you to admonish someone? Did you speak up, or stay silent?

_____

_____

_____

_____

_____

If you spoke to them, admonishing them about an inappropriate action or sin, what was the result? Do you believe God was honored by your response to His leading?

_____

_____

_____

_____

As with the verse memorization, if we work at it long enough and allow God to guide us, eventually admonishing and teaching others the truth of the Word of God will come naturally. We have to keep at it. We must never give up in our quest to build others in their faith. It is the sweetest gift we can give.

*Body Building* | DAY FIVE

# FOR ME TO FOLLOW GOD

What a journey this lesson has been. Perhaps you are now better equipped to live a Christ-like life and to share a community with others who seek the same lifestyle. In this quest for godly living, we each have two questions:

- **What are the goals of our Christian leadership?**
- **What is God's goal for my life?**

Yes, we are to accept God and His Son and accept the gift of salvation given us. We are to become more like the example Christ gave us through our spiritual development. *But we cannot stop with ourselves and our local church.* God wants us to reach out to the world with the message of Christ.

Throughout this lesson we have spent a lot of time discussing our dwelling places and the actions surrounding those places. We have seen the necessity for individual adherence to the Word of God as well as collective adherence to the Word. We have seen the need for encouraging others in the Word of God.

**APPLY** Are you changed as a result of your studies this week? In what ways?

_____

_____

_____

Do you have new goals or higher goals for your own spiritual growth? List them:

_____

_____

_____

Do you have a sense that God is calling you to serve Him in a broader capacity in your church and community? How?

_____

_____

_____

_____

_____

Are you more willing to admonish and teach others God's Word when prompted by the Holy Spirit?

_____

_____

_____

What we have spent the last ten weeks discovering will take a lifetime to implement. And that is the point that is made over and over in Scripture. Becoming Christ-like is a process. It is a process that will continue until we reach the pearly gates. No one perfects their quest on earth, because only Christ is perfect—yet we are in Christ and we will spend eternity in our glorious dwelling of heaven in our glorified bodies. *"Thanks be to God for His indescribable gift!"* (2 Corinthians 9:15 NIV)

Take time to encourage those around you in the Word and make a point to study the Bible on a regular basis. God will bring you to concepts and truths in your time of reading that will continue to spur you on to spiritual growth and maturity.

Spend some time reviewing the memory verses we have covered so far. Journal any thoughts about your time of study and how it has impacted you:

_____

_____

*God will bring you to concepts and truths in your Bible reading that will continue to spur you on to spiritual growth and maturity.*

_____

_____

_____

_____

_____

_____

_____

*Jesus, Our Cornerstone,* how I thank You and praise You for bringing me into community with others through Your holy name. May I be pleasing in Your sight; individually as a believer, and collectively with the body of believers. Help me to stay in Your Word, focusing on bringing my actions and attitudes within Your will. May I spur others on to Christ-like living, and may my life be a testimony of the impact Your truth has had on my life. Make me forever changed, and may You receive all the glory, forever. In Jesus' name, Amen.

# Self-Consumed

## The Dangers of Depending on Self
## 3:16 Verses: Romans, James

Over the past ten lessons together we have studied the history of Jesus' message, recognizing the foundational concepts of the Christian faith. We have discovered principles that we can apply to our own lives in order to pursue a life that reflects the teachings of Christ. It has been a thrill to share the truths set forth in the Bible about Jesus and what He means to us as Christians. Spurring one another on in faith is an honor and a privilege, and I encourage you to share what you have learned with others!

You will notice that our last two lessons together will have a different focus than the first ten. While we have covered some very positive aspects of our faith in previous lessons, we would be remiss if we did not study some of the warning signs of falling away, or losing our passion for God.

No matter how long or how passionately we live for Christ, no one is completely immune from the temptation of sin and the lure of complacency. Our world is flooded with unbelievers who are desperate to hear the truth of the good news of Jesus Christ. The response of the lost is usually summed up by their assumption that they are "good enough" people, and, therefore, their lives will be rewarded somehow in the afterlife. Even if they

*You will notice that our last two lessons have a different focus than the first ten.*

believe they are good people, without Christ they *will* perish. God has entrusted those who believe to share the truth with the lost. If Christians are not passionately pursuing God and sharing His Word, who will? Who will tell the lost? Because of this, the last two lessons of our study together will focus on warnings we must heed if we are going to continue to live a life that is Christ-like. These warnings will keep us from losing our impact on the lost world around us.

# JUST CHECKING THE BLOCKS?
# 3:16 VERSE: ROMANS

*"DESTRUCTION AND MISERY ARE IN THEIR PATHS."*

Building on the previous lessons, we will now begin to look into the factors that stand in the way of our Christian unity and our relationship with Christ. God desires to protect us from making wrong decisions and to keep us from falling away from the truth. Unfortunately, because of our sin nature, we battle temptations and shortfalls our entire lives. There are many factors that endanger our unity as believers:

- **Selfish ambition destroys unity.**
- **Sin separates us from unity.**
- **Strife and quarrels distract us from unity.**
- **Following a teacher more intently than we follow God squelches unity.**

When unity is broken, the path to destruction begins. We step out in a direction that separates us from God. My heart's desire is to continue to spur you on in your walk with the Lord. To encourage you in a more complete and balanced way, we must go through the warnings that Christ set forth in Scripture through the apostles, prophets and scribes God entrusted with His Word.

**APPLY** Before we begin to study the focus verse, think about your life experiences concerning unity and disunity. Which types of disunity issues have you seen occur in your groups of fellowship? Which factors led to the particular issues of disunity?

_____

_____

_____

_____

_____

After we have accepted Christ and "walked as a Christian" for a while, we might be tempted into thinking that we know all there is to know and have done all there is to do with regards to our faith. We might find ourselves echoing that all too familiar refrain, "been there; done that; got the t-shirt. . . ." There lies a trap that we must be careful to avoid. *Self-righteousness* is a dangerous condition that can leave us in the reality in which we are worshipping nothing more than ourselves. Finding our worth in what we *do*, in legalisti-

**Self righteousness is a dangerous condition that can leave us with nothing more to worship than ourselves.**

cally following the traditions of man, can lead us away from a heart that beats for God and a life that runs after Him.

**APPLY** Has there ever been a time in your relationship with God that you thought you had learned all there was to learn? Were you reluctant to continue learning and studying God's Word?

_____

_____

_____

_____

_____

How did you overcome these feelings?

_____

_____

_____

Have you learned more about God since that time?

_____

The desire to be like God in our *character* is good; we are to continue to grow in our faith and our desire to be Christ-like. We know that as believers, we are "in" Christ Jesus, and the source of all power and blessing comes from God alone. There is nothing that we in ourselves can do without God's equipping. When the people who were under the Law in the Old Testament followed their laws to the detail, they may have felt at times that they had "succeeded" in having a righteous faith in their own strength. The problem with this is that they were seeing the adherence to the Law as the ultimate marker of righteousness. Keep in mind who kept the Law but stood against Christ:

- **Many who were prominent in religious circles.**
- **Many who knew the Law.**
- **Many who were powerful in the world.**
- **Many who thought they had it all because they observed all the traditions and rules of the day.**
- **Many who felt they didn't need a redeemer.**
- **Many who were too afraid to stand up for what they knew was right.**
- **Many who were "good people."**

Christ's perfect sacrifice on the cross has become that once-for-all shedding of blood for all mankind. We are all under that new covenant made through Jesus Christ. We all have access to God and are able to worship Him and have salvation if we repent of our sins and believe that Jesus died for our sins.

We are equipped from on high, but in *no time ever* is that *our own* power, or are we righteous **on our own**. All status, righteousness, and acceptance by God are given to us through His Son's sacrifice and His Holy Spirit. Our faith is submitted under the authority of God the Father, the Son, and the Holy Spirit. Any benefit we receive is their gift to us and is at every moment theirs. Any power is and always will be God's. Not one of us can fully compare to Jesus in any form.

*Our faith sets us under the authority of God the Father, Jesus, and the Holy Spirit. Any benefit we receive is their gift to us, and is at every moment theirs. Any power is and always will be God's.*

Our first focus verse for this lesson comes from Paul's letter to the Romans. This verse is tucked inside a passage that was written to instruct the Jews of Rome to refrain from legalistic tendencies. Paul was warning that by focusing on works, they might miss the promise of salvation. No longer were adherence to the Law and animal sacrifice required for relationship with God. Now, with the Messiah's coming, salvation was provided to atone for sin. People simply needed to trust in Jesus in order to establish relationship with God. However, all people—Jew and Gentile alike—were now able to receive salvation. Jesus had fulfilled the Law, and His sacrifice was for all mankind.

Keep in mind that Paul had felt the hand of Christ on His life since that day on the road to Damascus. Paul knew that even though he had been a Jew of high standing before his transformation and had all the credentials of the religious elite, *even he* fell short of being righteous in his adherence to the Law. Paul knew his repentance and faith combined with the atoning sacrifice of Jesus was the only requirement for salvation. Paul realized that we are saved by God's grace and mercy. He wanted the world to know this vital truth.

📖 Do you remember our lesson on Philippians? Re-read Philippians 3:4–7, and write out Paul's credentials:

_____

_____

_____

Yet even with his lineage and titles, Paul was nothing without the saving grace of Jesus Christ. In the light of Paul's experiences, we can begin to look into the passage in Romans 2 and 3. Paul had great credibility in talking with Jews who clung to their religious traditions because he had served with them, trained with them, and worshiped with them. So now when Paul wanted to explain humanity's standing with Jesus, he could do so with conviction, sparking their interest. The readers in Rome knew that he understood their faith and ultimately understood their point of view. They knew Paul's letter to them was worth their attention and that his argument would be credible. In this passage, Paul answers the criticism of legalistic Jews in Rome.

📖 Let's begin our look at this passage by reading Romans 2:17–29. What does Paul teach the Jews in this passage?

_____

_____

_____

This passage gives correction to the Jews who knew the Law yet continued to sin. Paul meets them in their mind frame, mentioning many points from the Ten Commandments in his questioning of their "breaking the Law." The fact that the Jews knew the Law but continued to break it anyway brought great dishonor to God. We are guilty of the same thing if we habitually and knowingly sin while professing to be Christians.

Circumcision was the outward sign of the Jewish link to God, established with the Abrahamic Covenant. Without circumcision, there was no physical sign that the Jews were a part of that promise. Yet as they sinned, their outward sign of separation became an example of symbolism over substance. Paul wanted the Jews to see that with Jesus' provision of salvation in place, God desires an obedient heart more than He desires the legalistic

"But he is a Jew who is one inwardly; and circumcision is that which is of the heart, by the Spirit, not by the letter; and his praise is not from men, but from God."

Romans 2:29

approach of the Law. The Law had been fulfilled with Christ, and the grace of Jesus was open for all to accept.

Romans 2:29 gives us a wonderful statement to remember:

*"But he is a Jew who is one inwardly; and circumcision is that which is of the heart, by the Spirit, not by the letter; and his praise is not from men, but from God."*

We see in this verse that their heart condition needed to match their regulation keeping! The Law was not enough. Now, each Jew needed a heart that genuinely sought after God.

📖 Read Romans 3:1–2. Paul begins the chapter with an acknowledgement in verse 2 about the Jews. What does he say?

_____

_____

_____

Paul gives honor to the Jews and their place in history. He clearly states that the Jews *"were entrusted with the oracles of God"* (verse 2). Indeed, they were God's chosen people, entrusted to carry the Word of God from one generation to the next, which was a huge honor. Yes, they were a people that God loved and watched over. Yes, God entrusted them with the Scriptures. Yet they still needed Jesus to experience the fullness of what God had for them through the ministry of Jesus Christ.

As we have studied earlier, Jesus came to fulfill the Law—not to negate it. God is consistent, and those who follow Jesus and His teachings would naturally respect the laws of God and the Ten Commandments. Jewish Christians were not to abandon the Law: however, following the letter of the law in legalistic fashion was not necessary. When one lives a Christ-like life, the Law will be honored, because a Christ-like life is consistent with God's Law. Those who follow Christ will stay on the path that is in line with the Ten Commandments because Christ is the fulfillment of the Ten Commandments—the only person to obey all Ten Commandments at all times.

📖 Now look at Romans 3:3–8. Paul offers an interesting line of thoughts and questions in this passage. What does Paul want the Jews to understand?

_____

_____

_____

Paul makes several points here. In man's unfaithfulness, God is faithful. If man sins, God can still remove sin. God is righteous, even if we are not. Everyone is dependent upon God's righteousness. Such serious points of discussion are listed in these few verses! Paul probes his readers' deepest questions with concise answers.

Paul has a clear message: not being under the Law does not give the New Testament church permission to act in a lawless manner. Heresies abounded that taught that a person who sins just allows God's grace to show through. Can you imagine? Can you hear it now? The excuses might sound something like this: *Well, I know I should do something the right way, but I really want to go against what's right and please my desires. . . . that's ok, it'll give God a chance to show His goodness and mercy.* What a flawed sense of reasoning that is! When we knowingly go against God, He surely **does not** see it as an opportunity to be who He *already* is.

Unfortunately that same line of false teaching is alive and well in our world today. Some people may say that God's grace gives us license to practice sinful habits. We may hear people say we are under grace and that "God will love us no matter what." Though that statement is true, it does not mean that God will permit us to continually dishonor him without consequence. God chastens those he loves. Those who truly repent will follow God by turning from their old ways. Though we as Christians will not become sinless this side of heaven, our consciences will be seared when we do things that are not pleasing to God. We are saved by grace and transformed by the renewing of our minds.

Have you heard anyone say that as Christians we can sin without consequence because we are already guaranteed eternal life? What is your reaction to such a statement?

_____

_____

_____

How would you explain to someone the boundaries of grace and the necessity for repentance and forgiveness?

_____

_____

_____

_____

What does God think of sin? What does He think of the sinner?

_____

_____

_____

Let no one try to convince you that believers who remain in habitual sin are not accountable for their indiscretions. Beware of those who say that once we accept Jesus Christ as our Savior we have so much grace given to us by God that we are free to live lives marked by repentance.

God loves the sinner but hates the sin. God cannot be in fellowship with someone who has not laid his or her sins at His feet. We all need to check our hearts for sinful desires and actions in order to preserve a close relationship with God. Our fellowship with Him will be hindered until sin issues are addressed. We should go to the Lord daily with our sins and burdens, laying them at His feet and making sure we are not keeping ourselves from all that God has for us.

As a Christian, you might read today's lesson and say, "There's no way *I* would be like that! I wouldn't continue to sin! I love God *too* much. *I* have it all together. I am a great *Christian*." Be careful. We can be lulled into a

> **A life transformed will be a life that shows transformation.**

false sense of confidence, leaving ourselves exposed and unprotected from the schemes of the devil.

- We are <u>all</u> in the same process of faith.
- We <u>all</u> have more to learn.
- We <u>all</u> have new ways to grow.
- We <u>all</u> have new processes that God will bring us through.
- We will <u>never</u> get too old for growth.
- We <u>never</u> "get there."
- We will <u>always</u> fall short in our own strength.
- We will <u>always</u> need Jesus.

📖 With all these preliminary arguments out of the way, Paul uses verse 9 to zero in to the heart of the discussion. What does Romans 3:9 reveal? Who is under sin?

_____

_____

_____

Paul stressed that being a Jew was an honor, but such racial distinction did not make one any better than a Gentile. We all fall short; we all sin.

Memorize today's verse and praise God that He meets us where we are—in the depths of our humanity.

# WHO WE ARE WITHOUT CHRIST
# 3:16 VERSE: ROMANS

*"DESTRUCTION AND MISERY ARE IN THEIR PATHS."*

Before you sigh a breath of relief thinking how lucky you are that you are not a legalistic Jew in Paul's time, take a look at Romans 3:9 again. That verse very clearly says *"both Jews and Greeks are all under sin."* Where we find the term "Greeks" in the New American Standard, the New International Version interchanges the word "Gentiles." Anyone who is not a Jew is a Gentile. So, if you do not fall under the correction that the Jews are receiving in this passage, you are then a Gentile and thus fall short of righteousness without Jesus as your Savior.

Paul continues the passage with a wonderful list of just how much we need God because of our human shortcomings. Romans 3:10–18 give us every example of why we need God. Paul uses these verses which include Scripture references of the Old Testament to bring the point home.

📖 Read Romans 3:10–18. What is the overall message of this passage?

_____

_____

_____

*"What then? Are we better than they? Not at all; for we have already charged that both Jews and Greeks are all under sin"*

**Romans 3:9**

*Self-Consumed* DAY TWO

*Did You Know?*

### GOD'S WORD PRESERVED

Many times we see Old Testament passages quoted in the New Testament, but not in the exact wording. The scribe or speaker may not have had a copy of the text they were quoting on hand and may have quoted to the best of their ability at that moment. Even in such cases, it is amazing to see how the Holy Spirit has protected and preserved key concepts throughout the ages. The wonderful confirmation we have from God that He will preserve His Word is seen in how overall concepts have retained their core meaning throughout generations, regardless of how readily available the original text was.

Let's go through these verses line by line, tracing the thoughts back to their original reference in Scripture.

What does Romans 3:10–12 say?

_____

_____

_____

Now dig deeper into this passage's meaning by reading the verses that Paul references in verse 10: Psalm 14:1–3 and Psalm 53:1–3. How similar are these two passages in Psalms to the one in Romans? Is there any new information you gather from these two original texts?

_____

_____

_____

📖 The next segment of Paul's correction appears in Romans 3:13. Paul combines Psalm 5:9 and Psalm 140:3 to conclude this thought. Compare those two verses with the quoted portions in Romans 3:13 and then answer the questions below.

What part of Psalm 5:9 is in Romans 3:13?

_____

_____

_____

What part of Psalm 5:9 is *not* included in Romans 3:13?

_____

_____

_____

What portion of Psalm 140:3 is in Romans 3:13?

_____

_____

_____

📖 Romans 3:14 refers to Psalm 10:7. What additional imagery is seen in Psalm 10:7?

_____

_____

_____

Now we are to the point in the passage where we will discover the focus verse and the cross-reference. Quoted in Romans 3:15–17 is a passage that has its origin in Isaiah 59:7–8.

📖 Read Isaiah 59:7–8.

What a picture. If ever we needed a Savior, it sure would be now. Our focus verse is tucked into this listing of the unrighteous nature that all mankind has without the Lord Jesus.

Romans 3:16 in the New International Version mentions that *"ruin and misery mark their ways."* This concept comes from Isaiah 59:7–8. God's response to the need for salvation is to send salvation through Jesus. (It has been God's plan and God's response since the world began.) Look again at Romans 3:16 in the New International Version. *"Ruin and misery mark their ways."*

**APPLY** Can you remember a time when you have taken a situation into your own hands and not consulted God?

_____

_____

_____

What happened? Were there negative or even tragic results?

_____

_____

_____

_____

_____

_____

Have there been other times when you have taken a situation into your own hands without seeking God for guidance, and, if so, were the results positive?

_____

_____

_____

_____

_____

_____

There have been times in all of our lives when we have made big mistakes while living within legal boundaries, but not according to God's will. We go through the process, just not *God's* process. We catch ourselves trying to come up with solutions in our own strength or in our own wisdom, which may only bring us trouble and heartache. Why? We are limited, but God is limitless. Alone we are unrighteous, but through Jesus we become righteous. In our own wisdom we fall short, but with God and His counsel, we will make decisions that will bring a godly outcome.

As we become stronger Christians, clinging to His truth and upholding His ways, we need to study this list given in Romans 3. By dwelling on the characteristics of the unrighteous, we see a whole world out there that exists without a Savior. Jew or Gentile—the verdict is the same. None is righteous, no not one! We must be compelled to share the truth with the world around us. We shouldn't be afraid to say that we need a Savior.

## "DESTRUCTION AND MISERY ARE IN THEIR PATHS."

### Romans 3:16

📖 Romans 3:18 tells us why people go through life without God. What is the reason?

_____

_____

_____

Without the *fear of the Lord*, there is no reason to think that we might need Him. The idea of fear in this verse does not present the though of one being scared. Fear of the Lord is better described as a reverence, respect, and awe. To *fear the Lord* means that we hold Him in the highest respect. We don't want to experience God's displeasure with us or His punishment for our sin or shortcomings. Fearing the Lord means worshipping Him for who He is—a righteous and sovereign God.

Paul used the Old Testament references in this passage to make a point to the Jews. He knew they would recognize these verses from the Old Testament. By hearing the Old Testament verses applied to the Christian teachings, perhaps the people would finally understand how much they needed Jesus.

Paul showed them their unrighteousness because he had a desire to provide a solution to the predicament they found themselves in without Jesus.

📖 Romans 3:21–22 shows us a great comparison. What do the two verses compare?

_____

_____

_____

*"For all have sinned and fall short of the glory of God."*

*Romans 3:23*

Apart from any law, we all have access to righteousness through faith in Jesus. As reiterated in Romans 3:23, all fall short. There is nothing we can do to deserve this righteousness. None of us reach the goal of righteousness apart from God. There is no way to be righteous in God's eyes simply by trying to keep all the regulations. When we acknowledge that we cannot do it on our own, we allow Christ to stand in the gap for us. Then we find it possible to be in God's presence.

Romans 3:24–26 states that it is through Christ that we are justified and made righteous before God. Praise God for the gift of His Son! Through this justification, we are forgiven and are able to be in relationship with Jesus. We become more and more Christ-like with every passing day.

- ■ **In Christ we have our worth.**
- ■ **In Christ we have our being.**
- ■ **In Christ we have our righteousness!**

We cannot do it on our own, ladies and gentlemen. *Not one is righteous, no not one.* Our own path will lead to misery. When we get to the end of ourselves, God is there waiting. Run to Him! Dedicate your life to helping those who are still in the depths of their misery reach out to the God of the Universe who can provide them righteousness and eternal life through His Son.

# Who's Da' Man?
# 3:16 Verse: James

*"For where jealousy and selfish ambition exist, there is disorder and every evil thing."*

Unfortunately, in the world we live in, it's all about being "number one." As we discovered in the first half of this week's lesson, being number one without God leaves us in quite a lurch. In our second focus verse in this lesson, God once again tells us that **He** is number one, and *only* while we are functioning within that truth will we find success for ourselves. Our success is *always* a gift from God.

Success is achieved through wise choices and wise counsel. The wisdom we should seek is wisdom from God, not wisdom from man. God imparts wisdom to those who follow Him through the Holy Spirit. God equips believers to do that which will bring honor to Him. We should never seek wisdom for our own importance, ego, or financial gain. That type of wisdom is driven by selfish ambition.

Once again, we see that ours is an interactive faith:

- **We are gifted to build others up.**
- **We are blessed to be a blessing.**
- **We grow in our relationship with Christ in order to help others grow in their faith.**

Sounds practical doesn't it? Grow and help others grow. Isn't that what the entire Bible tells us in one way or another? Out of our faith in God should flow godly choices and godly wisdom. The Bible is filled with people, places, and whole lifetimes that have depended on man's wisdom. The outcomes for these self-made men and women along with those who depended on the Lord are quite predictable:

- **Focus on self—you miss God, and He doesn't bless you.**
- **Focus on God—He is with you, and He blesses you.**

Ever looked at the book of Ecclesiastes? Not a "light and peppy read" by any stretch of the imagination, but still recommended reading for everyone. In it we can see the impact and downside of self-reliance and following fleshly pleasures. The author, presumably King Solomon, had it all: wealth, wisdom, and a kingdom.

📖 Read Ecclesiastes 1:12–18. What is the topic of Solomon's thought here? What point does he make?

_____

_____

_____

> ## Our success is always a gift from God.

> ## "The fear of the LORD is the beginning of wisdom, And the knowledge of the Holy One is understanding."
>
> ## Proverbs 9:10

King Solomon describes the wealth of his wisdom. He also acknowledges how much grief and pain that very wisdom has caused him. He evaluates his life in other areas regarding works and wealth, and sums up his thought in Ecclesiastes 2:11. What does this verse say?

_____

_____

_____

*"Vanity and striving after the wind"*? Is this the kind of statement you would expect from such a wealthy and blessed man? Yet there are many other passages in the Bible that discuss wisdom, and we learn through these passages that wisdom itself is not bad, as seen in Proverbs 9:10:

> *"The fear of the LORD is the beginning of wisdom,*
> *And the knowledge of the Holy One is understanding."*

📖 Now go to Ecclesiastes 12:13, and write out what Solomon's conclusion is:

_____

_____

In this passage we should heed the warning not to search out wisdom and knowledge as a personal goal, for edifying yourself, is nothing more than *"striving after the wind."*

Incredible how we have the picture yet again of how everything the world and man have to offer pale in comparison to our standing in the Lord. It is all meaningless without God. Notice the focus in Ecclesiastes 2:11: **"I."** The writer was evaluating all he had done. This is an evaluation done in order to see *his own* glory, not God's glory. In his own strength and wisdom, all he had accomplished seemed meaningless. Only God's wisdom is perfect. Only bringing God glory will bring true fulfillment. Only God's path is perfect and full of joy.

Speaking of Solomon, more than a few times lately I have heard friends talking about how situations in their lives have reminded them of a story that concerned one of Solomon's rulings as judge. Before I talk about the details, take a look at the passage they have referred to in 1 Kings 3:16–28. (Yes, I am smiling at the fact that this very story begins with a 3:16 verse as well.)

Describe the argument that is mentioned in 1 Kings 3:16–28.

_____

_____

_____

_____

_____

_____

What was Solomon's initial solution to the problem?

_____

_____

_____

**Only God's wisdom is perfect. Only bringing God the glory will bring true fulfillment. Only God's path is perfect.**

What was the reaction of each woman to Solomon's first ruling?

_____

_____

_____

How did Solomon finish the discussion? What was his final ruling?

_____

_____

_____

Why did the first woman have such a reaction? Do you see the compassion she had for the child she loved?

_____

_____

_____

_____

_____

Now, imagine some attempts at self-proclaimed ownership that occur in our world:

- Someone wants something and is willing to do anything to get it.
- Someone thinks he deserves to be in charge.
- Someone wants to have her name out front.
- Someone wants to call all the shots in a situation.
- Someone tries to control a ministry that was never his to begin with.
- Someone wants all the credit for everyone else's work.
- Someone wants control so badly that she is willing to destroy the very thing she is trying to control.

Do you notice a theme in those statements? It all goes back to "someone" with a personal agenda. It goes back to selfish ambition. Thoughts are along the line of, *"I can't have something that I deserve"* or *"I think I need something someone else has, and I'll get it any way I can."* Praise God that Solomon had the wisdom in this case to be able to reveal the one mother with the pure heart. When it is our word against another, the only thing that will prevail is our blameless walk in the Lord and His promise to bring into the light the sin that is hidden in darkness.

In the account we just read there were high emotions and deep, troubled motives. The issues we saw in this passage involve the value of human life, the intensity of family bonds, and the desire to have a child so badly that a woman was willing to steal another woman's child to offset her own loss.

 Have you experienced something similar, but maybe in a different life situation? Has someone tried to take over, or take away, something very precious to you? Explain:

_____

_____

_____

*In I Kings 3:6–15, Solomon prays to the Lord for discernment and understanding. Because of Solomon's pure motives and godly desires, God gave him that wisdom, and added to it wealth and prestige.*

_____

_____

_____

How was the situation resolved? Did the opponent wind up winning the argument, or were you able to prevail?

_____

_____

_____

_____

Was the thought of letting go worse than the thought of destroying something precious to you? Do you relate more to the actions of the person taking over, or the person releasing?

_____

_____

_____

_____

**Sometimes the things we love the most are the very things we may have to be willing to give up.**

Sometimes the things we love the most are the very things we may need to give up. With the Lord's help, we can get through even the hardest times of separation from those things we release in order to help them survive. God is looking for the heart that is set on doing the right thing, and on those who are willing to put selfish ambitions aside to protect that which cannot protect itself.

Work on today's verse and pray to the Lord, asking Him to reveal any aspect in your life that is driven by selfish ambition or jealousy. If He reveals anything to your spirit, take time now to deal with it. Repent of any sin, and ask God to help you transform your attitudes, responses, and motives so that they are more Christ-like.

Self-Consumed  DAY FOUR

# CHANGING OUR FOCUS
# 3:16 VERSE: JAMES

*"For where jealousy and selfish ambition exist, there is disorder and every evil thing."*

Having set the stage in Day Three with some background on wisdom, selfish action, and absolute disorder and confusion (as seen in the actions of the women fighting over the child), we will move into a passage from James. I simply love the Book of James (along with the rest of the Bible) because God openly explains the behaviors we should have and the lessons we are to learn. It is very clear that we are often in need of a major overhaul in our actions and words in order to transform our earthly minds into minds set on God.

In a previous lesson we talked about James 3:10, which reads,

> *"from the same mouth come both blessing and cursing. My brethren, these things ought not to be this way."*

That verse is at the end of a wonderfully vivid and strong passage about the power of our tongue. The tongue is such a small part of our anatomy, yet it is able to cause more pain than just about any other weapon we could use against someone. James likens the tongue to a rudder, and it *"defiles the entire body"* (verse 6). What power our tongue has to bring honor or dishonor to God!

After this eye-opening teaching about our words, James discusses the different kinds of wisdom. As we learned with Solomon and the women he judged, wisdom from God is always good, while dependence on our own wisdom can be destructive. What does James have to say? Let's take a look:

📖 James 3:13 begins the segment on wisdom. How does James say we are to show our wisdom in this verse?

_____

_____

_____

📖 Verses 14 and 15 contrasted with verse 13 point out some of the characteristics of depending on self. What does James mention as the source, and the product of worldly wisdom?

_____

_____

📖 Now write out our 3:16 verse here:

_____

_____

_____

According to this verse, what does jealousy and selfish ambition produce?

_____

When we have lives filled with jealousy and selfish ambition, disorder permeates everything we do, and all sorts of evil things fill our lives. When we rely on self more than God, we allow Satan to have a foothold in our lives and rule our hearts.

That word **disorder** in James 3:16 is translated from the Greek word *akatastasia*, which means confusion. Wherever the world places earthly wisdom above God, there will be chaos.

📖 Look at Genesis 11:1–9. Here we see a scene of total disorder that resulted from man's wisdom. Describe the scene and why the people were brought into confusion:

_____

_____

_____

> **The tongue: such a small part of our anatomy, yet the words of our tongue are able to cause more pain than just about any other weapon we could use against someone.**

> **"Who among you is wise and understanding? Let him show by his good behavior his deeds in the gentleness of wisdom."**
>
> **James 3:13**

## Word Study
### EVIL

In James 3:16, we see that *"where jealousy and selfish ambition exist, there is disorder and every **evil** thing."* According to the *Key Word Study Bible* (NASB) the original Greek word for evil, *phaulos*, brings to mind our word "foul." Imagine the response you have to a foul smell, or something that is just not right. That is an apt description of evil. Evil is the exact opposite of anything godly or pleasing, including our jealousy and selfish actions.

The Tower of Babel. What a perfect example of rebellion and selfish ambition. The inhabitants of this city were set on making a name for *themselves,* and they were intent on going against the instruction and wisdom that God had for them. The people were going to build their own path to heaven. They were essentially trying to make themselves like God. As a result, God scattered them and confused their languages. Their earthly wisdom, used for corporate pride and self-worship, dishonored God and brought them disunity and strife.

The phrase *"jealousy and selfish ambition"* is also seen in Romans 2:8–9. What new insight do you gain from those verses concerning these two characteristics?

_____

_____

_____

We are all prone to jealousy and selfish ambition, and we must depend on the Holy Spirit to steer us from these tendencies. Daily reflection on the Word of God and prayerful self-examination are key. Paul knew this truth and continually addressed the dangers of the flesh nature.

In 2 Corinthians 12:20, Paul shares his fear of what he may find when he returns to the people in Corinth. What are his concerns? What is he thinking they might be like?

_____

_____

_____

_____

_____

As he preached and wrote to the people in Rome, Corinth, and many other places Paul also showed concern for those who followed the wisdom of the flesh. Paul's concern matches James' concern: those who wanted to follow Christ needed to live as Jesus did and follow His teaching.

Just as James 3:16 tells us the end result of man's wisdom (built on earthly measures) is godlessness and a lacking spirituality, verses 17 and 18 give us the result of godly wisdom.

James 3:17 reveals that, *"the wisdom that comes from heaven is first of all pure; then peace-loving, considerate, submissive, full of mercy and good fruit, impartial and sincere"* (NIV). How are verses 17 and 18 different from the wisdom and results described in verse 16?

_____

_____

_____

All these attributes listed in verses 17 and 18 are totally opposite of our 16 verse. Looking at that side of wisdom, we see bitter envy, selfish ambition, and unspiritual earthly wisdom that comes from the devil. Are you catching a theme here? Whenever wisdom goes against God, the devil is always involved.

The devil wants us to exalt *ourselves*, *our* knowledge, *our* pride, and *our* sense of wisdom over the God of all Creation! There aren't a lot of choices for us to make regarding the type of wisdom we will have. We choose self-idolization and importance, **or** we choose God. All humanity is caught up in this battle for power, and there are two sides. The side that seeks godly wisdom will enjoy victory, while the side that lives according to self will die in the darkness of their sin.

**What starts with God must end with God to truly be from God.**

What starts with God but ends with self or emptiness is a subtle excuse for worshiping self, and must be avoided with all our might! We *must always*, at every step of our walk of faith, keep God as our focus. Whether through prayer, study, fellowship, or counseling, God is the One whom we are to worship. All *true* help and comfort comes from our Helper, the Holy Spirit.

Beginning and ending our worship with God includes beginning and ending our day with God. It is good to involve God in our daily lives and decisions, allowing Him to guide us into right relationships, decisions, and actions. God knows what we need before we can think it, and He has a path for our lives that He will show us if we seek His direction.

📖 Our discussion here goes back to the critical concept found in Matthew 6:33. What does this verse say?

_____

_____

_____

Matthew 6:33 finds Jesus teaching that we are not to worry about our needs, for the Lord will provide. It is our job to simply seek after God, and He does the rest, including providing for our needs. Focusing on our relationship with God, and not simply focusing on gaining wealth, frees us up to be the person God calls us to be.

We would be very wise to seek God first and place Him in the top spot on our priority list. In doing so, we look to Him for our guidance. We will be content to be in His will. We will give Him glory at all times. When we rely on the wisdom of God, we are truly on the narrow path of faith. There is no danger of being led astray when we are obeying God's commands and living a life that is pleasing to our Savior.

> We must always, at every step of our walk of faith, keep God as our focus.

# FOR ME TO FOLLOW GOD

The downfall of Satan occurred when he wanted to be as powerful as God. Satan has spent every moment since his fall from grace trying to "woo" people toward counterfeit gods and away from the true

> **Satan wants us to get to the point where we think we are such a good Christian, or such a good person, that we no longer need God.**

God. Satan's goal is to keep people from the truth of Jesus Christ. He will use whatever lure he needs to use—even if it is packaged in a façade of joy, great worldly success, a false sense of peace, and a perception of harmony. Satan wants us to get to the point where we think we are good enough that we no longer need God. Yet Satan's lies lead to ruin and despair.

There are two ways to diminish the view we have of God's power. We can say we are as great as He is and in turn falsely elevate ourselves to His level, or we can say that He has no more power than we do—which underestimates the power of God, demoting Him to our level. Either concept is equally against all that Scripture teaches us and should be avoided. In the same manner, beware of false teaching that states that all gods are equal, and that our God is of the same caliber and power as another god. Beware of religions that acknowledge Jesus, but say He was just a great Teacher, one of many Prophets, or a just a really good guy. The Jesus who saves is Jesus, the Son of God. Tolerance is fine in some areas of life; love is wonderful in all areas of life; but standing up for the God of the Bible *is* life, and is essential for Christians.

📖 Read Matthew 7:13–23. What do you learn about the wide and narrow gate, as shown in verses 13–14?

_____

_____

_____

In Matthew 7:15–23, Jesus shows how to discern those who are truly with God. How does He show this? Describe the passage:

_____

_____

_____

_____

_____

As we see from this passage, the way to follow God is to stay on the path that is based on Him. There will be a lot of false teaching that crosses our paths, especially as the days go on. We will have to oppose any false teaching by standing strong on the Word of God. We have to be careful not to think to highly of our own knowledge and abilities. True strength and equipping comes from the Lord.

Take time to journal any additional thoughts or observations about this week's lesson:

_____

_____

_____

_____

_____

_____

*God of All Wisdom,* how I worship You and praise You for the wisdom You impart to those who cling to You! Thank You Lord for the discernment that You give and the wisdom that leads to true peace and knowledge. Lord, I fear You with all reverence and respect, holding You in a position of honor in our lives, homes, and churches. Lord I pray that You would keep me focused on Jesus and all that You have to offer me as a believer and that You would keep me from desiring the things of the world. Lord, I acknowledge no one is righteous without Jesus, and that righteousness only comes through Him. Thank You for the sacrifice of Your Son, and the provision of Your Holy Spirit. Thank You for sustaining me in my walk with You. Thank You for giving both Jews and Gentiles access to salvation through Jesus Christ. May I live a life that honors You in all things. In Jesus' name. Amen.

# Notes

# TWELVE

# Dangers of Complacency

## LEARNING FROM COMPLACENCY IN THE CHURCH

## 3:16 VERSES: HEBREWS, REVELATION

Lesson Twelve—what an adventure this has been! Has your outlook on Christ-like living changed as a result of this study? Has God revealed a deeper level of who He is and who you are in Him? I trust that a new level of transformation has happened for each person doing this study and that Christ-like living will be the end result. By learning new concepts and memorizing focus verses throughout the study, you have become better equipped to follow God and serve Him throughout our world.

As equipped followers of God, *do we still have a passion for God?* Do we see not only **how** and **why** God sent Jesus, but **how we can live** as a result? With all this equipping, we need to be mindful to stay on the "big picture path" God has for us. Are we totally committed to God's service or are we giving God our worship leftovers because we have been too busy? We have to be mindful not to lose our focus, but instead run after God, full steam ahead, and never looking back. We must finish the race with as much passion as we started. We need urgency to our passion and commitment to God. This week we will examine the dangers of unbelief and the subtle onset of complacency that can occur when a believer loses focus of who God is, why he or she desires Him, and why he or she follows God.

*We have all this information and all this Scripture, but do we have passion?*

# CAUGHT GRUMBLING
# 3:16 VERSE: HEBREWS

*"For who provoked Him when they had heard? Indeed, did not all those who came out of Egypt led by Moses?"*

This first focus verse from Hebrews can be summed up in two words: **DON'T GRUMBLE.** We who are steadfastly following God *should* understand this concept of not grumbling—but how do we fare when we are having a rough day? How do we focus on this statement when someone treats us less than perfectly? Or when we step in a puddle in our best shoes? What about when we are faced with a difficult situation, and instead of thanking God for all He has done, we complain instead?

**APPLY** Think of a time recently when you caught yourself grumbling. What was the grumbling about? Did your attitude and complaining solve anything?

_____

_____

_____

_____

_____

God never promises us a perfect life on earth. God does, however, expect us to have a grateful heart regardless. He wants us to thank Him for the blessings and provision that He gives us—even when we don't feel very blessed. Even the Israelites, God's chosen people, struggled with keeping their focus on their blessings from God.

**History Lesson:**
It is time for a Bible lesson from the Old Testament. Let's step back in time and put ourselves in the shoes of the Israelites. They were forced into slave labor in Egypt—away from home and under persecution. They were enslaved because they became too numerous and became a threat to Egypt. The Pharaoh thought he could keep this people under his thumb, but they continued to multiply even in slavery. So, Pharaoh treated them even worse. He had their firstborn sons killed to keep the families from multiplying. Even in this season of murder, God protected the Israelites and used one of the first-born males, Moses, to deliver His people from captivity.

Through a series of well-known events, Moses grew up under Pharaoh's roof and was raised with Pharaoh's blessing. On seeing an Egyptian beating an Israelite, Moses killed the Egyptian and fled to Midian. He stayed there until after the Pharaoh died. God remembered the Israelites, heard their cry, and made a path of deliverance through the calling and leading of Moses.

Moses saw the burning bush on Mount Horeb. There he was called by God to free his people, and obediently went back to Egypt to do just that. He was chosen by God to deliver the Israelites from bondage, and made his very famous "let my people go" demands to the Pharaoh. Plagues and destruc-

> **"In spite of all this they still sinned, and did not believe in His wonderful works."**
>
> **Psalm 78:32**

tion came against the Pharaoh; the first Passover occurred, and God led His chosen people to freedom under the leadership of Moses. God parted the Red Sea right in front of Israelites, securing their route to freedom.

After all that turmoil and abuse during their time of slavery, we would hope that the Israelites would forever praise the God that delivered them out of the hands of evil. Unfortunately, humanity has a funny way of testing God even in the midst of victory.

📖 Read Psalm 95. What is the focus of the psalmist's praise in this Psalm? What does the psalmist warn the reader about?

_____

_____

_____

There are two distinct sections to Psalm 95. Look at verses 1–6. What does the psalmist encourage believers to do? Why?

_____

_____

_____

_____

Verse 7 is the transitional verse in this passage. What is the statement given about God in the first portion of this verse?

_____

_____

_____

Now, describe verses 7b–11: what is the scene with the specific group, and what is going on with their behavior?

_____

_____

_____

Psalm 95 begins with praise to God and flows into a warning about a hardened heart toward God. In this passage we find great encouragement along with intense caution to stay in a passionate relationship with God. Such concepts are applicable to any Christian in any generation.

Psalm 95:9 talks about a time of testing. Compare to Psalm 78:18 and record how the people tested the Lord.

_____

_____

_____

📖 Read the entire passage of Psalm 78. It is a lengthy Psalm but it tells you more history about the Israelites. Write out any details you learn about their disobedience.

> "How often they rebelled against Him in the wilderness, And grieved Him in the desert!"
>
> Psalm 78:40

_____
_____
_____
_____

*Extra Mile*
### BAD ATTITUDE

If you want to look into more verses about grumbling, here are some great ones to look at:

- Exodus 17:3
- Numbers 14:36
- Psalm 106:24–25
- Luke 15:2
- John 6:43
- Philippians 2:14
- James 4:17

There are many, many more examples of disobedience, rebellion, grumbling and complaining in Scripture. If you have time, look them up using a concordance. It's enough to make us even more amazed that God would be mindful of us, considering how we react in our humanity.

The last portion of Psalm 95 describes the Israelites' rebellion, confirming the account of the rebellion we read about in our text from Hebrews. Psalm 78 gives us a lengthy explanation about the relationship between the Israelites and the Lord. Our discovery of Psalms 78 and 95 have given us a clearer understanding about the people God led through the wilderness and why their unbelief was so . . . well . . . unbelievable!

It is important to see that while we start out praising the Lord, going down the right path and knowing who our God is, caution and a guarded heart is required in order to remain in a healthy relationship with the Lord. We have to guard our hearts against the hardening that occurs through sin and disbelief. God is the Author of all things. He created everything. We cannot take for granted the blessings around us that God has provided.

Do you think that we, the believers of today's generation, are immune from this problem of grumbling and a hardened heart? I imagine the Israelites wouldn't have described themselves listing these problems, but we have many Scriptures that paint a different picture.

What happens to our ability to praise the Lord with a tender heart when unexpected circumstances catch us off guard and impact our lives in negative ways?

_____
_____
_____
_____

How can this negative influence affect our relationship with the Lord?

_____
_____
_____

Our focus verse from Hebrews 3:16,

> *"For who provoked Him when they had heard? Indeed, did not all those who came out of Egypt led by Moses?"*

describes the fact that those who followed the one called by God were rebellious. Take note—these were the *chosen ones*. These were the ones following a godly leader. These were the people who were the "believers" in their society, and even they experienced times of rebellion!

The Israelites were not content to go where God said to go without complaining. Their grumbling kept them going around that mountain, and God was not about to deliver them from their problems with the attitudes they had. This is a valuable lesson for us today. Just because we start out with every intention to follow Jesus and obey His Word, we are not guaranteed that we will finish our time on earth with the same zeal. We need to stay focused and continue growing in our faith.

Even in our world today, there are many Christians who are loving others and serving God while complaining about each and every detail as they go. They are serving God and bringing others to Christ, yet there is always something wrong.

- The money isn't there.
- The facilities aren't perfect.
- There is never enough time.
- "So and so" wasn't nice to me.
- There are never enough people to help.
- The supplies are not what we wanted.

If we aren't careful the "this and that" of life will become more important than how we are reaching others for God.

What factors are holding you back from fully serving God in your church or community?

_____

_____

_____

_____

_____

Does it honor God when we are not happy where He puts us?

_____

_____

What if we feel that we just can't serve Him or attend the place He has sent us to because it "doesn't meet *our* needs?" Are we justified in grumbling and not making God a priority?

_____

The excuse that "our surroundings aren't perfect and therefore we need not serve" gives the implication that *God* cannot meet our needs. The reality is that no matter where God calls us, He will sustain us.

God wants us to have faith and acknowledge His hand in our life, no matter what our situation is like and no matter what obstacles we face. God saves us and calls each of us to serve Him in some way. We all are called to minister to others in our sphere of influence, regardless if it is ministering to one person or to millions of people in our lifetime. "Ministering" in this sense means nothing more than reaching out to others with the love of Christ and the truth of the gospel—no special degrees required!

# THOSE ISRAELITES!
# 3:16 VERSE: HEBREWS

*"For who provoked Him when they had heard? Indeed, did not all those who came out of Egypt led by Moses?"*

By the leading of God, Moses led the Israelites out of captivity and into the freedom of the open terrain of the wilderness. Their journey did not lead them to an ideal location in their eyes, but God led them to the exact place that He desired them to be—which should have been more than acceptable to them. God was worthy of their praise, yet their praise was left unspoken. The Israelites hated the desert so much that they thought it would have been better to die in Egypt. What a tragedy! All they could remember were the pots of meat they had in Egypt, but somehow they forgot the slavery side of life there. The manna God gave them in the desert kept them alive for forty years. Even with this provision of manna, the Israelites went so far as to become fearful that they might die of thirst. Imagine! Would God bring the people out in victory, provide sustaining food, yet forget to supply the life-giving water needed for survival? God graciously answered their concern and brought water from a rock. Every time they grumbled, God continually met their *needs* but not necessarily their *wants*. Every time they grumbled, God continually heard and responded. He may not have responded in the way they expected or desired, but a response came.

📖 Read Numbers 11:1–9, and write down the scene:

_____

_____

_____

_____

The Israelites were not content with the manna that fell from heaven, even though there was constant provision. They did not lack nourishment, but they still allowed the *rabble* (foreigners among them) to influence their reaction to the manna. God provided what He knew they needed, yet they insisted they needed more. Suddenly, God's provision was no longer enough.

📖 Look at God's reaction to their grumbling, found in Numbers 11:31–35. What happened?

_____

_____

Apply this reaction to God's provision to the people around us today, who grumble in spite of God's blessings in their lives. I imagine that God will deal with them much the same as He dealt with the Israelites. God will undoubtedly show them that He is God, and He will have some sort of correction for them.

The moment we are delivered from the sinful life we lived before we knew Christ, we are thankful for salvation. Our initial reaction is excitement,

## Every time the Israelites grumbled, God met their needs ... not necessarily their wants

praise, and obedience. At some point in our faith walk, we are *all* prone to failing to praise God for delivering us and for His daily provision. We must remain alert.

**APPLY** Have you ever lost sight of God's provision and blessings while dealing with the details of daily life? How did you get back on track?

_____

_____

_____

_____

_____

We can sometimes get caught up in the day-to-day life that we lead, and forget that this all-powerful God is supplying all our needs. We may find that what we *think* we want or deserve is not always lining up with reality. We might even start to blame others and God for not giving us exactly what we want when we want it. Recognizing the Lord's provision in our lives and praising God for this provision will help us re-focus on the Lord.

Hebrews 3 reveals to us that as the people of Christ we can see how our journey parallels the journey the Israelites had with Moses. Much like the situation with the Israelites, how many times do we see ourselves "going around the mountain" one more time?

There have always been comparisons made between the choices and lives of Old Testament believers and the church of today. Whether in a "wilderness" moment or receiving manna from above, examples abound that apply to our lives. Much too often we are found grumbling and harboring dissatisfaction with what the Lord hands us as a blessing.

📖 Read Hebrews 3:14–19. What is the writer conveying here?

_____

_____

_____

The Israelites chose to grumble about their situation, lost sight of the blessings from God, and sat in a puddle of unbelief. Through their account we learn that no matter how strong our faith may be at one moment, we are always at risk of losing our passion for the things of God in another moment. For as we turn from God, our hearts get hard, and our Creator becomes displeased with us. God was clear in His correction of those who were rebellious in the Old Testament. Our God is all-powerful and very capable to use whatever actions He sees fit towards those who are disobedient to His will, no matter the generation or the era.

Just as Moses led the Israelites, Christ came to lead us, His children, in the ways of the Lord. Through the accounts of Moses and the Israelites we see an applicable parallel to our own lives. Even if we follow Jesus Christ for a very long time, and in very visible ways, we are not immune from the dangers of unbelief and rebellion.

> *Somehow in the midst of tremendous provision from God, the Israelites lost their focus.*

> *Grumbling is nothing more than unbelief and a lack of faith. Unbelief leads to disobedience and rebellion; a lack of faith may keep you from God's promises!*

📖 Look back at Hebrews 3:12–14. How does the situation with the Israelites relate to us, according to this passage?

_____

_____

_____

_____

> **"Encourage one another daily, as long as it is called Today, so that none of you may be hardened by sin's deceitfulness."**
>
> **Hebrews 3:13**

Hebrews 3:13 is a powerful verse! We are reminded to *". . . encourage one another daily, as long as it is called Today, so that none of you may be hardened by sin's deceitfulness."* (NIV) Through support and love from fellow Christians, along with correction and confidence, we are able to stand in the knowledge and peace of the salvation we have in Christ without being moved by the influences of the world. This will protect us from the condition seen a few verses later in verse 16. *Today is the day; encourage one another!*

Think of a close friend who needs encouragement in an area of life. What would you say to encourage him in the Lord? How would you help him stay on track?

_____

_____

_____

_____

_____

Make a point to call, E-mail, or talk with him soon and share a word of encouragement!

Without our sustained relationship with Christ, we are vulnerable to the same problems the Israelites had, and God will have the same displeasure with us that He had with them. Their disobedience led to unbelief and kept them from entering God's rest—a warning to us all!

- ■ **He created us.**
- ■ **He loves us.**
- ■ **He redeemed us through Christ.**
- ■ **He protects us.**
- ■ **He provides for us.**
- ■ **He heals us.**
- ■ **He blesses us.**
- ■ **He is our sufficiency.**
- ■ **He alone knows our true needs.**

We must thankfully and obediently do what He asks, and accept what He provides. Obedience is the key to truly believing and having a relationship with God. He knows who are His.

Memorize our focus verse, and take a moment to pray that the Lord will reveal to you any unbelief or rebellion in your heart—and ask Him to forgive those things. Renew your commitment to the Lord.

# WHO BROKE YOUR WATER HEATER?
# 3:16 VERSE: REVELATION

*"So because you are lukewarm, and neither hot nor cold, I will spit you out of My mouth."*

Ok, ladies and gentlemen, we have come to our final focus verse. What a journey we have been on together. What an amazing time of fellowship with each other and the Lord. I praise God for you, and am so blessed by your dedication to God and His Word!

I pray that we will all recognize the wonderful things He has done our lives. Today's focus verse from Revelation brings such a visual image to mind. God desires for us to be passionate about Him. Otherwise, we are distasteful in His mouth. It seems that the Israelites may have had such an effect on God while they were in the middle of their grumbling.

Imagine for a moment seeing a wonderful meal awaiting your presence. It is your favorite recipe; the food you love the most. You can't remember the last time you were able to experience the taste, and your taste buds are perking up and flooding your mouth in anticipation. The culinary delight has been in the cooking pot for a while, off the heat and quickly losing steam. The meal is your favorite after all, so you eagerly find a plate, piping hot or not. You serve up your portion, and sit down for a wonderful meal. The true taste is only wonderful when it is whisked off the stove the moment it is boiling, but you're sure there is still a touch of warmth to it, so you dig in. The first fork full that hits your tongue almost makes you sick! It is neither hot nor cold; it has been sitting there for so long that it is just room temperature, and less than palatable. What usually gives you joy now only brings you disappointment. The consistency is bad, the flavor is gone, and the overall effect of this meal is ruined. It has gone from something incredibly pleasing to something you can't even stomach. Think about how badly you would want to get it out of your mouth and into your napkin when no one was looking. Think of how strong your desire would be to wash your mouth out with refreshing water in order to get the taste out.

Now, look at our verse, Revelation 3:16 again:

*"So because you are lukewarm, and neither hot nor cold, I will spit you out of My mouth."*

The image is quite a vivid one, and it is an effective way for us to understand the dangers of complacency. When we are no longer passionate for God, we no longer bring Him joy.

 Have you ever had a case of the "blahs"? You know, when you just feel unmotivated? Unexcited? When everything seems dull and boring?

_____

_____

_____

## Word Study
## LUKEWARM

What does "lukewarm" mean? It is that temperature that is exactly between hot and cold. It is neither one nor the other. It has no noticeable temperature setting; it almost has no feeling to it, as it is hard to distinguish between hot or cold. What a visual reminder this is of having no feeling, no passion. It is as if the church referenced in this verse went unnoticed by God because they had no reaction or interaction with God.

How did you combat those feelings and become more energetic?

_____

_____

_____

_____

**APPLY** Ok, apply this same scenario to your relationship with God. Has there ever been a season in your life when you were not excited to go to church or build your relationship with God?

_____

_____

How did you get through that time in your life?

_____

_____

_____

_____

What advice would you give those who aren't thrilled about church? How would you motivate them to go and participate?

_____

_____

_____

_____

_____

### _Extra Mile_
### PRAISE PSALMS

There are many Psalms that deal with the majesty of the Lord, and praising Him. Some that would be good to study are: Psalms 19, 23, 33, 46, 47, 65, 67, 93, 98, 117, 138, 139, 146, 148, 149, and 150.

Everyone is different, and we all go through seasons in life when motivation and enthusiasm are a struggle. Staying focused on the God we worship (instead of the people with whom we worship) should help us become more interested in our walk with the Lord. Reading Scriptures like the psalms, that describe the goodness of God and His infinite blessings, will help us see how magnificent He is. Reading books about God, talking to other believers who are excited about their faith, and watching Christian programs that teach and uplift will also help motivate us. Listening to praise music is a wonderful way to prepare your heart and bring joy to your outlook. God is worthy of our praise, and He wants us to come to Him with excitement and joy. God can't wait to see us, and He wants us to be piping hot, right off the stove; he wants us to be thrilled to see Him!

Psalm 100 is wonderfully upbeat and applicable to our lives in a time of refocusing on God. When you are having a difficult day or are emotionally drained, take time to read this psalm or another passage of Scripture that will remind you of the awesome God we serve! Read Psalm 100 with me, and let's take a moment to go through what we find there:

> _"Shout joyfully to the_ LORD, _all the earth._
> _Serve the_ LORD _with gladness;_
> _Come before Him with joyful singing._
> _Know that the_ LORD _Himself is God;_
> _It is He who has made us, and not we ourselves;_

*We are His people and the sheep of His pasture.*
*Enter His gates with thanksgiving,*
*And His courts with praise.*
*Give thanks to Him; bless His name.*
*For the LORD is good;*
*His lovingkindness is everlasting,*
*And His faithfulness to all generations."*

What is the first thing this psalm says we are to offer the Lord?

_____

After giving Him praise, then what are we to do?

_____

_____

We praise Him, and then we serve Him with gladness. As we see in this psalm, once we have praised and happily served, we are to praise God again. In doing this, we will *"Know that the _____ _____ is God."* We will know that God is God! We will *know that we know.*

📖 This passage in Psalm 100 has a cross reference back to Deuteronomy 4:35. Check this verse out. It is such a view of relationship.

*"To you it was shown that you might know that the LORD, He is God; there is no other besides Him."*

God wants us to know who He is. He wants us to know that He is the only God and that He is in control. Back to Psalm 100, we see the psalmist describe our relationship with God. We know that God is God and that He made us. We gain perspective with this passage concerning the relationship between God and ourselves in the following way:

He is the Shepherd, and we are the _____ of His pasture.

What types of positive reaction are we to give God?

_____

_____

Why?

_____

_____

_____

Praise Him, praise Him! What a love story this is. We are His, and He is ours. The Lord is in charge, and we praise Him for that. He gave us life. Are you joyful about God?

**A Personal Moment:**
Our family has a wonderfully energetic golden retriever named Shadow. We got her as a puppy, a mere six weeks old. She has grown up with us and has known us her whole life. There is nothing new about us! You would think that with this time together, she would get tired of running to meet us

## Are you joyful about God?

when we walked through the door. But instead, sweet Shadow gets even more excited with each passing day. When we wake up in the morning, the poor dog can barely make it up the stairs because she is running so fast to say good morning. When we come home from running errands, she is so happy to see us that she literally bounces on her front legs, steadying on her back legs, with a half-jump, half-hop type excitement. Shadow simply can't wait to see us.

Our puppy always acts like it has been forever since she saw us last. Whether it has been five minutes or two hours, her excitement is the same. She can barely contain herself! She is overjoyed to be in our presence. Shadow wants to please us, to love us, and be loved by us—all the time. At any moment, all we have to do is call for her, or look at her and say "hi," and up to her feet she goes, prancing over to sit by us. She simply loves her humans. And her humans simply adore her. What a dog! What a blessing from God.

Now, I want you to put those "God goggles" on and see this story as if it were God interacting with us—as if He were us, and we were, in theory, the golden retriever.

What do you do when we get up in the morning? Do you run to say "Hi" to God? Do you begin your day in prayer and praise, thanking God for your blessings?

_____

_____

_____

_____

Do you happily include God in all the details of your day?

_____

Are you excited to see God, to talk to God, and to worship God?

_____

_____

Additionally, when you go to church, are you happy to be there?

_____

Unfortunately, more than once in my lifetime, I have caught myself responding to God as if I were a sedate basset hound instead of an energetic golden retriever—no excitement, and responding at a much slower pace. (Basset hounds are great dogs too, I'm just showing the difference in pace here.) God wants us to be excited to meet with Him every moment of every day. *Especially* when we go to church. Church is not a chore! It is a privilege. We should be joyful that we are able to meet together to worship our King.

 Take a moment to think about your relationship with God. Are you more like the golden retriever or the basset hound? Are you energetic about meeting with God, or does your personal devotion time and your time at church seem more like a chore? What things could you do to react to God in a more energetic and positive way?

_____

_____

_____

_____

_____

_____

_____

_____

_____

_____

Memorize today's focus verse and read Revelation 2:1—3:22 in preparation for tomorrow's lesson. Thank you for finishing strong!

# CHURCH TALK
# 3:16 VERSE: REVELATION

*"So because you are lukewarm, and neither hot nor cold, I will spit you out of My mouth."*

The Book of the Revelation of Jesus Christ to John is both intricate and absolutely overwhelming. The chapters masterfully point to the future and our eternal life with Jesus. Unfortunately, it is probably one of the most intimidating books of the Bible to a reader because of all the symbols and bizarre details. There are terrific study guides available that will take you step by step through the prophecies found in Revelation. I encourage you to take time to study the Book of Revelation if you haven't already done so.

📖 Were you able to complete the reading assignment at the closing of Day Three? If not, please go ahead and read Revelation 2:1—3:22 now, so that our discussion will flow more easily.

What details stand out to you in this passage of Revelation? Write your thoughts:

_____

_____

_____

_____

_____

*Did You Know?*
## REVELATION

The Book of Revelation was written by the apostle John much later in his life, while he was imprisoned on the island of Patmos, around AD 95.

Looking at the context of our 3:16 verse, we see that there is much to discuss. John is describing a vision in which God is addressing the seven *churches*. The churches! God shows John how the seven churches in Asia—all named by their location—were faring in their faithfulness to God. The

> **"But I have this against you, that you have left your first love."**
>
> **Revelation 2:4**

> **"Be faithful until death, and I will give you the crown of life."**
>
> **Revelation 2:10**

### Word Study
### NICOLAITANS

The Nicolaitans were a people who followed heretical views and enjoyed self indulgence and sexual immorality. Not much is known about them, but the reference in Revelation 2 to their following the ways of Balaam would imply that their sect ate sacrificial food, and partook in sexual immorality.

comparisons and corrections concerning the seven churches also apply to us today. We can see how we have fallen short in regard to our heart conditions toward God. We also see what God thinks of those compromises and sins, as well as how to repair our relationship with Him.

Which church is mentioned in Revelation 2:1–7?

_____

What does the Lord have to say about that church?

_____

_____

_____

How can we apply that rebuke to our own lives and church interaction today?

_____

_____

_____

_____

The second church, discussed in 2:8–11 had distinct issues. Jesus does not criticize it, but it does have definite struggles. What is this church, and what struggles is it going through?

_____

_____

_____

Verses 12–17 show us the third church description. Name this church, and how it grieved the Lord.

_____

_____

_____

In today's world, what do you think this type of compromise looks like?

_____

_____

_____

_____

_____

Revelation 2:18–29 gives us a lengthy description of the church of Thyatira. What is its issue?

_____

_____

_____

_____

What about the people described in verse 24? Are they different from the rest of the church there? How?

_____

_____

_____

_____

The next church referenced in 3:1–6 is the church of Sardis. What is the Lord's focus as He speaks to them?

_____

_____

Thinking of this church as representing the Reformation church of the 1500s and beyond, (using the chart found at the end of this section), how do we see the effects of Sardis' philosophy manifested in our churches today?

_____

_____

_____

How can we remedy such a blind complacency in our current day and church environment?

_____

_____

_____

_____

What will happen to those who remain godly in an environment void of passion?

_____

_____

_____

The church of Philadelphia mentioned in Revelation 3:7–13 has a distinct role in the listing of churches. What makes this church different from the rest?

_____

_____

_____

The church of Philadelphia avoided criticism from Jesus as did the church at Smyrna. Philadelphia, however, would escape suffering. Jesus' comments focused on encouraging them to stand in faith.

The last church listed in this grouping (verses 14–22) is the focus of our final 3:16 verse. What is the location of the church?

_____

_____

*"Wake up, and strengthen the things that remain, which were about to die; for I have not found your deeds completed in the sight of My God."*

*Revelation 3:2*

*"I know your deeds. Behold, I have put before you and open door which no one can shut, because you have a little power, and have kept My word, and have not denied My name."*

*Revelation 3:8*

How does Jesus begin his discussion of it? What does His first statement in verse 14 reveal?

_____

_____

_____

Jesus begins by proclaiming His sovereignty and His role in creation. What rebuke does this church receive?

_____

_____

Reminding ourselves of the focus verse and the visual image that comes to mind, can you see how God is displeased with our indifference?

_____

Is the lack of enthusiasm due to a lack of funds or resources? What does verse 17 reveal?

_____

_____

_____

*"So because you are lukewarm, and neither hot nor cold, I will spit you out of My mouth."*

*Revelation 3:16*

The people of Laodicea had everything they needed! They lived a life of wealth and comfort in a city that had a tremendous commercial value. Business was booming, people were collecting wealth, and their response to the Lord was minimal at best. The Lord was the last thing on their minds; they were indifferent. They didn't give Him the time of day.

The people of Laodicea would have understood the image of a not-so-palatable meal, but the image of being lukewarm had another distinct meaning for them. Ray VanderLaan, in his video series, *That the World May Know* (Focus on the Family), points out another wonderful idea about the lukewarm faith of the Laodiceans. The region around Laodicea had varieties of fresh springs close by—both wonderfully cool and bubbling hot. The Laodiceans dealt with the impact of living in between the two extreme water sources, where they experienced the pooling of both hot and cold water together, which possibly resulted in very poor tasting water. The drinking supply in Laodicea could have been greatly impacted by its location. If so, the Laodiceans would have immediately understood the meaning of lukewarm, substandard water.

In God's wonderful way of relating His truths, the Lord made it very clear that the Laodiceans' lack of passion and "lukewarm" behavior grieved Him. Christ speaks of removing the complacent believers from His presence. This image of lukewarm water being spit out gave an immediate, passionate response to such an indifferent interaction with Him.

The chart below provides a visual listing of the churches, what the Lord said about them, and an idea of the historical era each church might represent.

| Churches Listed In Revelation | | |
|---|---|---|
| **Churches:** | **Major Offense** | **Possible Era Represented** |
| Ephesus | Forgot first love | Apostolic church |
| Smyrna | Suffered for not bowing to Caesar | Martyred church |
| Pergamum (Pergamos) | Traditions of false worship | State church |
| Thyatira | Tolerated immoral prophetess | Church and State combined |
| Sardis | Outwardly alive, inwardly dead | Reformed church |
| Philadelphia | Obedient | Missionary church |
| Laodicea | Lost their passion | Apostate church |

God gave the churches a chance to change, rebuked them, and allowed for repentance. Several of the churches mentioned were on the right path. The correction of these churches became necessary when they allowed pagan thoughts and beliefs to join in with the truth. They compromised, added aspects to their worship that were inconsistent with God, and thus allowed sin to enter their worship. In our 3:16 verse we see something else that equals the tragedy of compromise:

**The Laodiceans lost their passion. They became indifferent.**
The folks at Laodicea were lukewarm. They had no passion! They were indifferent to say the very least. Through Christ's rebuke of this church, we can understand that He won't just frown and say something like, *"Oh what a shame, these people seem bored and complacent and overly comfortable with their current place of faith . . . what a shame. . . ."* No way. What an image we have instead of the God of creation spitting us out of His mouth!

Choose your metaphor—whether a bad meal or a mixed water supply—that helps you see how this complacency must have really upset God. Go ahead and think of that image. *We are focusing on this deeply so that this concept will change your life.*

- **May it change your worship.**
- **May it change your relationship.**
- **May it give you passion.**

Are you ready for a more engaged, passionate walk with the Lord? What would you say to God, regarding your desire for more of Him? How would you describe your newfound energy and commitment to your relationship with the Lord? Journal your thoughts.

_____

_____

_____

_____

_____

_____

_____

_____

_____

Now take a few moments (or a few hours) and spend time praying to God, sharing these very thoughts with Him. Each day we have the opportunity to experience a new vibrancy in our walk with the Lord, and we can all take time to recommit our lives to Him. It is a new day!

There is still a chance for the lukewarm—*in Laodicea and wherever you are today*. If you have lost your passion for God, find it again through the renewing of your mind as you read the Word. Praise God through song and prayer and simply sit in His presence and ask Him for a renewed faith. Walk as a new creation. Live as a passionate believer. Share the hope of Christ with others, and it will energize you even more.

Memorize this last verse, and praise God for your renewed walk with the Lord, and for the protection this gives you from the dangers of complacency. May we all live passionate lives for the Lord!

*Dangers of Complacency*  DAY FIVE

# FOR ME TO FOLLOW GOD

What a combination of issues we have dealt with in this lesson, from the seven churches to God's chosen people. Whether we are grumbling about His provision, or just acting like we could not care less, the Lord makes sure to remind us of His awesome power and love for us. The Lord has lovingly given us the Scriptures to guide us to the path of righteousness.

Now that our study together is almost completed, what are some of the next steps for Christ-like living?

### Live a Godly Life That Follows Jesus' Example
God looks for the faithful. God looks for the individual's continual spiritual growth. A godly life is more than a strict routine and a good seat up front; it is a lifestyle that reflects Jesus Christ in all we do. Incorporate what you have learned in this study into your daily life. Intentionally search the Scriptures for guidance on dealing with difficult situations. Every day brings new challenges and new opportunities to react in godly ways.

### Get Involved in a Church Community
Attend a church that boldly proclaims the good news of Jesus Christ, and teaches the Bible faithfully from week to week. I pray that you are already involved in such a church. Many wonderful churches in different denominations (and some with no denominational affiliation) deeply seek the Lord and His truth, so don't think you have only one option. Church is much more than a lively, emotional event with a great praise band. It involves going to a place where you can meet others of a like faith, worship corporately, and continue to learn how to love and obey your Savior.

The first church structure consisted of twelve men chosen by God to serve alongside Jesus, and the crowds of believers who followed Christ, repented of their sins and believed in His Word. Today, the church includes all who repent, believe, and live a life for Christ. We are the church.

### Stick to the Bible and the God of the Bible
Look for the preaching of the Word, as we first studied in Lesson 1, with 2 Timothy 3:14–17. Look for churches, pastors, and teachers who have heed-

ed the instruction described by Paul in 2 Timothy 4:1–4. In this Paul encourages Timothy with the following message:

> *"I solemnly charge you in the presence of God and of Christ Jesus, who is to judge the living and the dead, and by His appearing and His kingdom; preach the word; be ready in season and out of season; reprove, rebuke, exhort, with great patience and instruction. For the time will come when they will not endure sound doctrine; but wanting to have their ears tickled, they will accumulate for themselves teachers in accordance to their own desires; and will turn away their ears from the truth, and will turn aside to myths."*

Paul knew the dangers of complacency, compromise, and rebellion. He knew that those who were to lead people to the truth would have to be prepared to give an answer for the truth they believed. In the same way, as a body of believers, we must stay focused on finding teachers such as Timothy, who would uphold God's message at all costs—especially as compromise infiltrates the church.

## Stay Unified with Other Believers

There is unity among us through the gospel of Christ. True unity is only possible with Jesus Christ. Those who do not hold that Jesus is the Son of God, and that He died and rose again once for all sin—are *not* in this category of believers.

There are great strides being made in some segments of our society to have an *interfaith* relationship with others. Make sure you understand the difference between interfaith and interdenominational. Interfaith is very different than interdenominational. *Interdenominational* involves the interaction and cooperation of those Christian denominations that, while different in detail, all follow the God of the Bible—the God of Abraham, Isaac, and Jacob. All interdenominational unity should agree that Jesus is the only begotten Son of God.

*Interfaith* involves the inclusion of any and every "god" with our God. Whether we incorporate their beliefs in with ours, or simply compromise by saying our gods are the same, it is all false worship. The God of the Bible should never be lowered to the same level as any other "god" that man has chosen to worship. Refer to the first commandment for details.

Which of the seven churches seems closest to this description of the incorporation of false worship? Which church would be the interfaith model? How does God respond to this?

_____
_____
_____
_____
_____
_____

No true unity lies with this type of compromise. When we do not agree on the deity we are worshipping, we cannot be moving in the same direction. There is only one true God—the God of the Bible. When we allow pagan deities to be placed on the same level as our God, we are asking for trouble. Read the second and third chapters of Revelation again to see what happens to the *churches* that allow this to go on. Please don't ever forget that this passage is addressing the *believers*; it is a warning for us all.

Do you remember the speech Paul made in Athens, found in Acts 17? We talked about this passage in Lesson 6. He presented a wonderful sermon to the Athenians concerning the "Unknown God." The people of that day could go to their place of worship and find whatever god they felt like bowing to, but our Savior was not listed among the statues. There was a little monument dedicated to the unknown god, and Paul used that wonderful opportunity to share with them what they did not know. He shared with them the promise of Christ.

What if our God is unknown to those around us? How can we make Him known, and show the difference between our God and the many other gods of this world?

_____

_____

_____

_____

What impact can sharing the good news of Jesus have on those who do not know God?

_____

_____

_____

You may be wondering how sharing your faith with others and having a dedicated relationship with the Lord impacts our quest for the Christ-like life. Well, those things are an integral part of a Christ-like life.

To be Christ-like, we are walking as Christ has taught us to. Everything Jesus Christ did was in the will of God, led others to God, led them to salvation, and to a life eternal. Our goals, actions, and interactions should have the same heart motivations.

List the names of some people with whom you want to share God's Word:

_____

_____

_____

Dedicate your time and energy to sharing the life-giving truth of salvation with these dear precious souls! It will impact them in ways you cannot even imagine. God's Word is powerful, it is mighty, and it saves. Sharing Christ with others is the outpouring of a Christ-like life. As we live a life for Him, we cannot help but express who He is to others. May we all spill out the goodness of the Lord, and the powerful message of atonement for sins—wherever our feet may tread!

 *Dear Lord,* I pray I would have a renewed passion for You and Your Word. My prayer is that I would find You, Lord, in every place we seek You, and that You would reveal Yourself to me in mighty and powerful ways. I pray that You would strengthen me in my understanding of the Scriptures, and in all that your Word provides. May I be excited about living a life that is pleasing in Your sight, and may I obey Your commands and follow Your will. May my life never be the same from this day forward. May I share Your word with the lost world around me, and may everything I do bring You glory and honor. I surrender my life to You and to Your service. In Jesus' Holy and Righteous name. Amen.

Before we say farewell, I have to ask you…

- ❏ Do you get really excited about God?
- ❏ Do you follow Him?
- ❏ Do you read your Bible with anticipation of learning more about God?
- ❏ Are you involved in a thriving church community?
- ❏ Are you in agreement, or is your life absent of these things, or do you just want more?

If you have never experienced any of the things listed above, it is not too late to invite Jesus into your life.

- ■ He wants more than a momentary introduction to your life.
- ■ He wants a backstage pass.
- ■ He wants full rights to your life.
- ■ He wants all of you.
- ■ He wants you to surrender all you are and all you think you want to be, to His will.
- ■ God wants to be the ruler and joy of your life.
- ■ He wants it all.
- ■ Are you willing to give it to Him?
- ■ Are you ready to be passionate about your Savior?

- ■ I pray you are, and I am praying for you!

Much Love in Christ,

Jennifer

# 3:16 VERSES EXAMINED IN LIFE PRINCIPLES FOR CHRIST-LIKE LIVING

| | |
|---|---|
| **Lesson 1:**<br>2 Timothy 3:16<br>"All Scripture is inspired by God and profitable for teaching, for reproof, for correction, for training in righteousness." | **Lesson 4:**<br>Luke 3:16<br>"John answered and said to them all, 'As for me, I baptize you with water; but One is coming who is mightier than I, and I am not fit to untie the thong of His sandals; He will baptize you with the Holy Spirit and fire.' " |
| **Lesson 2:**<br>Galatians 3:16<br>"Now the promises were spoken to Abraham and to his seed. He does not say 'And to his seeds,' as referring to many, but rather to one, 'And to your seed,' that is, Christ." | **Lesson 5:**<br>Matthew 3:16<br>"And after being baptized, Jesus went up immediately from the water; and behold, the heavens were opened, and he saw the Spirit of God descending as a dove, and coming upon Him."<br><br>Mark 3:16<br>"And He appointed the twelve: Simon (to whom He gave the name Peter)," |
| **Lesson 3:**<br>2 Corinthians 3:16<br>"But whenever a man turns to the Lord, the veil is taken away." | **Lesson 6:**<br>John 3:16<br>" 'For God so loved the world, that He gave His only begotten Son, that whoever believes in Him should not perish, but have eternal life.' "<br><br>1 John 3:16<br>"We know love by this, that He laid down His life for us; and we ought to lay down our lives for the brethren."<br><br>1 Timothy 3:16<br>"And by common confession great is the mystery of godliness: He who was revealed in the flesh, Was vindicated in the Spirit, Beheld by angels, Proclaimed among the nations, Believed on in the world, Taken up in glory." |

**Lesson 7:**

Philippians 3:16

"however, let us keep living by the same standard to which we have attained."

1 Peter 3:16

"and keep a good conscience so that in the thing in which you are slandered, those who revile your good behavior in Christ may be put to shame."

2 Peter 3:16

"as also in all his letters, speaking in them of these things, in which are some things hard to understand, which the untaught and unstable distort, as they do also the rest of Scriptures, to their own destruction."

**Lesson 8:**

Ephesians 3:16

"that He would grant you, according to the riches of His glory, to be strengthened with power through His Spirit in the inner man"

2 Thessalonians 3:16

"Now may the Lord of peace Himself continually grant you peace in every circumstance. The Lord be with you all!"

**Lesson 9:**

Acts 3:16

"And on the basis of faith in His name, it is the name of Jesus which has strengthened this man whom you see and know; and the faith which comes through Him has given him this perfect health in the presence of you all."

**Lesson 10:**

1 Corinthians 3:16

"Do you not know that you are a temple of God, and that the Spirit of God dwells in you?"

Colossians 3:16

"Let the word of Christ richly dwell within you, with all wisdom teaching and admonishing one another with psalms and hymns and spiritual songs, singing with thankfulness in your hearts to God."

**Lesson 11:**

Romans 3:16

"DESTRUCTION AND MISERY ARE IN THEIR PATHS,"

James 3:16

"For where jealousy and selfish ambition exist, there is disorder and every evil thing."

**Lesson 12:**

Hebrews 3:16

"For who provoked Him when they had heard? Indeed, did not all those who came out of Egypt led by Moses?"

Revelation 3:16

"So because you are lukewarm, and neither hot nor cold, I will spit you out of My mouth."

## Ready, Set, Go!

I am so honored that you have endured this journey with me, and have read what I believe God has for each of us in His word. It doesn't stop here! Please continue in your faith walk, and grow in your knowledge, understanding and love of the God you serve.

Have you made a personal commitment to Jesus? Unless we have made that commitment, the journey is for naught. We can spend a lifetime in the pews of our churches, and never truly be in the Kingdom of God on the day we pass away. How do we get there? How are we sure of our salvation?

If you want to be absolutely sure of your salvation, please pray this simple prayer to your Father God:

"Lord, I believe that you sent your Only Son Jesus Christ to die for my sins. I believe that He died on the cross, and rose again three days later. I believe that He is sitting at the right hand of God now, and that His sacrifice was for my sins. I know that I am a sinner, and fall short of righteousness on my own. I ask forgiveness for the sins of my life, and commit my life to you today. I hold nothing back—please use me for your purposes, and fill my life with your Presence and your Spirit."

If your have prayed this for the first time, congratulations! Welcome into the family of God! I urge you to find a church in your community to be a part of. Get a Bible. Read your Bible. Pray and ask God to guide you in everything you do. And rejoice! You are His forever!

# Notes